PILGRIMAGE
TO THE
WESTERN FRONT

PILGRIMAGE TO THE WESTERN FRONT

BY THE MEN WHO WENT BACK TO THE OLD FRONTLINE

MIKE HILL

FONTHILL

For Dad

I must return to my old comrades of the Great War—to the brown, the treeless, the flat, and grave-set plain of Flanders—to the rolling, heat-miraged downlands of the Somme—for I am dead with them, and they live in me again.

Henry Williamson, *The Wet Flanders Plain* (1929)

Always there are wandering veterans on those lanes and roads about the Salient.

Will R. Bird, *Thirteen Years After* (1932)

Fonthill Media Language Policy

Fonthill Media publishes in the international English language market. One language edition is published worldwide. As there are minor differences in spelling and presentation, especially with regard to American English and British English, a policy is necessary to define which form of English to use. The Fonthill Policy is to use the form of English native to the author. Mike Hill was born and educated in Liverpool; therefore British English has been adopted in this publication.

Fonthill Media Limited
Fonthill Media LLC
www.fonthillmedia.com
office@fonthillmedia.com

First published in the United Kingdom and the United States of America 2023

British Library Cataloguing in Publication Data:
A catalogue record for this book is available from the British Library

ISBN 978-1-78155-913-0

Typeset in 10.5 pt on 13pt Sabon
Printed and bound in England

Acknowledgements

This book could not have been written without the help and kindness of a number of people: Ian Small and Chris Anderson, of the Commonwealth War Graves Commission; Ian Ference, curator, the Jordan/Ference Collection of Great War Stereography; Iain Lynn, Stuart Clewlow, Steve Snelling, and Richard Rayner; Great War collector Philip Woets; military historian and author Charles Fair; author of *Aisne 1918* David Blanchard; Chantal Callens, of Skindle's Guesthouse, Poperinghe; and Mark Warby, founder of the Bruce Bairnsfather Society and editor of *The Old Bill Newsletter* and the official Bruce Bairnsfather website www.brucebairnsfather.org.uk. Also Bruce Littlejohn and the estate of Barbara Bruce Littlejohn for kind permission to republish the cartoons of Bruce Bairnsfather.

Thanks to military historian Paul Reed, of the excellent Old Front Line podcast, whose kind words of enthusiasm came just at the right time, and also to Mark Connelly, professor of modern British history at the University of Kent. Prof. Connelly's book *Postcards from the Western Front* (McGill-Queen's University Press) was published in September 2022 and is the essential starting point for anyone interested in finding out more about the history of interwar pilgrimages. Another key reference is *Battlefield Tourism* by David W. Lloyd (Berg, 1998).

Many of the images reproduced by kind permission of the CWGC belong to the collection of Col. Herbert Thomas Goodland DSO who was the Imperial War Graves Commission's deputy controller after the First World War. He was responsible for the organisation of the IWGC and its construction work in France and Flanders. He remained in this post until June 1928 when he resigned from the IWGC and returned to live in British Columbia, Canada. He was awarded the CB for the efficiency he displayed while working with the IWGC.

Great thanks also to everyone at Fonthill Media and to Lindsey, Antony, and Daniel for their patience, once again.

The British Newspaper Archive, the Australian War Memorial, Trove and the Imperial War Museum's Lives of the First World War all proved invaluable resources.

Contents

Glossary of Terms

2LO:	London transmitter of the first national radio broadcasting network.
5.9:	German howitzer gun or artillery shell so named because of the 5.9 inches bore of the gun.
8 chevaux - 40 hommes:	legend on the side of the French cattle trucks used to transport soldiers around behind Allied lines.
9.2:	Allied howitzer gun or artillery shell so named because of the 9.2-inch bore of the gun.
AIF:	Australian Imperial Force.
APM:	assistant provost marshal.
Archies:	German anti-aircraft fire also known as Archibalds. Thought to derive from a music hall song called 'Archibald, Certainly Not'.
Auld Reekie:	slang for Edinburgh.
Baloo:	soldiers' slang for the French town of Bailleul.
Bayonet frog:	device, commonly made from leather, used to attach a bayonet to a soldier's uniform.
Big Bertha:	a type of 16.5-inch howitzer deployed by the German Army.
Bill Adams:	fictional character of an old soldier from the stage monologue 'How Bill Adams Won the Battle of Waterloo'. Adams was famed for talking up his role in uniform.
Blighty:	soldiers' slang term for Great Britain.
Blighty one:	slang for a wound suffered by a soldier which was sufficiently serious to merit being transferred home to Britain without being life threatening.

Boche:	derogatory nickname for a German.
Bully Beef:	canned beef rations.
Chasse guardée:	private hunting reserve.
Combing out:	process of conscription of men working in essential industries.
Coolies:	men of the Chinese Labour Corps recruited by the British and French governments to carry out manual labour in support of the soldiers and help with the clear up after the war.
Crumps:	shellfire.
Devil's Wood:	soldiers' slang for the French wood Delville Wood.
DORA:	Defence of the Realm Act
Douanier:	French customs officer.
DSO:	Distinguished Service Order.
Elephant shelter:	pre-manufactured, corrugated metal shelter used during the war.
Estaminet:	small French café selling alcoholic drinks.
Etaps:	soldiers' slang for the French town of Étaples where a large military hospital was set up.
Feldwebel:	German army rank equivalent to sergeant.
Fiacre:	horse-drawn carriage for hire.
Flying pig:	slang for a British 9.45-inch heavy trench mortar.
Funk hole:	a hole in the side of a trench used by troops as a shelter against enemy fire or as a firing point.
Herberg:	hostel or inn.
Hows:	howitzer shells.
HLI:	Highland Light Infantry.
Isaac Walton:	renowned seventeenth-century writer and angler.
Jerry:	soldiers' slang for the Germans.
Junkers:	German name for the landed nobility and upper classes of Prussian and German society.
Kultur:	disparaging use of German word for culture to describe their way of being.
Limber:	carriage or trailer.
Lousy Wood:	soldiers' slang for the Belgian wood Leuze Wood.
Mairie:	mayoral office in French.
Mars:	ancient Greek god of war.
MC:	Military Cross.
Minenwerfer:	German short-range mortar.
Minnie:	slang for a *minenwerfer*.
Monty-Bong:	soldiers' slang for the French town of Montauban.

Napoo: British soldier's slang from the French *il n'y a plus*, meaning 'none left'.
Nissen hut: prefabricated hut made from sheet metal.
Ocean Villas: soldiers' slang for the French town of Auchonvillers.
PBI: Poor Bloody Infantry.
Pillbox: concrete defensive position built on the battlefield.
Plug Street or Plugstreet: British soldiers' slang for the Belgian town of Ploegsteert.
Poilus: French infantryman.
Pop: soldiers' slang for the Belgian town of Poperinghe.
RAMC: Royal Army Medical Corps.
Red Tabs: British staff officers nicknamed for their bright red shoulder tabs and hat bands.
Redoubt: defensive fortification.
Royal British Legion: body created in 1921 to look after the welfare of First World War veterans.
RSM: regimental sergeant major.
St Barnabas Society: Catholic charity which set up a support network to help veterans on lower incomes to return to France and Belgium.
Signal form: document for sharing official communications.
Silent Cities: phrase coined by the writer Rudyard Kipling to describe the war cemeteries of France and Belgian.
Skindles: popular hotel in Poperinghe, Belgium, named after a hotel in Maidenhead, Buckinghamshire. There was also a Skindles in Ypres.
SRD: supply reserve depot.
Tammy: colloquial for Tam o' Shanter, a traditional Scottish bonnet.
Tattie-masher: slang for a grenade.
Tommy: slang for British soldier, abbreviated version of Tommy Atkins itself a generic name for a soldier thought to date back to the eighteenth century.
Verey lights: flares used for signalling and lighting at night.
Via Dolorosa: Latin for sorrowful road, the route taken by Jesus to his crucifixion in the Bible. Hence a painful journey for soldiers towards death.
Wachtmeister: German rank equivalent to a constable or officer.
Whizz bang: light shell fired from one of the smaller calibre field guns, referring to the sound as the shell came to explode.

White Sheet:	British soldiers' slang for the Belgian town of Wytschaete.
Wipers/Wypers:	British soldiers' slang for the Belgian town of Ypres.
Wound stripe:	stripe worn on the uniform of a soldier injured in the war.
Ypres League:	society formed in 1920 for First World War veterans as a body to share and coordinate remembrance.

Introduction

Throughout the darkest moments of the First World War, there was an enduring faith that one day it would all be over. For the men who served on the Western Front, the yearning for an end to the bloodshed came coupled with the dream of heading home for good. But some looked beyond the return to a life in Blighty, free from the rigours of warfare, to a day when they could venture back to the places where they had lived through such extraordinary times and see what peace looked like in the towns, villages, and countryside where they had known only death, destruction, and the hardships of war. Whether to satisfy a simple curiosity, confront their past, or fulfil some greater need to set eyes again on the communities of the old frontline once ravaged by conflict now free from war's mortal dangers.

During the long years of fighting, the idea that the battlefields would one day return to normal was not lost on the average soldier. The war was only in its third year when John Masefield, later to become Poet Laureate, wrote:

> All wars end; even this war will some day end, and the ruins will be rebuilt and the field full of death will grow food, and all this frontier of trouble will be forgotten.
>
> When the trenches are filled in, and the plough has gone over them, the ground will not long keep the look of war.
>
> One summer with its flowers will cover most of the ruin that man can make, and then these places, from which the driving back of the enemy began, will be hard indeed to trace, even with maps.
>
> It is said that even now in some places the wire has been removed, the explosive salved, the trenches filled, and the ground ploughed with tractors.

> In a few years' time, when this war is a romance in memory, the soldier looking for his battlefield will find his marks gone.

Masefield had seen at first-hand the devastating impact of the fighting while helping to treat casualties at a hospital for the war wounded in France. His book, *The Old Front Line*, was credited with being one of the first guides to the battlefields of the Great War when it was published in 1917.

In these opening words, he acknowledges the truth among those serving on the Western Front that the battlegrounds were already a place of vivid memory for the Allied soldier at a time when a resolution to the conflict was nowhere in sight.

When the armistice did come, on 11 November 1918, there was no delay in the war zone becoming a place for visitors eager to see the scenes of so much recent history. Within days, travel agent Thomas Cook announced its intention to take parties across to the battlefields; this tour industry was to flourish throughout the interwar years with dedicated bureaux set up to cater for the demand, many run by veterans who had such intimate knowledge of the era.

Mass-produced guidebooks had been published by Michelin during the war years and after 1918 they sold in large numbers with photographs of the desolate aftermath of the hostilities and recommended itineraries for visitors serving to fuel the interest.

For the curious, a trip to France and Belgium was a chance to see for themselves those places which had become household names back home during the four years of fighting. For the families of soldiers killed during the Great War, it was the first opportunity for most to visit the cemeteries, memorials, and hallowed spots where their loved ones gave their lives.

Alongside the grieving relatives and tourist crowds were the men who had served on the frontline and witnessed at first-hand the bloodiest conflict in history. For the veterans, the end of the war granted the possibility to revisit the places where they had fought, to relive their experiences and remember those they had lined up alongside and lost.

During the war, it was not unusual to see reference in letters sent home by the soldiers to thoughts of going back one day when peace returned to Europe, often with a vow to show loved ones those places where they had lived through such cataclysmic events. As early as December 1914, Capt. Maurice Edward Mascall, of the Royal Garrison Artillery, in a letter to his fiancée, Esmee, describing the events of the famous Christmas truce on the Western Front, expressed just such a desire to take her to the battlefields once peace was restored. He wrote:

> I think we must come here one day, you and I, and I will show you all the places where I have lived and slept and been generally uncomfortable.

> We will wait, though, until the place has been rebuilt and the birds come back to the woods.
>
> At present there are no birds of any of sort, and practically no sign of animal life at all, and a horrible sort of silence reigns, broken only by the crack of rifles and the usual signs appertaining to soldiery in large numbers. Lucky, lucky England that doesn't know what war is!

Some may have expressed such thoughts merely as a way of escaping momentarily to a life beyond the grim toil of daily warfare, but for many former soldiers, such hopes crystallised into a desire that would eventually take them overseas again.

The first journeys across the Channel were perilous adventures, with roads and railways still suffering from the aftermath of war, while the countryside was strewn with the dangers of unexploded shells and abandoned ordnance. As work got under way to reconstruct those stricken areas of France and Belgium around the frontline, and the red tape associated with travel relaxed, so it became both easier and safer for veterans to go back.

Regimental associations and organisations like St Barnabas Society, and the newly formed Royal British Legion and Ypres League, arranged regular trips for former servicemen and their families, often to coincide with the unveiling of a new memorial or the anniversary of a significant moment in the war. Awaiting them was a growing infrastructure of accommodation, transport, cafés, and museums, despite the very real dangers still to be found in what was designated the red zone.

Some veterans were content to join organised tours; others, with a more personal or offbeat itinerary in mind, could employ the services of a personal guide with a car, while it was not unusual to see old soldiers cycling the lanes of Flanders alone or tramping the fields on foot.

Such was the numbers of travellers heading over the Channel that just one year after the conflict ended, the writer Rudyard Kipling made a high-profile appeal for those visiting the battlefields to show due reverence to the war dead. Kipling had been a founding member of the Imperial War Graves Commission in 1917, two years after his eighteen-year-old son, John, was killed at the Battle of Loos. Writing in *The Times* in December 1919, he said of the Western Front:

> A number of people from all parts of the world are visiting and there is every sign that an immense number may be expected next year to visit the French and Flanders fronts and the cemeteries behind.
>
> A proportion of these visitors will be relatives or next of kin to the dead whose pilgrimages will be made with heavy hearts, but very many

> others will be drawn by curiosity and a natural interest in historical ground.
>
> But that ground, it should be remembered, is also holy—consecrated in every part by the freely offered lives of men, and for that reason not to be overrun with levity.
>
> It is inevitable that the handling of such multitudes of sightseers must be managed on ordinary tourist lines; so it rests with the individual tourist to have respect for the spirit that lies upon all that land of desolation and to walk through it with reverence. It is said that there is a tendency among some visitors to forget this obligation.
>
> Nothing would be gained by giving specific instances of what, after all, is more in the nature of unthinking carelessness than any intentional disrespect; but the Imperial War Graves Commission have asked me to express our most earnest hope that all who visit the battle areas will bear in mind that, at every step, they are in the presence of those dead through the merits of whose sacrifice they enjoy their present life and whatever measure of freedom is theirs today.

It is most unlikely Kipling's message was aimed at the ex-serviceman heading back to the old frontline, but it illustrates the environment in which returning veterans may find themselves back on foreign soil.

If tourism was shaping the memory of the war for visitors, then the drive to rebuild the scarred communities meant many former soldiers found what one general dubbed 'the vandal hand of peace' was moving quickly to wipe away the world they knew. And with the ever-present threat of death and injury the veterans had been so used to no longer looming over them, places of previous notoriety took on a new perspective in peacetime. As one returning ex-soldier wrote in 1931:

> Thiepval Ridge cost the lives of thousands of Englishmen. If you revisit the site you wonder how a hill of such small dimensions should have been the scene of such a terrible conflict.
>
> I know a man who went back to Thiepval, certain that he would be able to find the place where he had endured hardships for weeks on end. All he found was a field of beetroots.

As the devastation cleared, and there was less to see of the war itself, the acts of pilgrimage too changed with the unveiling of memorials and creation of new and ever-expanding war cemeteries for the dead being given up by the battlefields every day, all providing further incentive for the ex-serviceman heading back.

Across the two decades after the war's end, the numbers of people travelling to the Western Front went through peaks and troughs, but old soldiers were still making the journey right up until the outbreak of the Second World War in 1939. Indeed, some battle-weary men who, when the guns fell silent in 1918, had no desire to cross the Channel again found their feelings change with the passing of the years. As Maj. Charles Emil Salvesen, of the Royal Garrison Artillery, wrote in *The Ypres Times* in October 1935:

> When the Battery left the Salient in May, 1918, after 17 months unrelieved strenuous fighting, it heaved a great sight of relief. Not one member wanted to see the blasted place again.
>
> Yet, in 1935, when the project was mooted for a visit to our old positions—and alas the graves of our dead—the response was instant and eager.

While most paid homage to lost comrades, time was often spent tracking down former billets or the *estaminets* where they once enjoyed respite from hostilities, and hunting for the campsites, trenches, dug-outs, and other familiar landmarks from their days in combat. Some even sought out those locals who had stayed put during the war years and played such an important role in the lives of Allied soldiers. What greeted the veterans as they retraced their steps through old haunts spanned the emotions from mournful to disillusionment, from those who found solace to bitterness and anger, and from reverence to moments of great surprise and comfort as they confronted the past and the reality of a world in recovery. As one former soldier wrote in 1925 of a journey back to the Belgian town of Ypres, which had been almost destroyed by the fighting:

> The new Ypres baffles the imagination of anyone who saw the dry bones of the place in all the ghastly wreckage of the war.
>
> You may look in vain now for the former terrors of the town—the tottering asylum which never fell, the crazy, shell-gashed water tower, and the narrow death trap of the Menin gate. There is no litter of shattered glass and tiles, no heaps of splintered woodwork and tumbled masonry, no stench of corruption anywhere.
>
> The war—was there a war? It must have been long ago. And Ypres, the stronghold of the Salient? A fable, you would say, that exists in military histories, unbelievable, absurd.
>
> You cannot believe that you ever lived in its cellars, with their comforting disarray of purloined mattresses, signal forms, smears of candle-grease, cartoons from *Le Rire*, and pictures of vivacious ladies

> from *La Vie Parisienne*. Strange things have happened to Ypres since then.
>
> It was only when after midnight the town at last was deserted, and I wandered back to my hotel, that I found in the paved stones and the curve of a road something which had seemed irretrievably lost.
>
> I was conscious of a sense of desolation—of the atmosphere which hangs about streets after a great procession has passed.

For many, there was a great importance attached to pilgrimages as simple acts of commemoration and remembrance for fallen comrades and with that a desire to ensure their sacrifice was not forgotten.

In 1936, the novelist Ralph Hale Mottram, himself a wartime lieutenant, wrote:

> Our War, the War that seems the special possession of those of us who are growing middle aged, is being turned by time and change into something fabulous, misunderstood and made romantic by distance, as it recedes into the Past.

Mottram made several return journeys to the Western Front in the 1920s and 1930s and wrote extensively of his experiences. His report from the Royal British Legion's Grand Pilgrimage to the Menin Gate in August 1928 is among fifty personal accounts featured in this collection, spanning every one of the interwar years as we join those who were there to witness the First World War on a poignant journey back to the Western Front.

1

1919

It is summer, and it is peace. Now is the time to go 'on a pilgrimage', and the loan of a coveted motor makes all things possible. Before we are 'dispersed', 'disembodied', or 'demobilised', let us have one more look at those grim fields which we used to approach with unutterable aversion, and only saw through a swiftly raised periscope, with a wholesome respect in our beating hearts for Brother Boche, 100 yards away.

Was it only a year ago? Is it all an evil dream? In this warm, seductive sunshine, the war seems far, far away—a chapter of ancient history which no one has any wish to recall. The illusion grows stronger as we sweep along the familiar roads once crowded with the amazing traffic of the war; now empty, and quiet, and lonely, as they run between the trim and tidy fields. Scarcely a khaki uniform is to be seen.

The villages are as sleepy as a village should be. What do the villagers think of it all? I suspect there are not a few sore hearts among those girls on the doorsteps watching us somewhat wistfully as we glide swiftly by. The whole village is watching us. Only a few short months ago they accepted us as part of their normal life, and while they always received us marvellously well, it was only natural that they should sometimes wish we were gone, and they were back again to the old quiet, humdrum village ways.

Well, it has come at last. The war is finished, and the armies are melting away. The whole countryside is rapidly assuming its normal aspect. But things are not as the villagers expected them to be. Tommy has gone, and has left behind him a vast, sincere, unmistakable regret. That is what these long, kindly looks from the doorstep and the arrested plough mean. And it is good to think that the ancestral feud between France and Britain is buried for ever, and that there are tender memories to seal a genuine alliance of hearts.

St Omer is now almost as sleepy as an English cathedral town—as sleepy as when the exiled Stuarts held their court down there in the monastery, and Jacobites from England and Scotland listlessly walked its streets waiting to strike a blow for Prince Charlie.

What a change from the hustling days of 1915, when St Omer was GHQ. Then, the streets blazed with 'red tabs', British generals seemed as numerous as subalterns, and every now and then you rubbed shoulders with a man whose name will live in history.

There, at that gateway, stood Field Marshal French's Lancers, guarding their chief. There is the modest house where Lord Roberts closed his glorious career, 'within the sound of the guns'. St Omer is once more as it was, but it has added to its traditions a romantic page from the record of the Great War.

Out into the shimmering fields once more there is scarcely a trace of the war left in the back areas. The untidy litter of the camps is gone. The improvised tracks across the fields are disappearing. How swiftly Mother Nature plied her healing art. But beyond Cassel the first scars of the battlefields are visible. A long irregular line scrawled across the green fields, and piles of rusty wire by the wayside, and curious round depressions in the ruddy, newly ploughed fields, show that the trenches and the shell holes are being filled in, and will soon be obliterated by the miracles of the spring.

But close by the roadside, just clear of the ditch, is a little wooden cross all awry. Stop, get out, salute, for a brave man lies there—of the innumerable host of our glorious dead, he lies nearest to the sea. And this is the inscription: 'To an unknown British soldier, October 1914'. So, he lost even his name for the cause; and somewhere beyond the seas there are doubtless some aching hearts hungering for the lad who has been 'missing' all these years, whose fate will never be known.

Ah, well, he sleeps sound enough there by the wayside, and the grass is growing green over him, and the birds are singing above him in the blue, and the cause he died for, lives, and the world is free. On the Other Side, he, I am sure, has no regrets. Let those who are left be content likewise. *Dulce et decorum est pro patria mori.*

But now that the ravages of war begin to multiply. There are gaping breaches, and ugly shell holes filled with green slime; but how quickly the all-conquering plough is soothing the sorrow of the tortured soil. Here and there in the cultivated fields there are rough patches left. Live shells are buried there, and it will take an expert to remove them.

The ploughman is becoming wary. He knows of many ugly episodes. In a moment his share may touch a live bomb, which will blow him and his team to atoms. But he ploughs on unconcernedly, as indifferent to casualties in his queer, loose peasant's garb as when he was clad in 'horizon blue'. Peace has its heroes as well as war.

A few kilometres further on, the limit of achievement possible in a few months is reached. The outposts of cultivated soil are pushing gallantly into the wilderness, but the wilderness gains in extent.

Soon there are only isolated strips of upturned soil beside broken and ruinous cottages patched with wood and canvas, where the returning peasants are bravely attempting to reconstruct the old homes, from which they were so rudely ejected.

Even these cease as we reach the line, where not a single habitable house remains. The road is excellent, for many thousands of German prisoners have been employed to good purpose in repairing the wanton destruction of battle, and along these roads the returning tide of life will continue to flow. But it will take a long time.

Each village that we pass is more ruinous than the last. When we come to Méteren we reach the abomination of destruction. For Méteren was in the Boche lines. It was the limit of his advance in the terrible days of 1918. And Méteren is 'napoo'.

Not a stone of this pretty little town has escaped the havoc of war. Not a habitable house remains. The very foundations have been blown out of the yawning soil. It is as if an avenging hurricane had swept over it and blasted it with fire.

And mark this! As we crossed No Man's Land the aspect of the battlefield changed. The shell holes were more frequent—they lay almost lip-to-lip. But that was not all. The holes themselves were bigger, deeper, monstrous caverns rents of raw red earth singed with fire.

And the explanation is this—that we had suddenly passed from the zone where the German shells fell to that which received the deluge of British shells when we began the stern work which finished at Mons on November 11, 1918.

Let the munition workers at home mark that, and read on these churned fields how they helped to win the war. For it was British guns that destroyed Méteren and Bailleul, and there is no more complete destruction in France.

We spared the French and Belgian towns within the German lines as a matter of course, and the German forces enjoyed an advantage denied to us in the possession of these sanctuaries. But at a critical stage of the battle Méteren and Bailleul—from which all civilians had fled—were packed with German troops prepared to launch an offensive, and it was of urgent military importance that this offensive should be checked.

Accordingly, a concentrated fire of massed guns was suddenly poured upon these doomed towns, and upon the packed German troops within them, and we did the grim work so thoroughly that neither Arras nor Armentières nor Ypres nor Lens can show such an appalling example of the destructive power of modern artillery.

The Germans may be 'thorough', but when the Britisher puts his back into it he can be as 'thorough' as the Germans at need. Little wonder that the Boche morale gave way under that pitiless, amazing avalanche of high explosive shells. We suffered sorely in the early days of the war from lack of ammunition, but we paid the score with interest in the closing days.

The Boche must have had a rotten time all along the line while Haig was delivering the hammer blows which British industry enabled him to do. That was what won the war—weight of material, hurled by men who had endured with patience too sublime for words until the people at home woke up and supplied them with the tools they needed to finish the job. There, on that arena of inconceivable havoc, is the material evidence of the spirit that won the war.

How Bailleul—poor old 'Baloo'—has suffered. Fire has rained on it from heaven, like as upon Sodom and Gomorrah. In the blazing sunshine the raw ruins looked unspeakably ghastly. And the unmistakable odour of mortality told of tragedies they concealed. Standing there in the Grande Place it was difficult even to distinguish the sites of the stately edifices that gave such dignity to a very noble and spacious square.

The Town Hall, the church, the tall warehouses, and taverns have disappeared—of some not even the pounded fragments remain, for they have been blown out of the soil and scattered to the four winds of heaven.

How familiar and friendly 'old Baloo' used to be in 1915 on those days of respite when one rode out of the beastly salient to lay in stores of 'comforts' for the men. Where are all the old friends on whom one practised the first limping essays in French, who were always so helpful and friendly, who week-by-week grew into old acquaintances.

Just there lived the little maiden of 10, who never forgave me, but called me a 'monsieur merchant' to the end of the chapter, because I said incautiously but truthfully that her eyes were grey when the Irish doctor with a touch of blarney had previously declared them to be blue.

Where is she now? Her pretty home is a heap of irreparable ruin. And, by the way, there on that strip of broken pavement is the very spot where I condescendingly returned the salute of a merry young subaltern with a noticeable row of ribbons on his tunic.

'Do you know who that is?' asked my friend. 'No, but the face is familiar; he seems to have seen something by the "herbaceous border" on his breast.'

'That,' said my friend, 'is the Prince of Wales.'

And we turned and looked with interest at the boy who was showing so Royal a spirit—though he was a 'sair thocht' to distinguished generals in those days. 'I wouldn't mind so much,' said one of them, 'if he came by a "Blighty", or even got scuppered, for that is everyone's luck, but think what it would mean if the Boche roped him in—in my line.'

Ah, well it was awkward, no doubt, but Tommy will not forget that this future King persisted in sharing all danger with him and shirked no hardship or discomfort in 'doing his bit' and the British empire knows that when he comes to the throne—there will be a man there who has proved himself worthy to fill his father's place. It may be heresy in these democratic days, but there must be something in heredity after all.

Gangs of German prisoners and Chinese coolies (curious combination; the oldest and the most brand new '*Kultur*' in the world; which would you choose?) were working busily in the inextricable chaos driving roads along what were once streets—a dangerous game, as the numbers in the local hospital show.

Live shells and bombs are perilous things to come across in heaps of debris. And many ugly things come to light of which one must not speak. And, here and there, you meet little groups of sad faced people visiting for the first time what was once their home.

My friend saw an aged couple sit down by a hospitable War Department lorry in the street where they used to live. All their worldly possessions were in a little wooden box, but they had evidently been very well-to-do.

The poor old woman looked wildly round, and when her eyes fell upon the place where her home had stood she flung her arms about her husband's neck and sobbed as if her heart would break. And that human anguish (which is partly what war means) has been wantonly imposed upon hundreds of thousands of homes along the battle line.

How can justice be done if Germany does not atone for the misery she has caused? She cannot give back the dead, but at least she must be compelled to restore to the living the years which the canker worm hath eaten. Let justice be done though the Boche should whine! When he has paid for all the material damage he has done his debt to injured France and Belgium will still be immeasurable.

No one who has seen the stricken battle towns and villages, and contrasted them with sunny, prosperous, uninjured Germany, can understand how anyone can be so wrong headed as to require less than the uttermost recompense from those who are responsible for the war.

Talk of forgiveness! It is the sufferers—France and Belgium—who alone have the right to forgive. The spectators—and by reasons of her inviolate seas Britain is happily but as one of the spectators, notwithstanding her aching wounds—must see to it that justice is done.

Let us get out of this quarry and sepulchre which was once Bailleul. It is difficult to strike the right turning in this hideous confusion, though the way was once familiar enough, and the services of the once ubiquitous Military Police have to be requisitioned to discover the road to Ypres.

The huge asylum that was a visible landmark is riddled—like a sieve. The aerodrome beyond the asylum is ploughed deep by the plunging shells. We are now on the virgin battlefield, strewn with all the debris of the great agony.

The Chinese Salvage Corps has not yet come this way. It will be long before their grim job is finished. Pick up those three bayonets that lie side-by-side, still fixed in the twisted rifle barrels. One is British—strong and workmanlike; one is Boche, thick, clumsy, but powerful; one is French—'*La Rosalie*', long, slender, and deadly, but broken at the point.

They will be significant souvenirs, for there has been wild work here, where British and French charged shoulder-to-shoulder against the German line. Helmets riddled with shrapnel are everywhere—boots, haversacks, belts, rifles, broken wheels, bits of machine guns, rags of all description.

But look where you step. Bombs are strewn on the ground, and a touch may unlock the lever. And that tempting helmet—look carefully underneath it; it may be a booby trap, though I suspect the Boche who left it had other things to think of than reprisals at this particular point of carnage.

What a ghastly country it is now—that was once so sweet and smiling in beautiful summer days in 1915—like Kent with its rich hop gardens. That blackened strip of moor in the dip, with broken stumps of trees, is 'Plug Street'. These white smears on the convulsed soil are all that is left of Neuve Eglise and Dranoutre.

But what is that huge mound of raw earth smeared with yellow ochre stains that looks for all the world like a gigantic shale heap? Can it be Kemmel, that was the very image of Corstorphine Hill with its soft contours and trailing woods?

Kemmel it is, naked to the living rock, without a trace of vegetation, devastated by high explosives and stained with the fumes of poison gas. We held Kemmel against tremendous odds for nearly four years, and then lost it in a night, and it seemed as though Ypres was lost, for Kemmel dominates the Ypres salient as Corstorphine Hill dominates the plain of west Edinburgh.

But the tide of battle flowed no further. In a few weeks we were back on Kemmel, and the salient was saved, and in the interval, we had poured a deluge of fire and gas by day and by night upon its conspicuous slopes that made observation by the Germans precarious and almost impossible, and made of Kemmel Hill itself the ruin that we see.

At the dip of the road that ascends to the saddle between Kemmel and Mont Rouge we cross the frontier between France and Belgium. To the junction on the French side the road is macadamised; in Belgium it is pavé, venerable pavé at that, for it has been torn by shells, and has as yet been only hastily patched.

We go cautiously along the extended track of ruin that once was Locre. That mound of conical dust, with a curious pillar of masonry rising beside it, is all that is left of its stately, dignified church.

The cemetery beside it is indescribable—an appalling scene of incongruous devastation—for war has neither pity nor mercy nor reverence for the most human or the most sacred of things. Somewhere there Willie Redmond rests, for here he found a soldier's death.

Ah, if Ireland had but followed the example of one of the noblest of her sons. But the curse of Meroz rests on Erin, and history will tell with sorrow and shame how, in the day of the world's agony, she thought only of self (Sinn Féin) and made the great refusal.

Swinging round to the right beyond Locre we come to Hyde Park Corner, where the three main roads meet on the saddle between Kemmel and Mont Rouge, with the ugly bare pimple of the Scherpenberg, that was once a lovely clump of wood, staring down shamelessly upon the wan roads, so unfamiliarly empty and silent.

What a contrast to the dim summer nights of long ago, when the imperturbable Military Police stood in the middle of the endless stream of traffic making for Reningelst, or Vlamertinge, or Dickebusch, while the sinister shells went whining overhead, and the shrapnel burst with a vicious clatter, searching for the convoys, and the columns cowering in the shelter of the leafy trees, that gave at least the comfortable illusion of protection.

We are now in the famous salient, and down in the haze are the ruined towers of Ypres. Beautiful exceedingly is that wide landscape, shimmering under the summer sun, but the tang of blood is in the air, and tears are not far away.

For there is no other stretch of the battlefield from Switzerland to the sea—not even Verdun—which has witnessed an agony comparable to that endured in the Ypres salient. The crown of palms is well interlaced with cypress.

But we are not making for Ypres, meanwhile, but for Reningelst, to find a grave. We know that it is in the military cemetery there, but in the hurry of the morning the map references were forgotten, and it is not a hopeful quest.

The graves lie thick 'as leaves in Vallambrosa' in the salient. Reningelst that was practically intact in 1915 is scarred and riven now. That is a souvenir of the loss of Kemmel. But here is the cemetery—a neat blackboard marks the entrance, and we stop to pay our reverent tribute to the memory of brave men.

A footpath runs hard by a sluggish stream of clear water, green with cress, to a raised plateau of dry ground surrounded by trees scarcely touched by the withering shrapnel. And there they rest—the brave who died so greatly. What a forest of crosses, and each stands for a heart-stirring tale of derring-do and a desolate home far away. How closely set together they stand—it takes but little to cover a brave man at the last.

But where among all these crowded graves is the one we came to seek? Let the psychologist explain this. Numb with the long, intense, and varied emotion of the day, I walked aimlessly and without effort of thought through the interminable graves, as if led by an invisible hand, and stopped, and seemed to wake to consciousness as I read the very name I came to find.

And I remembered old experiments in thought reading, and wondered was it only an accident, or was there really some directing mind which brought me just there, and arrested me at the very spot I had scarcely hoped to find.

Ah, well they rest there in peace—in sweet and lasting peace till the Great Reveille comes. Let the sorrowful hearts at home be fully persuaded of this, that all that reverence and tender care can devise to do honour to the last resting place of our glorious dead is being done.

The cemeteries will be enclosed with a bold plain wall, and each grave will be marked with its memorial stone. A tall, massive cross will throw the shadow of its wide arms across the green sward proclaiming the victorious sacrifice and the deathless Hope.

And closing in the vista of the central pathway will stand the great Altar Stone of Remembrance, bearing on the face of it in strong bold lettering the noble and worthy epitaph—Their Name Liveth For Evermore.

And, there, the birds will sing their sweet requiem, with hope in the heart of it; and the trees will bud, and shed their leaves, while the generations come and go; and the gentle river will glide in long liquid lapses hard by the place of their rest. 'After life's fitful fever they sleep well'. It is peace.

'Honour, honour, honour'.

'Eternal Honour to the Brave'.

With hearts softened and cleansed by sweet remembrance we left our dead and took the *Via Dolorosa* from Reningelst to Ypres. God in heaven, how many brave men have trodden that way to find a grave. There they lie by the roadside—a solitary cross here—a little group of two or three there—buried where they fell in the lurid confusion of the night.

Ah, the piquancy of memory as one recalls the scenes when the words of deathless Hope were whispered at the dead of night, 'with the lantern dimly burning'.

A halt by the wayside gave a welcome opportunity to turn in to a little cemetery where many a gallant Scot is at rest; and I read on the cross before me, 'Private J B, 1st Gordon Highlanders'. Ah, I remember. A grey day, with low clouds, and we had brought the pipes to sound the coronach.

As we moved slowly to the wail of an old lament, that recalled, there on the plain of Ypres, the Braes of Lochaber, a hundred men came running out of the dug-outs by the roadside, and fell into line, and followed us reverently and formed a guard of honour by the grave.

They were a company or Argyll and Sutherland Highlanders just arrived from home. The service had only begun when the loud drone of an aeroplane emerging from the clouds overhead arrested attention, and the black crosses on the wing were unpleasantly visible.

A sharp order to scatter sent every man to cover, for no group of men was safe from the searching shells directed by those spying eyes. There is the very tree against which I flattened myself and wished it were more substantial—it is only a stump now.

And the shrapnel, I see, has swept poor JB's grave, for the cross is perforated. Perhaps that was done, two nights afterwards, when the English padre found a soldier's grave beside the comrade he had come to bury. It was eerie amid such scenes and incidents to think it might be one's own fate to fill that open grave, ready and waiting for a tenant still in the fullness of life.

At the crossroads there flashes out of the stored chambers of memory a vignette of a very different character. It was a dark October night, and three divisions were on the move—horse, foot, and guns—all making for different directions through that central road. What a chance for the Boche gunners if they had only known it, but the friendly cloud of night baulked them of their prey.

Though the confusion seemed inextricable, the lines moved with wonderful speed under the skilful direction of the traffic sergeants. But at the corner stood a hospitable *estaminet*, now only a mound of bricks. It was crowded with men, and a flood of light streamed from the open door, and behind the counter a smiling girl was busily serving glasses of beer to very thirsty men.

Out in the street the passing column rested, and looked wistfully at the door, but it was not their luck to leave the ranks. And I see by the lamplight a perspiring Tommy, in full field equipment, resting on his rifle, and looking round at his mate, as he says—'I say, Bill, it just does your heart good to look at it!'

'Move on,' cried the sergeant, and the humourist shouldered his rifle and passed out of the yellow lamplight into the night. Cheerful, obedient, invincible Tommy!

How the forest of crosses has grown in Brandhoek since gallant Colonel James Clark, of Edinburgh, was laid there. But the padre understands, for he can recall days when from early morning till late at night he buried the dead till all feeling died out under the numbing routine of duty. Grim work.

And here is Vlamertinge Church—though only a ragged shell remains—with the cemetery beside it. On such another shining day as this Norman Stewart, of the Royal Scots, found there a soldier's grave.

As the pipes went wailing by, a little, wizened old woman rose, like the Witch of Endor, from one of the cellars and followed us, gathering the wildflowers by the roadside as she went; and when the service was ended and The Last Post sounded, she came timidly to the graveside and strewed her flowers upon the dead for an unknown mother far away.

Perhaps she, too, knew Mary's sorrow; at least she understood in her ruined home what is meant by 'the honours of war'.

Round Vlamertinge corner the white road runs straight into Ypres between fields of green grass. It ran between rows of tall houses in 1915. But the street has been blown to atoms long ago; we used to watch the German 'crumps' falling regularly every day as if they had been fired by clockwork.

So complete has been their work that not a vestige of the street remains. The debris has been removed to serve as metal for the roads, and now the green sward covers the site were scores of comfortable homes stood only five years ago.

Nearby here the children used to sell cigarettes and chocolate to passing soldiers, running laughing into the cover of the dug-outs when the glittering shrapnel burst with a vicious clatter overhead—as if it were a shower of rain.

But, now, even these amazing children are gone, and the desolation is complete. Trees are uprooted, broken, twisted, only stumps, with all the bark pulled off them, remain. Right and left of the roadway the shell holes lie lip-to-lip—a tumbled, festering wilderness of rank green grass and slimy pools.

And there, staring wildly over the gaunt and ghastly landscape, are the ruined towers of Ypres. It is the abomination of desolation. And this is what '*Kultur*' has given to the world.

In one terrible night a bombardment of massed guns which had found the range set the town on fire, mutilated without pity the historic edifices, and slew hundreds of men, women, and children. It was evident that Ypres was doomed by the unspeakable Hun, and that night there streamed out of the western gate the saddest procession that mortal eyes ever saw.

More than 10,000 people—the old man with but a day to live, the mother with her infant born an hour ago, young and old, rich and poor; with the roaring flames and the crashing shells behind them they streamed out into the night towards Vlamertinge and Poperinghe—homeless, ruined, many of them grievously injured, all of them rooted out in a moment without warning from the place which was theirs, and flung to the mercy of the soldier, seeking shelter where they could find it, and a crust of bread from the passers-by. Such is war!

In a cottage behind our lines a gentle lady, with two girls of 10 and 12 years, found a livelihood by brewing coffee for our men. Her husband was killed, her house was burned, their flourishing business vanished, the property in which they had invested their savings was destroyed.

She was homeless, penniless, and a widow, and she had begged the hospitality of a relative on a Flemish farm, but the wretched miser charged her rent for the room she occupied.

It was with grim satisfaction that one observed that the avenging shells had reached that unhospitable house and taught its owner effectually the necessity of human sympathy. The worst of war is not destruction, and wounds, and death, but the ugly human nature it so often brings into the revealing, accusing light. But thank God there is another side.

Soon there were no civilians in Ypres, for the Boche set methodically to work to destroy the whole town without mercy. He pounded the Cathedral and the Cloth Hall till they have ceased to be even picturesque ruins.

There is nothing of the 'imploring beauty of decay' about these gaunt masses of masonry. They are rare and ugly, like the debris of a quarry. But the Boche did not achieve his purpose. He did not drive the British from Ypres. They burrowed like rabbits into the ramparts and the cellars of destroyed houses. They even used its torn and littered streets by night for their transport.

And though there is not a stone of its dreadful streets but has been drenched with the blood of brave men, they stayed there till the end—till the thunder of the guns rolled eastward, died into silence, and the shells fell no more, and Ypres—or at least the site of it—was free.

No German has set a foot within its ramparts except as a prisoner of war. Ypres is the symbol of British endurance, and tenacity, and invincible will. Not a habitable house remains. It is a waste of irreparable ruin. But the sunlight of victory shines on it today. *Laus Deo*!

It is a singular sensation to drive out through the main gate, where men used to go at dead of night in constant imminent peril of their lives. And the deadly crossroads known as 'Hellfire Corner', where God knows how many thousands have met their fate, are wan and eerie under the glaring sunlight. For four years no man dared to stand where we stand now.

There is the crumbling communication trench where they pressed on in haste, or huddled together in fear, while high explosives deafened and blinded them, and the shrapnel fell like rain. Note how Hellfire Corner is the focus of the curving rim of crest a mile away.

A board by the roadside is marked Hooge, and across the road is a forest of crosses, and the gate bears the script 'Hooge Military Cemetery'. It is the only trace of the village that once stood here. Not a stone remains.

There by the wayside is the yawning crater where there was wild work on that June night in 1915, when 400 Boches went skywards, and before the debris fell to earth the British had leaped the chasm, and held it against the bitterest assaults. That protruding mass of masonry is all that is left of the stables of the *château* where the British and German lines were only five yards apart. The *château* is gone.

Look northwards across Bellewaerde Lake to T Wood and southwards Zouave Wood and Sanctuary Wood to Hill 60 and the Bluff, and then at the churned mound of raw earth known as Stirling Castle, and remember that men have died there by the hundred thousand. The miracle is that any survived.

What a landscape! It is like a chart of the craters on the moon. No words can describe the hideous desolation. Not a tree remains; not a yard of soil has remained undisturbed.

Millions upon millions of shell holes filled with green shining water, and an inconceivable litter everywhere—stranded tanks, broken wheels, rifles, rags, barbed wire, live bombs—and rats, long, lean and ugly, scampering over the fetid mounds.

Will this land ever be put to wholesome uses again? Look hard, and remember that Germany must pay. The marvel is that men kept their reason in this Gehenna. Yet here they lived up to the waist in water in the awful winters, grilled by the hot sun in the not less terrible summers, always with deadly, incessant fighting taking its daily, hourly toll of human lives.

Yet here they lived stoically, and jousted in the jaws of death. It was just there that a Jock, reading from a scrap of newspaper, announced that Italy had come into the war, and slapped his thigh as he cried, 'Man, it's just great! There'll be ice cream barras frae here tae Wypers'. (In those days the legend ran that the historic pronunciation of 'Wypers' was derived from a most distinguished general, and that it was the measure of his mastery of the French language!).

Let us get up to the German trenches that are dug deep on the rim of the ridge. There is the whole salient at our feet—spread out like a map—every field and hedge, and village, and road, under direct observation. If we are to build a monument to the men who saved Britain in the Great War, this is the site for it.

Here let us build a Cairn of Remembrance which will mark to all time the scene of the greatest epic in the history of our race. For it is here alone that one can understand what human nature is capable of enduring under the miraculous spell of grand ideals.

Visits to the devastated areas are not joy rides. They are stern educational pilgrimages. Before the grim realities of war are obliterated by the merciful wizardry of Nature, and the patient cooperation of human industry, it were well that as many men of public influence as possible should see with their own eyes what the horrors of war mean.

Only those who have seen can understand the magnitude of the crime against civilisation of which Germany was guilty when she launched her legions upon an unsuspecting world.

And those who have seen must tell, with a tongue of fire or a pen dipped in righteous wrath as the case may be, the things that they have seen—lest the people should forget, and again be taken unawares.

It was because of a strong conviction that there is need to tell the story that it was a peculiar and congenial privilege to conduct such live wires as the ministers of St Giles and the New North through scenes which have brought mingled sorrow and pride to innumerable Scottish homes.

A long swift run brought us to Ypres in the light of a sunset of memorable splendour. The western sky was ablaze with diffused scarlet, and a full moon looked over the torn crest of Hill 60. Beautiful exceedingly was the martyred city.

The splintered towers and the jagged masses of masonry threw long and deep shadows across the great square. Silhouetted against the flaming sky the gaunt fragments of once stately buildings seemed like the skeleton of a dead city. Not a soul was to be scene. Not a sound broke the uncanny stillness. It was peace.

The vivid afterglow lay bright upon the battlefield as we swept through the Menin Gate, and paused for a moment at Hellfire Corner to give time for the thronging memories of that Aceldama to surge through heart and brain.

Down in the hollows of Zonnebeke and Zillebeke the shadows were gathering fast, and a thin blue haze veiled Sanctuary Wood and Zouave Wood like a shroud; but the curving crest was bathed in light from the wan ridge of Passchendaele to Kemmel, far in the south, changing momentarily, as we watched it, from amethyst and ultramarine.

The silence was awful—there is no other word. No sound of 'streams inaudible by day' broke the stillness—no cry of beast or bird—no laughter of happy children—no echo of the sweet domestic activities of the evening hour.

We were in a dead world—like Dante's landscape of Hell. But all of a sudden from some PW camp far down in the valley there came the poignant penetrating note of a violin like a whisper from another world, and it seemed as if the wings of 'an exceedingly great multitude' were winnowing the shining air behind that invisible barrier that lies between Life and Death.

Another pause by the great crater at Hooge where Briton and Boche—only five yards apart—wrestled in the death grip for four long years till the weaker grew stronger, and prevailed—for so it was decreed.

Deep, deep are the thoughts of the men to whom it fell to prove in that cockpit of the war that Right is Might. Great is Truth, but when proclaimed by the spoken or the written word it does not always prevail.

There are occasions when its invincible strength must be demonstrated by the way of the Cross, and Hooge is one of those sacred places of Humanity where the will of God has been manifested through suffering that the nations may know themselves to be but men. But let us get away from the brooding thoughts and exchange a cheery greeting with the old coachman of the *château*.

He is the first to come back to this desolate wilderness, and there he is, smoking an evening pipe at the door of his wooden shanty on the very lip of the crater. He is glad to talk for a little with friendly folk, and he will point out to you the foundations of his stable and coach house protruding through the soil, and tell you the hair-raising tales of 1914 when the battle raged first over the ridge, while French and Haig pored over their maps in the great hall of the *château*, as the first act in the drama of Ypres began.

The stately *château* is no more—the very masonry has been blown to the four winds, and the site of it is indistinguishable from the rest of this tortured soil. The beautiful gardens have vanished. Of the long umbrageous avenues only a few blackened stumps mark their location.

Fields, copses, cottages—all the elements of a beautiful and opulent landscape, such as you may see outside the battle-zone, have been totally erased, and as far as the eye can reach there is nothing but churned pock-marked soil, with pools of green slime in the festering shell holes – of life the only sign is the rats! Myriads of them!

Long, lean, and ugly they go scurrying along the broken duckboards, and dive into the holes like frightened rabbits. I ask the old man if he is not afraid to live all alone in that appalling wilderness. He smiles grimly and puts his hand in his pocket and draws out a loaded revolver.

He has come to stay in this no man's land of civilisation well knowing the risks. But it was his home, and better times will come. He is the pioneer, and he means to stay. All honour to him, and those who will follow him to repair the waste places and transform the wilderness once more into fertile smiling fields.

The red glow of evening is dying swiftly in the west as we breast the crest of the ridge and look back over the darkening salient bisected by the long white ribbon of the Menin Road. The full moon rides gloriously in a cloudless sky as we glide down across the scene of the first Battle of Ypres through Gheluvelt to Gheluwe.

There are many German cemeteries to right and left of the road. The heavy wooden crosses flash out of the moonlight as we sweep by. These tell their own tale. Before we reach Menin, we are out into a kindly cultivated inhabited country once more. This, too, tells its own tale.

Behind the British lines the towns and villages are destroyed, and the country is wasted as far as modern artillery can range. Behind the German lines the devastation is strictly limited to the immediate battle zone.

There are certain solid advantages in fighting in an enemy's country where the frightfulness of war can be practised without compunction, and the Germans made the fullest use of them. All the more honour to the men who prevailed in spite of an unequalled handicap.

As we entered the interminable suburbs of Lille we noted how thoroughly all bridges and culverts were destroyed by the retreating Germans—so thoroughly that Lille, the Manchester of Northern France, is still comparatively isolated and its commercial renaissance greatly retarded. But the town has suffered little, except in the central area, which was ruthlessly burned by the Germans early in the war.

Though Lille was within the range of our guns we spared it, and the Germans enjoyed the priceless advantage of this great sanctuary right behind their lines. Few people were in the streets, though Lille is known as 'Little Paris', and used to revel in the nocturnal habits of the gay metropolis on the Seine.

But nearly five years of military law administered by the Boches have left their mark, and the streets were empty at an hour when, before the war, they would have been teeming with gay life.

It is not always easy to find a bed in Lille. The Germans looted or commandeered without scruple, and swarms of returning refugees find Lille the nearest point of approach to their desolate homes. But fortune favoured us at the second attempt, and we were ready for an early call on the morrow.

It is extraordinary to note the change that has passed over Lille since the Armistice was signed. I regret to say that I am not the Scottish chaplain who was one of the very first to enter Lille, and who was kissed and cuddled along three miles of streets till he arrived in a helpless state of dilapidated happiness to receive an overwhelming ovation in the Grande Place which would have been more than sufficient for General Birdwood himself, who has been given the proud title of 'the Liberator of Lille'.

But I visited the town at a sufficiently early period to see its wan and desolate war aspect. Great magasins with shattered windows and boarded up, and a pitifully meagre display of goods, gave a curiously woebegone appearance to the spacious streets.

Grass grew in the residential quarters, and even in what used to be busy thoroughfares. The people were white-faced and careworn as if awakened from a long night of troubled sleep. The wine of liberty has revived Lille, and it is today humming with the returning tide of happy vigorous life, though it still awaits the resuscitation of its great industries.

The Germans cleared the factories of all machinery, and what they did not remove they destroyed. It will be long before the Manchester of France is working again at full pressure as before the war, and the destruction of the railroads in all directions has specially affected its recovery.

But an enterprising people is working wonders. The wooden boards have disappeared, and the windows of the splendid shops are glazed, and crammed with every variety of goods. The cafés are open, and doing a roaring trade. The streets are crowded, and the bright faces and gay attire are curiously reminiscent of the Paris Boulevards.

Lille is rapidly coming to its own, though a glance at the local newspapers discloses some anxiety over this hectic prosperity and the delay in re-establishing the vital industries, which are the only solid guarantee of permanent wealth.

As we sweep out through the south-western suburbs of Lille the evidences of war reappear. Rows of streets are gutted and roofless. We are running parallel to the frontline, a few miles in rear of the German trenches. It is a sweltering hot day, with a clear atmosphere, and we pick up as we go along many a famous battlefield.

That gentle eminence—scarcely an eminence—on the right is the Aubers Ridge which we failed to take for lack of ammunition in 1915. Had it fallen we should have taken La Bassée in the rear, and the key of Lille would have been in our hands.

The long dark patch of broken tree stumps on the left of the ridge is the Bois de Buisson better known as Neuve Chapelle Wood. Many a gallant Scot has found a last resting place in its sombre recesses. It was there in the spring of 1915 that the British Army found its feet. I suppose it will be recorded in history as an unsuccessful battle because the main objectives were not attained.

But those of us who were in close touch with the men noted the curious effect produced upon the spirit of the Army; and will always regard Neuve Chapelle as a moral victory which had far reaching results.

All the way from Lille the road rises gently, and as we approach La Bassée, looking down upon Festubert and Givenchy, we note that we are on a raised spur of ground that projects, like a promontory, into the surrounding plain.

It is that position, and the line of the deep canal, that made La Bassée an impregnable fortress in the German lines. But though we never set foot in La Bassée, till the hour of the great advance had sounded, we contrived to make things thoroughly uncomfortable for the defenders during their four years of occupation.

The town is a wilderness of ruin. The cemetery in the heart of the town is one of the ghastliest spots to be seen in France. Shells have ploughed up the graves, shattered the monuments, and worked hideous havoc in what must have been a sweet, sequestered God's acre.

Three women black clad in deep mourning were searching for a grave among the broken monuments. I spoke to them, and learned a pitiful story. It was a mother, accompanied by her two daughters, visiting the burial place of her son.

She and her daughters had fled before the German advance, but her son delayed his escape till it was too late. He was only a boy, but the Germans used him savagely. He refused to work for them, and with a number of others, was set up against a wall and shot without pity.

'Have you any other sons, madam?' I asked sympathetically. 'My only other son was killed in 1915 down there at Neuve Chapelle, within sight of home.' 'Where is your home, madam?' 'There, sir,' and she pointed to a street of inextricable chaos—a heap of pounded rubbish over which wild shrubs were starting to grow.

Both her daughters were married. The husband of one was blind; the husband of the other had lost an eye and a leg. In that grim cemetery it was a tale of unrelieved tragedy that stirred the heart with bitter wrath against the perpetrators of this monstrous wrong.

Ruin, sorrow, and death fall upon the innocent because of the vaulting ambition of a few men far away, and justice will never be satisfied, and the world will never breathe freely till the guilty have atoned for the abominable crime.

From La Bassée to Lens the road leads right across the battlefield of Loos. A wide, gently undulating landscape where the lines of the trenches in the white chalk soil could be followed by the eye for miles—a wilderness of vivid green formed of self-sown crops—and poppies—dense masses of scarlet poppies, like vast splashes of blood upon the stricken field.

The minister of the New North kept crooning to himself, 'and from the ground there blossoms red life, that shall endless be.' Ah, the comma is right. Immortality is not pale spectral existence in Hades. It is 'red life', full blooded life, and the lads who died here know that now.

It was not on a blazing day such as this, but under dismal clouds and against pitiless rain that the Jocks of the 9th and 15th Divisions charged there against the German lines, broke them, and over them on September 25, 1915.

That is the Hohenzollern Redoubt, and Hulloch, and Fosse 8, and Fosse 14, and, down in the hollow, the village of Loos itself. But look how, here as at Ypres, that cruel crest, that lies between us and Lens, dominates the battlefield, and that crest was held in strength by the Germans.

Reverently we looked over that wide green plain with its myriad scarlet poppies and blue cornflowers glowing in the summer sun, for we thought of the Scottish homes for whom this place will be forever sacred.

And look, there on the crumbling crest of the parapet of a trench is a thistle—a Scots thistle, with its sturdy leaves and flaunting purple flowers, glistening in the sun. In spite of Burns we did not 'spare the symbol dear', but reverently transferred a sprig to our pocketbooks 'for sweet remembrance' sake'. Truly they sleep well who died for freedom here—with the Scots thistle blooming on their graves.

In the faraway Hebrides, in the glens and straths, in the villages and cities of Bonnie Scotland, let them not mourn over much for those who fell here at Loos. These men were worthy of their race.

They did not die in vain. Their sacrifice is already blossoming with red life which is giving new hope to the world. It is the Dawn of a New Age, and here is Pisgah where they viewed the land from afar, but were not permitted to enter into it.

And like Moses, too, so many of them rest in unknown sepulchres here at our feet. But what does it matter? They did their stern duty and died greatly in the doing of it, because God took them, and in our hearts 'their name liveth for evermore'.

—SCOTTISH CHAPLAIN, WRITING IN JUNE–JULY 1919.

*

Ypres! Noble, magnificent in its ruins—a name engraved on the hearts of thousands of English men and women; the resting place of dear ones, and the end of many cherished hopes. The object of my journey was to visit the isolated grave of my son, and to try to locate the graves of comrades who fell in the early days of 1915.

Let me at once acknowledge the universal kindness received from every official with whom I came in contact, and their willingness to supply me with all the information at their disposal. With the assistance of the officers of the 68th and 188th Labour Corps I was able to trace the graves of many of the fallen, and to take photographs of the crosses.

The magnitude and importance of the work carried on by these Labour Corps on our battlefields is little known to the man in the street, and it should bring comfort to the hearts of many to know that every effort is being made to trace the bodies and establish the identification of our fallen.

Each Labour Corps consists of a commanding officer (usually a captain), 10 to 20 officers, a chaplain, and 600 to 1,000 men—a formidable command, indeed, for a captain, who acts as his own adjutant and quartermaster.

All the officers, and those of the men whom I saw, are keen on their work. They recognise its importance, and, from my personal knowledge, no body of men more deserve the thanks of the nation.

The area is cut up into sectors; each sector is subdivided; every yard of the ground is closely examined, and upon any indication of a grave search is made, and if a body is recovered it is reverently removed to the nearest cemetery and given burial with military honours.

I was allowed to attend such a service, and the consecration of a cemetery. After the officer in charge of the cemetery had drawn up his company, the chaplain consecrated the ground and then took the burial service, which we all know so well; the bugler sounded the Last Post, and the men returned to their work.

A few months ago this place was the centre of the deadliest struggle history has known; today it is in a position of awful isolation, amidst the desolation and ruin of a once happy and prosperous country.

Another instance of the unfailing efforts of the Labour Corps was the endeavour to trace the remains of an officer buried in my presence in the early months of 1915. Every landmark was wiped out, but the farmer who once occupied the farm where my friend was buried happened to be in the place and was able to point out the size of his farm, now completely gone, even to its foundations.

In this manner I was able, roughly, to locate the position of the grave. These good fellows, six of them, dug for two days, and when I left they had not yet succeeded in their search, but as I was positive the body was there they are continuing the search in their own time until they succeed.

The grave of my own son was easily located. I was present when his body was taken up; with the chaplain; an officer, and a bearer party, we left him on the Frezenberg Ridge in a cemetery on the site of the place where he fell in 1915. These cemeteries are usually 100 yards off the main road, containing generally from 300 to 600 graves, in positions well selected and in ground well kept.

During my stay as a guest of the Officer Commanding 68th Labour Corps, two bereaved women, a mother and a widow, came over, each to find the unknown graves of a son. Hospitality was extended to them with the same kind heart, and every effort will be made to send them back with the knowledge that their boys have been found and laid to rest in 'God's Acre'.

Let me give a word of warning to those intending to make the visit. Keep to the main roads and do not satisfy your curiosity by invading the country; it is dangerous, and there are sights that it is not good to see.

Avoid moving about after dusk; on no account touch or search for loot; unexploded bombs and duds are lying about on every side. Medical men and hospital accommodation are scarce, and the doctors have no time to patch up civilians.

Finally, let me urge on those who have no other reason for visiting the battlefields than that of curiosity to keep away. There is a lot to do and little time to do it in. Let the officials clear, unimpeded, this war-ridden country, and let our dead be reverently placed in their last resting place before the craving of the man in the street to see what has been going on is gratified.

—Field officer, writing in September 1919.

2

1920

On April 13 with three companions I arrived at Amiens on the first stage of a week's trip round the battlefields of northern France and Belgium.

The idea was to visit most of the places which had become familiar during the year of 1915–16, the period above all others when our armies were composed of the men who had joined up in the first rush of enthusiasm at the beginning of the war, when conscription and 'combing out' were unknown and DORA was yet in her infancy.

We were lucky in being provided with a car driven by an English chauffeur who had himself served in France during most of the war.

Directly one landed at Boulogne the flood-tide of memory was let loose and even now it has hardly begun to ebb. At Amiens we saw with regret the damage done in 1918, but were glad to see that the cathedral had been so little hurt.

The whole scene brought up at once pictures of those 'joy-rides' in August and September 1916 when many of the 1/19th were lucky enough to make a pilgrimage there from Brèsle. The next day we started off to visit the Somme country. The first village I sighted was Franvillers, where we spent a week of reorganisation in October 1916.

After that the familiar sights came thick and fast. The fields over which we practised for High Wood, the hills round Brèsle where we did night attacks behind a creeping barrage of drums, and then Albert itself. A few wooden houses and one new brick house are all the habitations in Albert since 1918.

We photographed the ruins of the cathedral and spent some time among the ruins. It was for my companions their first sight of a ruined town and I do not think any of them will forget it.

Before going on I insisted on visiting Aveluy where there were some indications of the camp in which the battalion spent Christmas 1917 and certainly some of the pickets in the horse lines. The village itself is, of course, in ruins.

We then turned back through Albert and made our way past La Boisselle to Contalmaison of which there is nothing visible at all except three steps of the church. From there we went on through the Bazentins.

The machine-gun dugout at the 'circus' which served as HQ after High Wood has gone but a curious shaped tree which I remembered was there. I could not find Col Hamilton's grave, presumably it has been moved.

Over what was Brigade HQ on September 15, 1916 some sort of a house has been erected. We then went on through the utter desolation of these grisly fields to High Wood itself. The undergrowth of broom and small shrubs has mercifully covered much of its ugliness but of the original trees only forty bare poles are still standing.

I found without difficulty the 47th Divisional Memorial Cross, and then came upon the remains of the shelter which served as joint HQ for all the battalions of the brigade. It was a litter of bomb-boxes and bits of timber, but there is no doubt it was the right place.

We wandered about waist-high in the undergrowth gradually finding the trenches, and then I saw some graves outside the wood, and on going over to them I found they were mostly those of officers and men in the regiment.

Captains Henderson, Gauld and Davis; Lieutenants Pleydell-Bouverie, Cooper and Rowson; RSM Ridout, CSM Bolton, Sergeant Deighton, Corporal Toole, Privates Whybrow and Prewer (the latter my own orderly) were some of the many names I saw.

For me it was, I think, the most touching moment of the week. The longer we stayed there the more we became convinced how important a tactical feature the wood presents. The observation in each direction is wonderful.

One of the most interesting parts of our journey all through, to my mind, was to go into the German positions and see how completely they dominated ours in almost every place.

On our return journey that day we visited one of the German 'Big Berthas' near Bray. It is believed to have shelled Amiens, Arras, and Béthune, and was captured eventually by the Australians.

The next day our first objective was Eaucourt L'Abbaye and the Butte de Warlencourt, certainly the scene of one of the most interesting and thrilling situations in which the battalion found itself during the war.

I could not find any graves belonging to the Regiment in the neighbouring cemetery, but here again as at High Wood we were struck at once with the tactical importance of the 'Butte', though in itself it is not a place of any size at all.

From there we went on through Bapaume—a terrible sight of ruin and decay—and eventually crossing the Canal du Nord by a wooden bridge reached Flesquières after skirting Bertincourt, the scene of a certain dinner on December 10, 1917. Flesquières had a personal interest as it was the last spot in which I served with the battalion.

The village appeared capable of being rebuilt more than most of the places in the neighbourhood. We could make out the line of the trench which we held in front of the village in January 1918. Then we went on to our furthest objective, Bourlon Wood.

Time was pressing and rain was falling so we did not go into the wood, but round the left side of it into the village. In spite of its fearful shelling and the gas, the wood looked more like a wood than the woods of the Somme country or Ypres and will probably recover, but there is something grim and menacing in the way it frowns down on all the country round.

We went back in one stage from Bourlon to Amiens which must be one of the widest strips of devastated country. In almost every village there are a few inhabitants living in anything which can be made to look like a dwelling and endeavour to eke out their existence with vegetables, poultry and a cow or two.

But one wonders what joy or happiness can ever come into the lives of these people again. There is no town within reach of many of them. Supply trains are few and far between. There are no schools, churches, or places of entertainment. Education for the children and relaxation for their elders must be non-existent.

The feeling in the minds of all our party on this and every day was that those who lived in peace and safety in England could never know what the war had really meant to France, and that nobody can blame her in any demand which she makes for reparation or future security.

The next day we cut through the back areas having lunch at Doullens and picked up the real track of the war again at Arras. There the Hun seems to have deliberately set himself to destroy the more beautiful parts of the town while leaving the meaner quarters comparatively unhurt, though, of course, suburbs like St Catharine's have suffered badly. Here the work of reconstruction was going on apace, but nothing can replace the noble buildings of ancient Arras.

A remarkable sight was a French fair in full swing with its attendant booths and swing-boats for the children, while the workmen went stolidly on mending the roads and houses beside them. Arras would not be a pleasant place to walk about in at night, the square is full of yawning gaps leading to apparently bottomless pits.

On leaving Arras we could see Moreuil and its familiar church and *château*. I wondered if any of the elegant handiwork of Sergeant Sewell and the pioneers remained. Then we came in for an appalling storm of hail and rain which, however, eventually proved a blessing in disguise. For as we reached Cabaret Rouge the sun came out and the view of Notre Dame de Lorette, with Ablain St Nazaire in the foreground, was wonderful.

We left the car in Souchez just where battalion HQ dugout, near the foot of the ridge, used to be in 1916 and then climbed right up to the craters. I managed to identify our old frontline near the top of 'Robineau' and then we stood on one of the craters—possibly 'New Cut'—and looked right out into the blue.

We could see for miles past Lens and away out towards Douai, and behind us to the Servins and Mont St Eloi. It was a splendid moment to be there and I could have stayed for hours. Some French girls who were on the crater told us they were natives of Souchez and had been deported in 1914, but repatriated in 1916.

All too soon we had to descend the ridge and make our way through Aix-Noulette, past 'Colonel's House', and the quarry where battalion HQ was in July 1916. We could see Bully Grenay and Fosse 10 on our right and the slag heaps of Noeux-les-Mines and Ruchel in front of us.

Eventually we arrived at Béthune which, like Arras, has suffered more in its better quarters than in the poorer districts. The big square has practically no buildings left except the remains of the belfry. With pathetic and unconscious humour the inhabitants had put up noticeboards to announce that such-and-such a shop had 'removed' elsewhere!

Saturday, April 17th was devoted to the Loos district. We started through Philosophe (already busy again) and Vermelles and then skirted the Hohenzollern Redoubt. I did not actually see 'Bart's Alley', but nobody who spent part of Christmas Day 1915 in it is ever likely to forget that health resort.

This part of the country struck us as more depressing than almost any other. It could never have been beautiful, and the scars of war take longer to heal in a chalk soil naturally, while in many places the barbed wire was still standing or at best only raked into heaps.

We then went on into Loos, of which there is little left. We could get a good idea of the topographical aspect of the battle. It takes more than a war to wipe out Hill 70, the Green Crassier and the Double Crassier. The sight of the latter recalled some chilly days in February 1916. Was there not a wonderful plan for pushing a trolley of explosives along the northern arm of the Crassier?

We turned to the left over Hill 70 into Lens itself, a place one had always wondered about and seen perhaps through glasses from the Lorette heights or the Bouvigny Woods. Here was destruction deliberate, naked and unashamed, but at the same time more obvious activity in the work of reparation. In the very centre of the town, on what used to be the principal church, stands a board '*Lens veut renaître*', a typical motto for the unconquerable spirit of northern France.

From Lens we went over the reverse side of the Vimy Ridge, honeycombed with Bosche dugouts, through Roclincourt where there is part of the officer's club still standing and the London Irish transport lines, and then on into Arras for tea.

It was strange to find ourselves the only English people in the café and but for the scarred walls and cracked mirrors it might have been a pre-war scene. That evening we came back through Estrée-Cauchie, passing the camp where 1/19th and 2/19th were able to exchange greetings in July 1916 and then through Ranchicourt and Houchin back to Béthune.

The last two days were to be spent mainly in the Ypres salient, so we set off on April 18th in the direction of Armentières, passing La Bassée, where the 'leave train' still stands on the rails, and the brick-stacks of Cuinchy. Then on past Neuve Chapelle to Armentières and from there across the frontier near Neuve Eglise.

There we made our way to Wytschaete and stood at last on the lip of the Messines ridge and began to realise how every movement on the lower ground must have been visible to German eyes for the greater part of the war. Here, as on the Somme, one could get some idea of the havoc played by modern artillery.

No tree showed signs of life and no two bricks anywhere seemed left upon one another. Then we descended into Ypres passing a light railway which carried civilian passengers along the road east of Château Segard and Swan Château!

Here the aspect of the country had changed so much that it was difficult to get one's bearings except by some such spot as 'Shrapnel Corner' or 'Woodcote House'. The remainder of that day we spent in Ypres—the only spot which seemed spoilt by the genuine 'tripper'.

Here small boys with picture postcards and girls selling chocolate bombarded us with their attentions. The Belgian authorities are doing their best to leave the Cloth Hall and Cathedral in their ruins as a permanent memorial of British heroism.

We spent two nights at Poperinghe in what used to be the Officers' Club, but is now an hotel most excellently managed by the enterprising ladies who own 'Skindles', which name it bears now. The last day of our tour was spent in such places as Boesinghe, St Julien, Zillebeke, and last but not least The Bluff.

Here I found the old tunnels, fallen in it is true, but still easily recognizable. I could stand at the entrance to battalion HQ and almost hear the voice of RSM Trezona sending off ration parties. I am sure the stretcher bearers will grieve to know that there was some rubbish visible in some of the neighbouring shell holes!

Then on up along the 'Wynd' we went, which, at the top, is apparently a natural pond, so no wonder we failed to drain it! At last we stood right on the top of 'A' crater and looked out on all sides at the scarred and battered country beyond.

This was certainly one of the most impressive sights of all. The effects of war upon nature are shown here in all their hideousness, and while we stood there, to make a final scene to carry away in one's mind, some Belgian engineers exploded a dump of shells near Ypres with the dull familiar roar, without which the place would not have seemed real.

I began this article meaning it to be quite short, and my pen has run away with me. My only excuse is that this was, I think, the most interesting week I have ever spent. I would like to urge all old comrades to lose no opportunity of taking their friends, and especially the younger generation, to visit some at any rate of these spots.

It is only by seeing with their own eyes the devastation of France and Belgium that they can ever realise what they have been spared. Then perhaps they may catch something of the spirit of the men who died for them, for surely that unconquerable spirit amongst all the horrors of trench and mine, of shells and gas, is the greatest legacy that they have left to the race.

—Maj. Charles H. Fair DSO 19th Bn, London Rgt, 47th London Division, writing in April 1920.

Fair was a housemaster at Haileybury College, Hertfordshire, and following the outbreak of the war signed up for the Honourable Artillery Company in August 1914. He received a commission the following month and rose through the ranks to major in 1916. He was awarded the DSO the same year and would go on to be mentioned in despatches. After the war, he returned to teaching and served with the Home Guard during the Second World War.

*

I have seen Ypres again. It is being rebuilt, all except the Cloth Hall and the Cathedral. These are to be left just as they were when you last saw them, so that Time may not forget entirely the desecration and Sacrifice of War.

You would hardly recognise the old square through which we hurried past on many a fateful night. All around it wooden cafés and restaurants have sprung up like mushrooms. There is something tawdry and garish in these painted shanties which ill consorts with the tragic solemnity of the ruins.

With a feeling of relief one turns away to read the fine notice which the Burgomaster, R Colaert, has had posted up so that all may see. It reads: 'The Burgomaster and City Council of Ypres urge you to remember that the ground you walk on is hallowed by the sacrifice of 250,000 British officers and men who were killed or wounded in four terrible years of battle endured in the salient of Ypres and whose heroism Belgium can never forget.'

Much work is being done in the clearing away of debris and in the laying of new foundations for the future Ypres. You remember the derelict aspect of the shell torn square by the railway station. That is already transformed into a lawn with beds of roses! The pluck and industry of the Belgians is in fact beyond all praise. Such a spirit as theirs will obliterate the devastations of the Hun in less than 20 years.

I wandered along Cambridge Road thinking of that June morning five years ago. The outlines of the assembly trenches we squeezed into were still recognisable. A few gaunt stumps indicated where Railway Wood had been. But to pick out definite trenches on the Bellewaerde battlefield is no longer possible.

The ground is already half-reclaimed and the young corn grows where Y15 gave us shelter. The lake is dried up. The Château at Hooge is nearly rebuilt! Wherever do you think? Why, on the edge of the Hooge crater, which is now a lovely pond, with bushes planted all round and rustic seats and masses of iris.

Even the top of a concrete dug-out is made to serve as a little pier. Thus had Baron de Winck, by converting the hideous into the beautiful, triumphed over the tragedy which wrecked his home.

Sanctuary Wood, Zouave Wood and Maple Copse were all so completely annihilated that I did not even attempt to trace out any of our old haunts, nor to search for the famous Warrington Avenue. The most distinctive of our old trenches were the Ns, which I could see quite clearly as I motored down from Wytschaete to Kemmel.

Everyone who has a chance should endeavour to visit the battlefields. The cost of a holiday to Ypres is not as expensive as it might appear, because for every pound you get 45 francs or more. You learn many things from such a visit especially if you happened to be knocked out earlier in the war.

You learn, for instance, to appreciate still more the appalling nature of the task which we were up against. If you go to Frezenberg and stand on one of the derelict tanks which lie half-buried in the ground there, your eye, sweeping over the vast Passchendaele battlefield sees line after line of those concrete pill boxes which will remain an everlasting monument to the grit and valour of the British race which overcame them.

Again, you will have the satisfaction of realising in the happy faces of the peasants and of the repatriated Belgians that our sad losses and all the appalling weariness of the war—the aching wound, the painful pack, the bitter nights—have brought peace and joy to thousands and thousands.

And finally, you will see for yourselves that the graves of our comrades are not being neglected, and that though it will take many, many months before the various cemeteries are transformed into beautiful and noble resting places, that work is well in hand and the final results will be worthy of the dead.

There is one criticism, however, that I must make with reference to what we are doing in the way of memorials on the fields of France and Flanders. Wherever one goes one sees Canadian, Australian and American commemorative monuments on the more important battlefields but never an English one. I believe the English ones are in hand, but it is a sad pity that they have been so long delayed.

The French attach the very highest importance to such commemorations, and they themselves have erected in Paris the most glorious commemorative picture that, I suppose, has ever yet been painted. It is at the Pantheon de la Guerre. In this panoramic picture there are no less than 40,000 portraits of the principal people in the allied countries who took part in the war.

There is, of course, our King and the Prince of Wales, Lords Haig and Beatty, Edith Cavell, Captain Fryatt and a host of others. But standing out far and beyond all these, mystic and profound, is the figure of a woman draped in black, instinct with sorrow and courage, kneeling before the Cenotaph to the dead.

—LT-COL. GEORGE ROWLANDSON CROSFIELD CBE DSO, 1/4TH THE PRINCE OF WALES'S VOLUNTEERS (SOUTH LANCASHIRE REGIMENT) TERRITORIAL FORCE, WRITING IN JUNE 1920.

Crosfield was a member of the Territorial Army and after the outbreak of the First World War joined the The Prince of Wales's Volunteers (South Lancashire Regiment) Territorial Force, crossing to France in February 1915 as its second-in-command. He received the DSO 'for conspicuous gallantry and good service' in March 1916 and was promoted to lieutenant-colonel. The same month, he was wounded during an attack on German lines at St Eloi which resulted in his leg being amputated. He went on to be commissioned into the Royal Flying Corps and passed as an observer in early 1918. He was a friend of Earl Haig and after the war Crosfield served as national chairman of the Royal British Legion.

*

A striking feature of the cemeteries in Flanders and France is the enormous number of Yorkshiremen buried there. At New Irish Farm I officiated at the re-burial of a West Riding soldier, who had been found under the debris of the parapet of our old frontline trench near St Jean.

A visit to Bard Cottage Cemetery, near bridge four, on the canal bank, about a mile to the east of Ypres, is of great interest to Yorkshiremen. I began this cemetery myself three years ago one winter's morning by burying three men under fire, and by a strange coincidence I see it again almost completed, and it is now under my charge.

In one corner lies the grave of a well-known Wesleyan chaplain killed in action on April 10, 1917. I saw many graves representing battalions our city and country are justly proud of—7th Battalion West Riding Regiment, 1/5th York and Lancs, 7th York and Lancs, 1/4th King's Own Yorkshire Light Infantry, 21st West Yorks, 4th Duke of Wellington's West Riding Regiment. Artillery Wood, Pilckem Ridge, Poelcappelle all have their quota.

I was much interested in Polygon Butt and Wood cemeteries. At the Butt the Australians have erected a fine monument in the shape of a pillar approached by a triumphal way, with steps and ornamental walls. It is a landmark for many miles around.

Standing on the Butt you can see Ypres, and what seems like a rolling sea of old trenches, earthworks, pill-boxes, and shell holes. There is nothing like it in the world, a monument for generations to gaze at standing erect in the centre of the greatest battlefield in history, keeping watch over the thousands of our men sleeping there.

A little distance away is the Wood Cemetery, and there near a battered and almost obliterated village cemetery stands a gaunt cross of wood, just two huge trees formed in the shape of a cross. It is even more impressive than the monument of stone, and to it is still nailed a board with a pointing finger bearing the legend, 'To battalion headquarters'.

Almost under the shadow of this great cross in a weary land can be seen a little white wooden cross to the memory of the brave Hallamshire Major of the 5th York and Lancs killed on March 8, 1918, and to the right and left are the graves of many men who came from the Sheffield district.

—Revd George Kendall OBE, senior forces chaplain, writing in June 1920.

Kendall headed to France in 1915 to serve as an army chaplain and that summer was with the 12th Division at the Battle of Loos. In 1916, he survived a gas attack at the Battle of the Somme. After the end of the war, Kendall returned to France and Belgium to oversee the exhumations of the war dead and the provision of new war grave cemeteries. It was in this capacity that he was charged with finding, exhuming, and preparing the bodies from which the 'Unknown Warrior' was chosen for reinterment in Westminster Abbey. The major whose grave is referred to by Kendall was Maj. Charles Frederick Willis.

*

For anyone who spent any reasonable time at all in France during the war to revisit the old spots and dream about battles fought and won is certain to bring great disappointment, because the old spots, as such, no longer exist.

One of the wonders of the post war period has been the way in which the battlefield areas in both France and Belgium have been recovered from the havoc of war. With a few exceptions, in distinctly localised battle areas, such as Ypres or the Somme, all the trenches are filled in and untraceable. Even on Passchendaele one sees men and women busy ploughing the land.

The credit for this wonderful recovery is, of course, entirely due to the French and Belgian tradesmen and peasantry. On all sides, instead of clamouring for an eight-hour day, the workmen were putting in from 14 hours to 16 hours a day, and even then complaining that the hours are too short.

Complete towns were in course of erection, with whole families working at almost break-neck speed. We watched one house being erected near Ypres, on which were working grandfather, grandmother, father, mother and the grandchildren.

Trades unionism appears to have been thrown entirely overboard in both Belgium and France for we saw almost as many women helping in the building of houses as men, and the children also doing their share.

On every side were seen brick kilns, in fact, every field that was not growing corn or vegetables was being excavated to make bricks. The French houses are being built in a much more substantial and permanent form than the Belgian.

Most of the new Belgian homes are erected in skeleton form of wooden beams, and filled in with brick four and a half inches thick. One really good Fleetwood wind would demolish the whole building.

In France, however, as I have said, the houses are being built much more substantially. Building land in towns and in the villages is being sold with the promise of the indemnity for the damage done to it by the war, if and when the Germans pay up.

Thus you buy a pile of bricks, which once was a home, as though it were a house, on the understanding that you can claim for the house when the Germans see fit to pay their indemnity.

One was very surprised to see at Givenchy, on what was the site of the old frontline trenches, a small compact village, including a school and town hall. Both the French and Belgians appear to be far too busy reconstructing to worry over labour or other troubles.

At Bully Grenay, a mining village near Lens, I was quite surprised to be recognised by an old fellow prisoner of war.

This old comrade is a French miner, and had been traveling home to Bully Grenay in another compartment of the same train that I was in. Getting out at his destination, and walking along the platform, he caught sight of me looking out of the carriage window. In true French fashion he saluted me as though I was his long-lost brother.

As I did not recognise this very affectionate Frenchman dressed in his Sunday best, one can imagine my surprise at his behaviour. At last, he said, 'Were you not a prisoner of war?'

'Yes,' I replied. 'Did not I serve you as batman at Heidelberg?' he next asked.

Then, looking hard at him, I did recognise him. By this time everyone, as is the way in France, was taking the keenest interest in the pantomime in which I was one of the principal figures.

My good comrade was just rushing off to fetch his wife and children and all his friends to be formally introduced, when the whistle blew, and the train steamed out of the station, and the last I saw of him he was haranguing a crowd of admirers and explaining in a high key who and what I was.

—Revd Leslie Napier Forse, chaplain Loyal North Lancashire Rgt, writing in October 1920.

Forse was chaplain of the 4th Bn Loyals until his capture by the Germans on 9 April 1918 during the Battle of Estaires. A Cambridge graduate, he had been engaged on the battlefield with his batman and a regimental doctor during a five-hour bombardment when a group of Germans appeared from dense fog and took the three of them prisoner and they were taken to be held at Heidelberg. The former curate of Fleetwood Parish Church and South Shore Parish Church, Blackpool, he was repatriated the day before the war ended in November 1918. Forse returned to the battlefields in France with Major Arthur Houghton MC to investigate plans for a memorial for the 4th Bn, of the Loyals.

3

1921

Ruin everywhere. Heaps of crumbling brickwork to show where once houses stood; masses of rotting timber and twisted fragments of rusted iron; irregular lines of trenches across fields of weeds, pitted with gaping holes and littered with the rubbish of war; here and there the skeleton of a horse, a lonely grave or so, a track of broken duckboards, a discarded rifle, a shattered tank—the Somme country today is very much as we left it in 1918.

Rain was falling when we arrived at Albert—a rain soft and gentle as a woman's tears. It seemed as if all the mothers who once lived in Picardy were mourning their lost sons and vanished homes.

We were the only two to leave the train at Albert, and the porter seemed surprised to see us. A few of the inhabitants have returned to the town, a café has been erected, some temporary shelters have been built, there are a score of workmen repairing the road and filling in the shell-holes in the pavements—the porter could not understand why anyone should leave the sybaritic pleasures of Paris to see such things as these. I did not satisfy his curiosity.

Memories. That broken wall is all that is left of our billet where we rested before going up into the trenches on the morning in July that saw the opening of the Somme battles; here, behind the mount that represents the Cathedral, is the site of the little shop kept by a kindly Frenchwoman. She was killed on the night of the big raid during the March retreat. In one of those cellars some of the best pals a man ever had died violent deaths. We found their graves up on the Bapaume road.

There will be roses blooming again in Picardy this summer. Cuttings from English rose trees have been planted round the sides of the cemeteries near Fricourt, by the lake at Ovillers, and round the roadside, one close to the crater at La Boisselle. Already the buds are showing.

A black collie dog attached himself to us as we were walking along the track that leads to Artillery Road. There was a collar round his neck, and on it were these words—'Mascot of the 10th Fusiliers'. One of ours. We took him with us to Mouquet Farm.

An optimistic farmer has ploughed up the corner where we had Kay Dump and the track has disappeared, but that collie turned off into the fields at the exact place where we always turned off. He must have accompanied the Fusiliers scores of times into the line to have known the way so well.

Many of the trenches between Mouquet Farm and Thiepval have been filled in, but nothing is growing on the land. Perhaps high explosives and millions of gas shells have so poisoned the ground that crops cannot live in it.

Thiepval itself has been swept up and used to fill in the holes in the road. Only a notice board indicates where the village stood, but not even two bricks are left to give a clue to the exact site. There are only 33 stumps of trees remaining in Thiepval Wood. I counted them. All are dead.

We walked to Aveluy and returned to Albert by the road that runs past the old baths. There is another large cemetery where the long range guns used to be hidden. In none of the Somme cemeteries did we see any of the headstones which the Graves Commissioners propose erecting.

As the train left the station, on its way back to Paris, Kitty stood up and looked out on those poor battered homes and pitiful wooden crosses. Then she burst into tears.

—Sapper Frank Heathcote Briant, Royal Engineers, writing in May 1921.

After the war, Heathcote Briant worked as a writer.

*

Three years of my war service were spent in the Somme country—long enough to learn to hate every track, every trench, and every dug-out. No one cheered louder than I when that November day came and the last gun fired its last shell. I detested every yard of the old trenchland.

Yet I have returned to those poor shattered acres and have made my home in the midst of them. And I believe that I am beginning to love them—just a little. I am a battlefield guide.

My headquarters is the heap of crumbling brickwork that once was Albert. A few of the inhabitants have returned; temporary shelters have been erected; we boast three hotels; we have a wooden shed we call our railway station.

Some of my clients ask to be taken for a general tour, but the majority seek only particular graves. The former listen eagerly to my yarns; the latter wish but to be guided to the cemeteries and then left alone with their dead.

Battlefield cemeteries in the Somme country are neat and well-kept. They are bordered with English roses and planted with flowers from the homeland. The white crosses of wood are still in place, for the authorities have not yet sent out the stone head pieces recommended by the Imperial Graves Commission. It is nearly three years now since Armistice—I hope someone has not blundered.

On some of the graves I have planted seedlings sent out to me by parents who could not afford to undertake the journey. London Pride is their favourite flower.

Visitors are stupefied when they see the frightful havoc caused by high explosives, 'I never realised that it was so terrible as this.'

I take them up past the great mine crater at La Boisselle, over the shell-pitted fields to Thiepval, and show them the blackened rubble and twisted metal that once was pretty Picardy cottages, the scattered graves in old time gardens, the splintered stumps that represent a wood, the broken tanks at Mouquet, Trônes Wood with its monolith to the memory of the men of the 18th Division who died violent deaths for the possession of this tiny copse, and the iron gate swinging in the wind by the roadside. I tell them that it is all that is left of the hamlet of Montauban.

The Somme lands remain very much as we left them back in 1918. The men of the parties bite hard on their pipes and swear softly to themselves; the women break down in tears.

Melancholy work? I think not. Day after day I am telling the story of how the boys of Britain died that the world might be free.

—SOLDIER, WRITING IN AUGUST 1921.

*

There is something about your childhood days that lures you. Something calls you from the past, and you have to go. Charlie Chaplin had to come back and see Kennington not because Kennington is so glorious, but because he lived and struggled there once upon a time.

I, in my small way, longed to go back to the scenes in France and Flanders, where I romped about in the mud, and where, on bright summer days, I watched the shells flying overhead. I had to go back to Plugstreet Wood.

I have just come back, and (I fancy also like Charlie Chaplin and his Kennington) I was slightly disappointed. Time glosses over things, removes defects and irritations, and leaves just a slightly untruthful halo of pleasing memory.

For instance, I found myself bursting to go back and see the spot where my colonel said to me, 'Bairnsfather, if you don't want to come to the battle with us, say so; you'll find a whisky and soda in my dug-out, and cigars in that shell-hole by the fire bucket.'

I also so clearly remembered a sergeant major saying to a friend of mine (a ration party private), 'Let me carry these sheets of corrugated iron for you, old man.'

It was all these little touching memories that finally overcame me and forced me to leave for a tour of the battlefields. But there was also one other great magnet. I had always had an ever present desire to return and see the exact spot where, in 1914, I took to the mud, and where in a few weeks' time I drew my very first war picture.

It is perhaps difficult for anyone who reads this to realise how much the lure of this question was to me. I longed to find the exact spot, and stand alone there, in darkness and rain pondering on the past, the present and all that happened in between.

To stand and contemplate what was at the start a hopeless outlook; to meditate upon the acres of pictures I have since evolved, the host of episodes and adventures; to brood upon the fact that, as a damp and cheap second lieutenant, I sat congealed in mud, and somehow thought out the phrase, 'If you knows of a better, 'ole go to it' (which I have never heard the last of since, and which a few years after I was to hear in Alberta and Arizona, from London to San Francisco, from Wigan to Sydney)—this, I say, was my greatest desire.

I determined that I would go back, like a murderer to the scene of his crime, and stand among the surroundings which saw the birth of Old Bill. Once there I knew of many little places I wished to see besides, all connected with some happy boyish episode in the dim and soothing past.

The place, for instance, where I openly defied Newton's law about the apple, and obeyed one provided by a 5.9 instead, thereby temporarily securing my removal to a hospital in England. This was just one of many landmarks.

Anyway, the lure of all this suddenly overcame me, and the week before last I went, and saw, and—the French hotel keepers conquered. The battlefields begin in the lobby of your hotel as you are leaving, but of that anon.

I felt that really to bore down into the depths, and see all I wanted to see, the ordinary system of examining battlefields by train and hired car was useless. Mine was a weird and ardent pilgrimage, which would necessitate time and mysterious byways. So I took my car to Amiens, and launched out from there.

After my 1,000 franc lunch (including tips to all the hotel staff, augmented by some borrowed from a hotel next door), I filled the car up with the world's worst petrol at about 1,000 francs a tin, and set off up the Albert road.

Although I wished to see all the battleline, I felt I could not take proper interest until my solemn pilgrimage to Plugstreet was over. Accordingly I set off up the Albert road, on my way, via Arras, to Armentières.

My first impressions of the one-time war area came at Albert, and the first thing that occurred to me was that if one could only turn on the noise and people the land with draggled, khaki-clad soldiers, everything would look exactly as it did in war.

Rebuilding was at zero. The air, robbed of all danger, was also robbed of all war reality, and I felt that those who visit now, and who were unacquainted with the same spots in war, could never really visualise it.

The difference a large shell exploding anywhere within a hundred yards' radius of your car can make to your imagination is extraordinary.

Albert was a fair sample of a hundred other places of the same size and style, just a gaunt, crumbling wreck, its shaken foundations and yawning, roofless cellars scoffing the would-be rebuilder. I paused but a few minutes, and drove on.

There is no need to describe more than one small portion of the battle area. Describe a hundred square yards, then multiply it by the distance from Ostend to Switzerland, and you have the picture.

Houses in all stages of tottering destruction, cellars, cellars and more cellars, some with bits of house left on them, others black, jagged and half filled with rusty, tortured ironwork in fantastic shapes. In fact, just the same old picture that the war presented in its prime!

Along the broken cobbled roads, through Arras, Lens and La Bassée I went as night came on. On either side the dead and shattered poplar trees and mangled houses. Here and there a pathetic endeavour at rebuilding; and ever too frequent a graveyard, with its long rows of crosses.

Along the roads thousands of miles of rusty barbed wire rolled up into ugly heaps; rusty corrugated and perforated iron; shell cases, floorboards, broken concrete—all the stupid and pathetic relics of that stupid and pathetic thing called war!

As I drove along those dull miserable roads I could not help thinking how painfully ridiculous it all had been, and how terrible. How half the civilised world had elected to sit glaring at the other half across a ploughed field for a number of years, then called it off, and gone home to strikes, penury and unemployment as a result. Darwin may have been right about evolution, but I'm not sure it isn't working backwards.

It was late when I left that one-time horror, La Bassée. It's not much more than a horror to look at now. The broken cobbled roads gave my car more of a vibro-massage than I cared about, but still I persevered.

Late in the evening I was drawing near Armentières. Oh, those long, cobbled, poplar-lined roads! How I could picture the long lines of muddy soldiers, how

I could hear the tramp of feet and rattle of mess tins in the darkness! The wind moaning through the old barbed wire seemed to hum that Angelus from long ago: 'It's a long way to Tipperary; It's a long, long way to go.'

And everywhere the singers lie beneath their wooden crosses, just labelled and catalogued by a grateful though unregenerated world....

For a student of shell-shocked architecture I recommend Armentières as a useful study. Things are not quite so flattened out there as, say, in Ypres and yet there is not a thing that isn't broken. A wild disorder of crumbling brick and twisted iron, blackened by smoke and fire.

A few inhabitants creep about among these relics, and call it 'living in Armentières.' Late that night I took a stroll round the town. Among the tall, gloomy buildings in all their various stages of destruction, here and there one finds a mended *estaminet*.

I prowled around the dark streets, and peered in at one of two brightly lighted windows. Just the same dear old *estaminets* that Old Bill loved so well. The fierce-moustached manager, with his pneumatic-looking wife, red wine, beer, and a highly decorated organ playing tune after tune to an assortment of dull-looking visitors. It takes a lot out of an organ to overcome the cracked and battered gloom of Armentières.

I went back to the hotel, had some 150-under-proof beer, and went to bed, looking forward to tomorrow and Plugstreet Wood.

While at the hotel I gathered from the assembled few in the bar that one of my embryo drawings could still be discerned on the walls of a farm. In fact, it had become a sort of thing to show tourists who persevered sufficiently into the back of the beyond part of the trenches. I was most elated at this, and more than interested to see the place again.

In 1915 I stayed—or rather was incarcerated—in a farm known as 'La Plus Douve,' and here on many a warlike and humid night I drew rough sketches on the plaster walls. It was in this punctured edifice that I drew 'Where did that one go?'

After breakfast (1,500 francs) I set off up the Plugstreet road. About a mile out of Armentières one crosses the border into Belgium. This apparently simple process happens like this. You drive up the Bizet road, and suddenly become aware of a Chauve-Souris-like soldier, prancing in the middle of it.

You stop, from a mixture of intimidation and curiosity. I leant over the side of the car and gathered that my papers had to be examined, and, in fact, I must allay all suspicion before proceeding further.

I went into the *Douane* and unfolded my papers. I don't understand them very well myself—the official understood them less. I shall never forget the plaintive expression in his eyes as he gazed at them, just like a sheep with toothache. He looked up piteously at me, and seemed to say, 'Do tell me what I do with these, and where I have to sign.'

My heart bled for that Customs official. I showed him where to sign, and told him what suspicious things I had not got with me. His eyes filled with tears of gratitude, as I helped him through his day's work. I left him and resumed my journey.

I was now nearing the site of my very earliest war adventures. I could see ahead the hazy outline of the great Bois de Ploegsteert. It was up this very road that one dark and sticky night in '14 I wandered along with my battalion to take my seat in the alluvial deposits, on behalf of civilisation.

I had my car driven up the slope of the hill to the left of the wood. The old familiar bullet-swept slope, now quite safe, was lying there still and calm under the evening light.

Now came the last stage of the pilgrimage. It was about 500 yards from the top of this slope down among the fields that I would find my Mecca. A poor and furrowed lane ran down in that direction, impossible for motoring.

I got out of the car, told my man to wait, and wandered off with ever-quickening step. Friends of mine had told me frequently that I would never be able to trace out my original landmarks, owing to the subsequent riots that had broken out over the same ground.

Down past the wood, now a prairie of burnt out wooden stumps, down among the low lying fields and ditches, with the speed of Sherlock Holmes following up a clue with his lens, I discovered the site of one dug-out after another.

It was here the Colonel lived, it was there the sergeants lived. Here was where I had to make a machine gun emplacement one night, and here was that awful corner they used to snipe at.

At last I found the spot I had come to see. I looked down into a fast-disappearing slot, now covered with grass. Tangled and rusty barbed wire lay all around. It was here, in 1914, that out of sheer despair I broke out in picture form. This was where, on a rough sheet of paper, I scribbled out an idea; and a hundred yards away, in a hole under the floor of a cottage, I drew the picture in a suitable form to send to a paper.

I turned and went to the cottage, or rather to where the cottage stood. It had entirely disappeared, except for a few bricks. It would require an expert archaeologist to trace out that cottage.

This was the end of my journey. I stood awhile, and pondered. 'Down this very road and to this very spot I came in 1914. How we used to envy those who got shot each night and taken away. Now, here I am in 1921, still alive and just going to have lunch in Messines across No Man's Land.'

No, I couldn't quite conjure it all back. I think if I had got my man to shoot at me with a rifle all the time I was thinking, I might have done better. I turned and left those scenes of my boyhood and wandered back slowly, to lunch, and the road to Ypres.

I had 'lunch' in Messines in a 'rebuilt' *estaminet*. The rebuilding consisted mostly of procuring old corrugated iron left behind in the late trenches, and nailing it all together like a patchwork quilt. A very temporary appearance is thus formed.

Perhaps there is wisdom in the Belgian ideas! Who knows? Can it be that they say to themselves: 'What's the use? We've had Marlborough, Napoleon, Wellington and Hindenburg around here; why rebuild permanently? One of these guys, or another one like them, is sure to come crashing along this way again. In fact, when the next war comes along it's sure to be here.'

The famous Salient made a great name for itself in the war, but it will take History and Time to carve its full meaning and reality on the mind of Humanity. I once was a reluctant but a curious member of a group bent on holding it. I remember my ideas and views then. I know, on my revisit, what I think of it now. My one really big idea about the late war is, 'Why the—the Germans didn't win I don't know.'

I went to the first gas attack at Ypres. My colonel invited me. I think he had received an invitation from his brigadier, who had got a few invitation cards to spare from Divisional Headquarters. I wish I hadn't gone—but I went; and the other day I drove around, looking at the scenes of the escapade.

Geographically speaking, of course, the place was absurd. Heroics superimposed on hereditary dullness saved us. We were far too unimaginative to lose that salient. I remember noticing in the middle of a pouring wet night that we had the most slender arrangements for its welfare. I remember that our attack was about as venomous as a fireworks display.

If I—or any of my friends—had been able to whisper a few things into Ludendorff's ear he could have taken the place easily. If all the lions in an arena intellectually combined to spring simultaneously at their solitary trainer they'd get him, wouldn't they? Well, there you are. The wonderful courage and domination of the British soldier completely baffled the delicatessen-fed 'cannon fodder' of the opposition.

On leaving the Plugstreet area, I drove, via Messines and Locre, into Ypres. It is impossible for anyone who has not lived in wartime in the area known as the Salient to imagine or grasp its horror.

The countless unrecorded and unheard of minor encounters; the night raids; the bombing parties; the desolation; the nauseous atmosphere; the danger and hopelessness; the episodes and adventure; the battles and stories which everywhere soak this tract of land through and through, make me, reading some of the names on the map alone, drift off into a sea of wonderful and painful memory.

My Salient times were comparatively short. I can only guess as what prolonged life—or rather, living death—at Passchendaele or Hooge were like. In a weak moment I agreed to go to a battle at St Julien, and in a very vulgar way they dropped a 5.9 in a place that necessitated my leaving the field.

All I can remember (it isn't much, compared to some people's adventures in the Salient) is that, soaking wet at 3am on a dead-strewn road, heavily shelled, we marched along in time to be decimated at 4am.

This is so feeble and so pleasurable a Salient episode that I almost hesitate to mention it.

Well, anyway, up this very road at Ypres I went the other day. A wild and desolate road! It runs to St Julien, which came in for a severe dose of warfare.

I think they must have had another war (they haven't mentioned it around there lately), or else they've been mighty slow about clearing up the last one. The country looks as wild and messed up as ever it did. The roads are only just possible in a car. One really wants a Ford to go to St Julien.

I persevered, however, and found the site of my last battle. A large and slightly sloping ploughed field, leading down to Pilckem Wood. I looked steadfastly at it, and tried to frighten myself into a real feeling about the war.

No good! It all looks so futile now. Just the ploughed field, with a peasant or two scratching about in it. One or two birds overhead, and a charming sunset! It takes too much out of you to imagine the same scene enveloped in all the horrid past.

Vast crowds of the enemy rushing out of the wood, not one of whom, scarcely, would know what the war was about, and why started, if you stopped and asked him.

Our men rushing forward in the open, and crumpling up under machine gun fire, like tallow candles in a crucible steel furnace. The long lines of dead, the shells, shell-holes and destruction.

Can it be that all this happened to enable people to make money by hiring out cars to people who want to 'Tour the Battlefields?'

I was vibrated off down the road through Wieltje and St Jean, back into Ypres again. This was the road long which my battalion went on the night of April 24, 1915, to take part in the first gas attack, the third battle of Ypres.

I was in the battalion at the time (having failed, since the start of the war, to get a job checking overcoats at Havre). It had been unanimously decided that I must be with my battalion, so I appeared on the morning of the 25th in my comedy sketch entitled 'The Gas Attack.'

I ran about and fired things in all directions, and helped as much as I possibly could to advance the British lines about 35 inches, and subsequently assisted in preventing our line being pushed back 34 inches.

In doing this I met my Waterloo, and in due course was met at Waterloo—or Victoria or Charing Cross, I forget which—and wafted temporarily out of the war.

You can imagine, therefore, with what curious eyes I regarded this horrible little road.... The Salient and its immortal defence was bound up in such humble little tortured roads.

I feel ashamed to mention any part that I took in its holding, when I know all the wonder-deeds of wonder-men who did things there. I lost many, many friends of mine in that Desert of Death. A real understanding of that terrible place only leaves you with shame that you are not represented by the Cenotaph!

With sombre thoughts I returned to Ypres, had lunch, tipped the neighbourhood, and drove back over the border into France from Ypres, via Locre to Bailleul, and thence to St Omer.

I stayed the night in a pub there, and the started for Paris. I felt that a little Paris would do me good after the Salient, and besides, I wanted to give away what money I had left in a really good hotel.

—Capt. Bruce Bairnsfather, 3rd Bn, Royal Warwickshire Rgt, writing in October 1921.

In September 1914, Bairnsfather rejoined the Royal Warwickshires a decade after first serving with the regiment. He was sent to France with a machine gun unit and while on the Western Front Bairnsfather drew sketches of trench life. In 1915, *The Bystander* weekly magazine began publishing his drawings which proved hugely popular both back home and with fellow soldiers on the frontline. In April 1915, he was badly wounded by a shell explosion and transferred back to England for treatment where he was diagnosed with shellshock. Bairnsfather spent the rest of the war in the Intelligence Department on the Home Front. He continued drawing cartoons with his Old Bill character remaining hugely popular and earning him a worldwide reputation.

4

1922

If I had been travelling in the year 922 instead of 1922 I'll warrant I would have made better progress than I have done so far. It is exactly a week since I started out from Todmorden to travel the mere 1,000 miles or so that separated me from Berlin, and I am only 200 miles nearer my destination.

The annoying wait for my British passport, the special journey to Liverpool to secure same, the cross examining, the photographing and all that sort of thing, is nothing compared with what I have experienced in London whilst waiting for the German Consul's visa.

When I first asked for the 'visa' (which is the equivalent of permission from the German Government to enter their country) I was informed that I must first obtain permission from the Berlin police to go there.

This, they told me, might take several days to secure. I telegraphed immediately to the directors of the school in Berlin to which I am going to get this for me. The telegram afterwards cost me five shillings. Four days afterwards I received a reply to the effect that police permission could not be granted in advance.

The Consul, when I passed the letter on to him, calmly informed me that he could not grant me permission to travel to Berlin without police permission. In that ridiculous position I found myself. I could not travel without a 'visa,' and the Berlin police refused to grant permission unless I came for it! Seemed like a stalemate.

The Consul, apparently a very busy man, shrugged his shoulders and advised me to wire again. And that is how the matter stands. I am stranded in London, amusing myself as best I can whilst the Consul and police fight it out between them.

The first few days of waiting I spent with some French friends of mine in Picardy. (A 'visa' is not required for British-born subjects travelling to France, thank goodness!—one worthy achievement at any rate of the Peace conference).

Many ex-soldiers of the then 2nd–6th will remember their old billet at the farm of *Monsieur* Beck-Minne on the road to Trois Rois, near Cassel, where our regiment spent Christmas in 1917. Old *Monsieur*, *Madame*, their daughter Adrienne, and the farm labourers who said their prayers together in the early morning before the day's work began.

I found the farm much the same as when we left it five years ago. *Monsieur* and *Madame* were sat by the fire when I entered. They recognised me at once, and threw their arms round me, kissing me on one cheek and then the other—for we were great friends in the old days, and I have dropped them many a line since.

No, they had not forgotten the little red-haired sergeant who presented them with a watercolour painting of their beloved farm, and signed it after it was finished 'Billy,' 'Christmas, 1917.' It is still hanging in a frame in the large room.

During the whole of my stay there I was treated as an honoured guest, and lavished with good food, red wine and cognac. Instead of sleeping in the barn I was given the guest's bedroom, and was saluted by the farm hands as I passed to and fro. It seems I was the first English ex-soldier to visit them since the war.

I cannot pretend to elaborate here the feelings stirred within me by this little trip to Picardy. The landing at Boulogne, the local train to St Omer, and the journey on foot through the forest of Clairmarais. Every field and farmhouse meant so much to me. All along the dusty road that winds through Coin Perdu and up the hill to the windmills I saw familiar faces.

I entered the old *estaminet* at the sign of '*Entrons ici il pleut la bas*' (Let's go in here, it is raining over there) and rested a while. Further on I reached another familiar little tavern (the sun shines for everybody). It was in this tavern, whilst sipping grenadine, that I heard the first scrap of news from Trois Rois.

Monsieur and *Madame* Beck, my old friends, were in mourning over the recent death of their eldest son. He had died through a disease contracted during the war. Whilst I was with them I tried to comfort them as well as I could; but *Madame* had loved her son very much, and it is hard to forget. I found her in tears several times during my stay.

Now I am back in London, the trip seems already remote. I feel to be in a different world again. The little circle I drew in Picardy, through Boulogne, St Omer, Hazebrouck, and Calais, and the little peeps of a simple French life I have consigned to my treasure house of golden memories.

—Sgt William Holt, 2nd/6th Lancashire Fusiliers, writing in February 1922.

*

A good many men who have almost, but not quite, forgotten their campaigning days and the scenes of battles not so long ago, will have their memories revived by such accounts as they may see of the tour now being made by the King and Queen of Belgium.

Their Majesties will be able only faintly to visualise Ypres as those remember it who saw it in 1916 and 1917. The Belgians are showing even more energy, and less sentimentality, than the French in the work of 'reconstruction'. In the sublime phrase, quite seriously used by an old Territorial Gunner, a very distinguished gentleman who attained the rank of general, 'the vandal hand of peace is destroying the battlefields!'

But though the chaos of the atomic debris of Ypres is being largely sorted out and rearranged, enough of the historic ruins remain to enable the Royal visitors to realise what intensive shellfire can do, if it is kept up for three or four years, night and day.

Most men who arrived on the Western Front found themselves sooner or later in Wipers. They will remember with mixed feelings, which grow pleasanter as time rolls on, the old '*via crucis*' from Poperinghe, through Vlamertinge, past the asylum, with its regular frieze of dead horses, into Ypres. A few thousand British hearts have beaten rather desperately close down on that road at different times!

It abounds in landmarks. There is the Goldfish Château, with its queer old gardens and sculptuary, all suffering more or less from 'Blighty Ones'. A good many gentlemen now pursuing their humdrum avocations in this country have 'bivvied' on those fields across the road, and drawn their densely populated army blanket closer when the whistles sounded the alarm for another Jerry aeroplane raid.

In the latter end of 1917 particularly the road into Ypres was admirably equipped for studying the psychology of mixed shellfire and bomb dropping. Inside Ypres proper their Majesties will view the still gloriously majestic ruins of the Cloth Hall, though here the 'vandal' hand of the restorer is hard at work one hears.

A search of the domestic treasures of ex-service homes in this country might reveal almost enough souvenir tiles taken from the smoking ruins of the old Hall to repave its central aisle.

But nothing can reconstruct the picture presented by the Ypres Square that terrible day the German batteries first opened out upon the doomed city, and the entire population rushed from its evening meal, fleeing down the broad road, with its stately avenue of Flanders poplars in those days, from the wrath that had come. The flight from burning Pompeii cannot have equalled the civilian terrors of that time.

If the Royal tour is reasonably prolonged, under capable direction, the King and Queen will certainly have a look at the famous ramparts where brigade and divisional headquarters had their overpopulated dug-outs, and the sappers slept and smoked in the intervals of deadly occupation up the line, with their hospitable kitchen in a cellar across the shell-holed road and, next door almost, their drying room, a huge ruinous apartment where grim figures, wet through from the saps, sat by a great wood fire that, according to local legend, never went out for four years.

Presumably their Majesties will motor through St Jean, the utterly demolished village just outside Ypres going towards the line, which was our counterpart to the German holding of St Julien, equally a smothered ruin, behind the enemy's lines as they ran when the third battle was begun.

St Jean was once rather a nice little place for a picnic, but it became unhealthy. The writer lay on the mustard-gassed grass by the roadside in St Jean, near the little cemetery where many comrades of the Liverpools rested from their campaigning, one sweltering July afternoon in 1917, waiting for a limber to carry him down the line as a gas patient, and watching the burial fatigue packing our dead into a cart.

St Jean was rather 'hot' in those days, humming with shells and bullets, and smelling like the seven circles of Dante's Inferno rolled into one. It was from St Jean the night wiring parties and other fatigues started up the line, ghostly and silent spectral companies, as seen through the darkness by the faint light of far off Verey lights, keeping open order once Liverpool Street trench was reached.

Farther on along that broken road, swept by the German machine guns, ploughed by occasional shell salvoes, is Wieltje dug-out, probably the most ambitious underground affair of the kind ever attempted by the British engineers.

It held a full brigade before the 1917 stunt, but the men slept in a way that would have made a tinned sardine sick. Its long galleries must by now be completely flooded, because pumping day and night was a necessary fatigue to make Wieltje fit for heroes at any time.

Away in front of Wieltje, past Garden trench and the deep Admiral trench, where a Jerry airman machine gunned my shaving water tin one morning, is the pathetically torn and twisted domain of No Man's Land, across which our boys advanced, each carrying a miniature Woolwich Arsenal of military equipment, through the early dawn mists of July 31 to open the attack on Jerry's reputedly impregnable positions at the start of the Third Battle of Ypres.

The terrain is flower strewn and bespangled with beautiful colour today, but the stricken and splintered tree stumps still stick up, which caused a gallant commander of tanks, when pressed by a certain fiery Divisional General to 'get forward', to inquire pointedly, 'Do you take me for a dammed airman, sir?'

—SOLDIER, WRITING IN MAY 1922.

5

1923

Sometimes, in despondent moments, we talk as if peace with all its burdens were scarcely an improvement on wartime. To an old soldier a Channel crossing is one tonic for such a mood.

Chance had it the other day that I came down from Amiens to Boulogne, and thence crossed to the white cliffs of England, by the same route as I travelled on my first leave from the Front, eight years before to the day. The same way, but what a difference!

The journey from the trenches to the boat, joyous as one was at the prospect of a week in Blighty, was not a wholly pleasing pilgrimage. I see myself, a lance corporal, with all my soldierly gear on my back, chafing at the delays at Boulogne, the smallness of our rations, and the chilling discomfort of the so-called Rest Camp, where we had to spend at least one night.

Our needs were few in those days—something to stay the pangs of hunger, two blankets, and room to lie full length at night—but they were often as unattainable as *pêche melba* in a listening post.

But here I was, after eight years, speeding over the battlefields in comfort in the Loire express, and then, for a modest 10 francs, after a night's sleep lulled by the rhythm of the train, having a breakfast of coffee and rolls, omelette, veal, cold beef, grapes, bananas, and marmalade. How times have changed, thank Heaven!

The greatest contrast of all was on board the Channel boat. In the war years, the boat was as distressing to the rank-and-file traveller as Ellis Island is today. The troops were herded under the decks, no lights were allowed, and you had to wear a lifebelt the whole of the time.

You had the uncertainty of getting home, an uncertainty which rumour magnified. To encourage you there was the story of the boat which crossed tempestuous seas and was actually off the English harbour when she was recalled to France by wireless, with all leave cancelled.

But now, what a jolly, bustling scene it is, when the 'Engadine' is about to leave. There is gay chatter about the crowded decks, and a cheering whiff of luncheon, and the rasping and pause, rasping and pause, spaced out monotonously, of the luggage crane, clawing great loads of bags and trunks into a swinging net, to the dismay of tourists who see their frail suitcases swung from shore to boat, with a force that threatens to smash every bottle of *Eau de Cologne* hidden in them.

As we waited on the sunny deck (for the Paris train was an hour late), it was pleasant to watch the picturesque activities along the Boulogne quay. It was the end of Fish Week, and the ships were all a-flutter with flags.

A triumphal arch of fish barrels decorated the quay, and the open yellow tramcars were rushing crowds of holidaymakers to the seafront. A little book was being sold under the advertisement, 'Boulogne in Wartime, interesting to Britishers.'

I thought of my first crossing, and of the men from my own battalion who were my companions on the journey home. There was dear old 'Pal' Stirton, a butcher in civilian life, and the kindest soul I ever knew in the butchery of war.

In the billets he was ever singing Harry Lauder's songs, in that melancholy, nasal whine affected by the Scottish ploughman. In action he was self-possessed, and tenacious. After that leave we came back together, and he was killed on September 25, in the Battle of Loos.

And now the doings and death of such a man are 'interesting to Britishers.'

Well, thank heaven, they are not yet utterly forgotten, and for many a year to come, returning holidaymakers from the Continent will spare a thought for the legions of the lost as they see the close ranked war graves.

Poor old 'Pal' Stirton! But for you and men like you—dear old soldier comrade—these happy English people in their gay holiday clothes, and with their cameras and alpenstocks and golf bags and tennis racquets, would not be crossing the Channel today, after being received in every part of Europe with the respect due to that monarch of the monetary system, the English pound.

—L/Cpl Andrew Glen, Royal Highlanders, writing in September 1923.

L/Cpl James Christie 'Pal' Stirton served with the 4th Bn, Royal Highlanders.

*

If the survivors of the 8th Norfolks could have assembled at night on the outskirts of Carnoy, not many of them would know, when day came, where they stood. Nor would the men of Suffolk, Essex, Berkshire, and other counties, who served in the 18th Division.

The ground from which their attack on Montauban was launched, and the fields over which it was pressed, seem to have been replaced rather than to have changed.

Before the 18th Division was thrown into the Somme fury it held trenches about Albert, at La Boisselle, Carnoy, and Maricourt, for nearly a year. I went over part of the old line the other day, cycling from Albert to La Boisselle and then to Becourt (where the Norfolk cemetery is) and Carnoy.

Albert, I was told, now has 14,000 inhabitants. Everyone works, but many years will pass before it is a place of comfort again. Most of the population live in huts or patched-up buildings.

The gaunt remains of the cathedral have not been demolished, and hard by a little church has been built. At the apex of its roof is a small replica of the figure of the mother and child that once crowned the cathedral, and that remains a vivid memory to many East Anglians.

There was an open space of grass in Albert when the 18th Division billeted there, lined by trees and girt with stone posts and chains. At one end was the monument of a French soldier. There is no grass there now, and part of the monument has gone; but the posts and chains remain, and the stone support of the monument.

At one end stood a café much used by the Norfolks and Suffolks. The building was obliterated, but another of wood is in its place, and, though you may not recognise him, the old proprietor is still there.

North-east of Albert, where the road, cut by a railway, runs straight to La Boisselle, I saw what might have been the scar of an old redoubt. Running along the right of the road is a chalky ditch, the remains of a communication trench the 8th Norfolks helped to dig seven and a half years ago.

La Boisselle, once a home of craters and trench mortars, and as cruel as any piece of old trench line, is now a cluster of comfortless huts and workshops. Almost touching the road is a mighty crater. Near this spot hundreds of East Anglians have held their breath at the roar of mortars, and the trembling of the mined earth.

The hamlet of Becourt I reached across a new track. I could not get my bearings there at all. I saw the Norfolk cemetery, and the graves of men killed at La Boisselle. But these graves have surely been moved from what we used to know as Becourt cemetery in 1915–16.

Nor could I trace the old *château* where the reserve company used to have its cooker, nor the little wood through which we reached it. Near the cemetery are chalk trenches, half filled in. A little iron-covered dug-out is still there. Jam tins lie outside it, and there is a petrol tin (the Army's water jar) and the case of a trench mortar.

Another empty mortar case, one of the tin can sort, stood upright on a heap of chalk. I wonder if it was put there by a visitor of the 8th Norfolks, a mark of the respect the battalion used to have for the full ones.

Through Fricourt, then past Mametz on the left, and on to Carnoy. I went to the north-east of the village. A cross to the officers and men of the Essex stands by the road. Not far from the cross is a crater, where a heap of concertina wire has been thrown.

Maricourt on the right, Mametz on the left, and a good mile ahead the goal that was well won and well held—Montauban. The silent fields seem to close tightly down on what they once saw.

A train came puffing down the valley behind Carnoy. The tiny railway line is still used. Beyond was the Péronne road. Leafy twigs have sprung from the trunks of tall trees that border it, but the treetops and the few remaining branches are dead. It is the same in the ruined woodlands, though the ground there is now covered in undergrowth.

This was the first battlefield of the 18th Division. Delville Wood, Thiepval, and the others I did not see; nor the billets of Buire or Bray. The craters and the wilted trees will be the last scars of the fields where for 12 months before the Battle of the Somme the 18th Division waited and made ready. The cemeteries, all but Becourt, new to me, are silent gardens now. I saw the graves of many friends.

—Sgt Alex Potter 8th (Service) Bn, Norfolk Regiment, writing in September 1923.

Potter was working in local government when the war broke out and within weeks had volunteered for the army. On the opening day of the Battle of the Somme, he was shot in the leg just minutes before the rest of his battalion went over the top. After the war, he settled in France and worked as a journalist writing for newspapers in the UK. During the Second World War, he was interned by the German Army. This article was written after the first of eleven pilgrimages Potter undertook to the battlefields of the Somme between 1923 and 1939.

6

1924

In appearance it is only a very ordinary road, straight as a die with a border of erect poplar trees accompanying it from start to finish. Probably you would find its exact counterpart a dozen times within a search of a 20-mile radius. Yet to those who soldiered in the Ypres salient—their number must be hundreds of thousands—the road to Poperinghe, or 'Pop' road, is as familiar and as unforgettable as the Strand or Piccadilly.

It is the only main road which leads rearwards from Ypres, and so it became the main artery which pumped an endless stream of men, guns, shells, rations, and a thousand other things into the hungry maw of the salient. All day it slept peacefully in the sunlight, little disturbed by the small parties who brazenly tramped its surface.

But at dusk the road woke up, and by dark it had become a turbid stream of humanity and horses, motors and mules, with a forward current and a rearward current jostling each other in its narrow breadth.

Occasional bursts of shrapnel would stab the darkness and whine amongst the tree branches. A few gaps in the stream of men, a temporary stoppage to drag the injured to the roadside, a little congestion and a deal of swearing, and the stream would roll on as slowly and surely as if nothing had ever happened, until the first streaks of dawn flushed the sky. Such was the 'Pop' road I knew—knew well, every stick and stone, gatepost and tree, so many times had I slogged along its ill-set pavé.

Substantially I found it the same old road I had hankered after. True, it had been re-metalled in places and dozens of unpretentious erected-while-you-wait shacks squatted in the neighbouring fields, but the old familiar landmarks still met me on my tramp and jogged the mind back in an instant, to those stirring days when their advent conveyed more significant meaning.

Presently came Vlamertinghe, new risen from her ruins with workmen putting the finishing touches to the church spire. Adjoining the church is a large military cemetery, the first one to be finally completed. The many thousands of plain headstones, row upon row set in the greenest of close-cropped turf with beds of brilliant and sweet-smelling flowers, give the enclosure a dignity and sacredness which could not be surpassed.

On the road again, past the watering tanks and the large mill which was used as a dressing station until a half-hour's tramp brought me to the straggling village of Brandhoek, once the centre of a dozen or more rest camps snug hid in the thick copses which encircle the place. It seemed strangely silent and deserted now, for my memories were of crowds of khaki, laughter and light and oh! blended warmth and all the comforts of 'home' that really matter.

After the miseries of the trenches this was really 'home.' Here the iron grip of self relaxed and men became civilised beings again for the brief period of their rest. Of necessity the hub of all this social revival was the local *herberg* with the large dancing room and execrable piano.

Even if the heat had not proved so physically insistent, 'old time's sake' would have driven me to its inviting door. The same bare room and crude bar counter, the same battered piano and, miracles never end, the same buxom Marie smiling welcome!

She did not remember me personally—how was that possible when ten million troops had crossed her threshold?—but she knew the regiment and we talked with the happiness that comes with the unexpected meeting of old friends again.

From here to Poperinghe every yard of the countryside brought back old memories with a rush. Tiny cottages where we had bartered 'bully' for hand-made lace or feed of eggs and chips; the lane leading through the hop plantation to our old transport lines (what a row there was when some of those hop poles went for firewood); the short cut across the fields to dodge the 'red caps' when we had visited Pop passless; the tapering archery pole and the railway station at the entrance to the town; the crooked narrow streets with the same old shops and the same splaw-footed inhabitants.

Across the Grande Place—once a fair target for long-distance shooting—to a restaurant where I had celebrated my first leave with a memorable feed of duck and green peas and champagne; I dined there well.

Curiosity must need lead me to the old furniture depository which the Divisional Concert Party had turned into an excellent theatre. Many the night we had forgotten the war in the topical humour and broad farce we had enjoyed there. An enjoyment none the less even when abruptly interrupted by the order 'All lights out' and the German planes high above commenced to drop 'eggs' all over the town. Now it has reverted to its original prosaic use.

What more fitting than I should return to Ypres by railway along the identical line which five years ago we traversed at night, lightless and at snail's pace, with our engine smothered beneath a tarpaulin to hide the tell-tale glare from the fire-box?

—SOLDIER N. F. E., WRITING IN MAY 1924.

*

It is approaching the anniversary of the first big battle fought by the Australians in France, so I decided first to visit Pozieres. What were the chief landmarks in Pozieres in 1916? The concrete pill-box in the village and the shattered windmill alongside the road in the direction of Courcelette.

I found them both. The pill-box nearly overgrown with nettles and weeds, had an inscription in French warning against interference. The windmill was a mound of earth, with portions of trenches in which the nettles were rank. But it was exactly the same shape as when last I saw it, after the capture of the main German line in front of Pozieres, except that its base was then covered with the bodies of dead Germans and Australians.

I went inside the pill-box. Despite the adjacent memorial of the First Division and the warning notice of the French authorities, the villagers of Pozieres had entirely disregarded any sentiment attaching to the pill-box.

The inside appeared to be used as village latrine, and the place was indescribably filthy. The entrance to the dug-out beneath the windmill and the fragment of trench remaining by the windmill were in a similar abhorrent condition. These are the only two remnants of the Pozieres battlefields that remain, but no woman, visiting the death place of husband or son, could enter either the windmill or the pill-box.

Nearly 10,000 Australians were killed at Pozieres. The scene of such intense and costly fighting is naturally sought out by many relatives, but they discover only the disgusting spectacle described.

The state of these places is no reflection on the Australian Graves Section, still working in France. This staff is small in numbers, and is fully occupied in the tedious work of completing the permanent cemeteries. But it might have been thought that the villagers of Pozieres, mostly the original inhabitants who fled from the Germans, would have had a feeling for the memory of men who actually, with rifle and bayonet, recaptured the area.

Among the ancient Hell track from Sausage Gulf to Pozieres, where the military was once concentrated in row after row like shark's teeth, there are scarcely any landmarks left. La Boisselle mine crater, of course, and the chalk pit at Contalmaison, and there is still some lumber at Gordon Dump where weary ghosts of diggers, perhaps, come at midnight for boxes of bombs and tins of water to be carried to the frontline.

Sausage Gulf used to look more like a traditional battlefield than any other part of the line—galloping limber, swiftly-moving ambulances, frenzied horses from some shelled battery, dead soldiers, and a curtain of smoke. Every tree, every telegraph post, smashed by shell-fire.

Today I saw huge red brick, red tiled barns and farms standing where the ancient cookers used to park; and the battlefield consisted of crops of potatoes and rye and clover. With poppies everywhere, of course. There are singular depressions everywhere in crops, indicating shell holes that have not been properly filled in, or maybe a collapsed dug-out which had been buried and forgotten.

I watched a farmer ploughing at Pozieres. The share dragged something out of the ground. It was the web equipment of a British or Australian soldier. The farmer merely disengaged it from the ploughshare and threw it aside, and went on ploughing.

At the same spot on the next furrow the share turned up more stuff—a British rifle, with bayonet fixed but broken off short, a German tin hat, a gas helmet, and other matters. Evidently the complete gear of a British and a German soldier.

The British soldier must almost certainly have been an Australian. I took the relics away with me; but the farmer showed me heaps of stuff which he had ploughed up, and removed from his fields from time-to-time—lengths of barbed wire, water bottles, and a green, mouldy Australian hat.

I saw a remarkable discovery near Pozieres. The Tank Memorial stands alongside the main Albert–Bapaume road. At present a water pipe is being laid from Albert towards Bapaume, and the entrenchment for it has just been dug as far as Pozieres.

The trench is about six feet deep. Exactly in front of the Tank Memorial the evacuators came upon a buried tank. Evidently the monster, after becoming disabled, had turned on its side and sunk deep into the mud.

It is not proposed to excavate it (it having been ascertained that there are no dead inside it), so when the water pipe is laid the tank will be covered up again. An inscription on the Tank Memorial reads, 'Near this spot tanks were first used in 1916.'

—Australian soldier, writing in July 1924.

*

To England the war was summed up by that one little word, Ypres—the Gate of Flanders. Almost every unit that sailed from England found itself at some time or other in that little hell on Earth, and every survivor would add his weight in favour of peace as long as he remembered the name of that sinister town.

The achievement of the people of Belgium in reclaiming so soon the war-wasted lands for agriculture and rebuilding their annihilated farms and villages and cities, was indeed one of Peace's 'renowned victories.'

In 1917 sitting in shell holes with comrades under sheets of tin, we used to amuse ourselves by planning conducted tours of the Salient when the war was over—all except those who roundly declared that they had seen enough of the unmentionable place to last their time.

I took the pilgrimage in earnest some time ago, looked up my old maps and diaries and planned an itinerary. I must visit Hill 60, and all those other beauty spots, Zouave Wood, and Sanctuary Wood. Sanctuary! What a joke? I would take a stroll (without a tin hat) on that nightmare of all highways—the Menin Road, though imagination still boggled at the idea of any living thing 'taking a stroll' on that road.

Then to Dickebusch, where they fired the first round, and on to Vierstraat, where the ammunition lorries caught fire and there was mischief to pay. Then on to Kemmel and up the hill to Wytschaete. Wytschaete, with its memories of the inferno of June 7, 1917, when the mines went up! I would look at all these fond, familiar spots again and put up in Ypres itself in a real hotel with whole walls.

The hotel was there all right, and the tourists. And a cinema. The harvest of barbed wire had been safely gathered in, and the horrible swamps were under cultivation. It was a shock to find the train passing through Ypres, right into No Man's Land.

One felt—and others had confessed to the same feeling—something queer and indefinable about the new Ypres after dark. It seemed peopled by the ghosts of vanished armies. And well it might be!

The Hotel Britannique is a modest wooden erection opposite the Cloth Hall, comfortable, well found, and fitted with electric light, a telephone, and real peacetime waiters. Next morning we started off through the ramparts where the Menin Gate stood (and where a triumphal arch is to be erected to the memory of the British dead) out on to the Menin Road. Queer to see trams and motors running along it.

On to Hellfire Corner. All is peaceful, most peaceful of all the small British cemetery by the roadside, beautifully kept. Turning south I was soon in Zillebeke. Soon! That was the amazing thing about the whole

Salient. You jumped a night's journey in a few minutes, just because you did not have to wait for hours till the strafing of the next crossroads died down.

From Zillebeke across country to Yeomanry Post, the site of a beautiful new farm, and then on to Zouave Wood, but the old battery position takes a bit of locating, for there are no trenches, no duckboards, no dead mules to steer by—only a splendid new road which knew nothing of the war.

Hill 60 still bears traces of trenches and concrete observation posts, but we cannot explore the tunnels, for the entrances have fallen in. On the summit is a small and already mutilated monument to a British division.

In Verbrandenmolen the old haunts are fairly easily located, but gone are the two great mushroom-like structures on the skyline which had to be occupied at any cost. Down the valley to La Chapelle Farm, and here were found almost intact our old shelters of elephant iron and concrete now serving as stabling for '*deux vaches*' and '*deux chevaux*.'

Then we reach Spoil Bank, where the telephone exchange used to be. What a job it was to keep the lines working between there and La Chapelle! Forward to Voormezeele, peaceful enough now, but a death trap then. How well were those crossroads marked down by the enemy's guns.

Hunger and a tram rattle us back to Ypres, and next morning we explore Dickebusch, where I am greatly surprised to find that little remains of the church which we left standing in June 1917, and no trace at all of the farm in which we were billeted.

I had so hoped for a chat with the old lady who did our washing. But the tide of war had ebbed and flowed through the village, and church and farm alike are engulfed. In the military cemetery here we found the graves of the first of our battery to lose their lives. From here we walked to Vierstraat, where traces of our trenches are visible, but where also a prosperous farm is growing again. What marvellous energy these people are displaying!

From Kemmel we had a splendid view of the Flanders battlefield. Here and there are pill boxes in various stages of decay, and the woods that formerly clothed this slope appear to have been wiped out by fire in the last stages of the campaign. From Kemmel we take the tram to Wytschaete. Here things are not quite so advanced.

Building is held up by subsidence due to the collapse of the great German tunnels, some of them 50 feet deep. Wytschaete gives us the only scene reminiscent of the war, for they are blowing up ammunition here. Topping great bursts, and what a day for observation! At the end of the road leading from here to St Eloi we noticed a sign which we Englished as 'Smoking forbidden. Danger of death,' so we took the Vierstraat Road.

We looked in vain for the mine craters, unless that great claypit, where men are making bricks by the thousand, is one. We spend the remainder of our visit wandering about Ypres, noting the building that is going on feverishly everywhere. The Cloth Hall and the Cathedral are muffled to the eyes in scaffolding.

There was a strange fascination about Ypres which gripped one even in the midst of its agonies. I felt it even in the midst of relief at being transferred to the comparatively peaceful Somme in 1917. As we came through St Omer, on the homeward journey we met a young Englishman whose job was breaking down ammunition in Houthulst Forest. We asked him if he were crossing to England that day. No such luck, he said, sadly. It sounded like a mournful echo across the years.

—Lt Samuel Worrall MC, Royal Garrison Artillery, writing in September 1924.

7

1925

From Hill 60 the gaunt ruins of the Cloth Hall and of the Cathedral of Ypres stood out black against the blood red sunset sky. Between the Hill and the crumbling city were fields, where, as the War went on, more and more poppies made splashes of colour like blood amidst the unharvested wheat.

They grew near the dug-outs in the railway embankment near Zillebeke Lake, where you could snatch a hurried bathe on hot summer afternoons before the German shrapnel churned up the water near you and drove you to cover.

Before many months had passed the larch woods became a nightmare, for the trees were splintered and ghastly; but in the fields you could lie amongst the corn and poppies and succeed, for a few brief moments, in escaping from the filth of war.

You forgot the mud, the lack of sleep, the loathsome, unburied remains of gallant, cheerful youngsters who had fallen in the First Battle of Ypres. The drone of shells flying overhead and the boom as they burst among the humble little houses near the Rue de Lille, was almost soothing.

Everything was forgotten but the poppies and the wheat, the busy movement of God's insects amongst the grass stems and the blessed smell of sun warmed earth. If there be anything to be said in favour of war, it is that its degrading horror heightened the enjoyment of those few moments of forgetfulness in Flanders' fields.

When night came, the fields were haunted and accursed. The poppies were trodden under foot by tired, overburdened men on their way to the trenches, by tired overburdened men on their way back to rest for two or three days before they returned to the senseless waiting of war. Men fell in shell holes and over strands of telephone wire.

When someone was hit by a stray bullet the long file of men halted a moment until the stretcher bearers had been summoned, and then tramped on again hardly wondering whether their companion of a few moments before would get back to England and cleanliness or whether his body was destined to form one more pitiful mound in the green ramparts of Ypres.

No time to worry about anything except food and sleep. No time, thank God—for that way lay madness—to ask oneself why there should be this red harvest of keen young men. At the most, one looked vaguely ahead to the time when it would all be over, when there would be peace and decency again.

And then down some narrow communication trench to the miserable dug-outs of the frontline, where star shells, mockingly reminiscent of the November rockets of one's childhood, lit up the shell pitted destruction of the fields of Flanders. At any rate one's children would not have to know all this.

The poppies have lost ground again, for the fields of Flanders are recultivated, and the plough has hidden the shell holes and trenches. Nieuport is still three quarters destroyed and barbed wire still straggles over the sand dunes of Coxyde and La Panne, but the houses on the Grande Place of Furnes are rebuilt, and by the end of 1922 quite half the work of Belgian reconstruction had been done. And done well.

You will find nowhere rows of ugly, little houses, all exactly alike, such as one might expect when rebuilding has to be done in such haste. Outside the Menin Gate of Ypres, for example, is the delightful garden city of Ligy, much on the lines of the garden cities of England, by which, indeed, it was inspired.

Little steep roofed Flemish houses stand peacefully round the central square, the *plaine de jeux*. Between Dixmude and Ypres there are dozens of as pleasant little farms as a man could wish to see. Only the shattered poplars by the roadside recall the past.

And Ypres itself has become a city of dust and new bricks and motor lorries. The Grande Place, of course, remains much as it was at the moment of the Armistice, for the Cloth Hall has been left in majestic ruins as a national monument.

There are two wooden buildings misnamed 'hotels' and a few sellers of postcards and souvenirs, but through half-closed eyes one can call to mind once more the Grande Place of wartime.

In the Rue de Lille I found again the ruins of the church behind which I sheltered when an aeroplane began bombing on my first day 'up the line' and from which I was driven by shame at the sight of a little girl who passed, whistling, up the street when the noise was at its worst. But most of the other streets were unrecognisable.

I left the car at a place we used to call 'Hell's Corner,' just at the level crossing, and set off on my pilgrimage to Hill 60. On my right were the remains of the Railway Dug-outs, with the little pond where everyone used to wash his dirty linen.

Transport Farm, formerly brigade headquarters, was rebuilt, and by the second level crossing was the first British cemetery I had seen. An old man pushed a lawnmower to and fro between the white graves and I stood near the hedge and watched him a while.

The sky was blue, with white puffs of smoke like the bursting shells of 'Archies,' but the hum of the lawnmower recalled to me the playing fields of school, on quiet summer afternoons. Perhaps all the young fellows buried beneath the smooth turf dreamt, too, of schooldays, and were content.

Everywhere new houses had sprung up on the ruins of old ones. Klein Zillebeke was a flourishing village, and the children from Verbrandenmolen were playing near Blauwport Farm where, for the first time in my life, I had been called upon to bury a fellow soldier and a friend. A signpost announced that a little path to the left, in full view of Hill 60, led down to the Larchwood Dug-outs.

Almost unconsciously, I walked along the railway line until I heard a train coming round the bend behind me—what was formerly the only safe way to Hill 60 was now the only dangerous way!

I rambled about on the slopes of the Hill as much as I dared—there were no longer any Germans to snipe at one, but most of the land was ploughed and a farmer stood watching me suspiciously from the doorstep of a new farm built where many a time I have spent all night digging support trenches.

But the trenches and traverses and dug-outs had gone, and only on the odd pieces of uncultivated land were there rusty helmets and cartridge clips and strands of barbed wire.

On the top of the Hill, which had always been in German hands in my days, stands a monument. At its foot were three girls and a man, an ex-officer, who was describing the troubles of 10 years ago.

The girls smoked cigarettes through long cigarette holders and laughed and chatted as though someone were pointing out to them the horses in a paddock. Was it for this that hundreds of men died on Hill 60, were left hanging like ghastly scarecrows on the enemy's wire, lay in helpless agony in No Man's Land?

I stumbled down the slope of the Hill to the quiet of the Larchwood Cemetery, where I recognised only too many names on the tombstones.

For the first time for many months I prayed, prayed that the immense sacrifice had not been made entirely in vain. Away to the west, the sun sank in glory behind the ruined Cloth Hall of 'Wipers'.

—VERNON BARTLETT, WRITING IN MARCH 1925.

Bartlett was twenty years old when war broke out and signed up for the army in August 1914, joining the 1st Battalion, Dorsetshire Regiment, as a lance corporal. In May 1915, Bartlett was hit by splinters on his head, hand, and thigh at Hill 60 and was transported to Rouen by hospital train. Just a few hours later, his battalion was moved closer to the lines to replace a battalion that had been decimated in the first poison gas attack. His battalion met the same fate, and when he returned a week or two later, he found that so many fellow officers had been gassed, wounded, or killed that he was in command of a company. Later that year, he was the only man pulled out alive when his dug-out received a direct hit. He was invalided out of the army soon after and became a journalist for the *Daily Mail*. Having served in the war, Bartlett was selected to interview men who came home wounded from the Western Front. In 1917, he joined the staff of Reuters, which sent him to cover the Paris Peace Conference after the war. He continued to work as a journalist for the rest of his life and served as an MP for twelve years.

*

There were five of us in the car. My companions were the ex-captain, who commanded the second last British camp in France, and has stayed on in France as a civilian; the London ex-sergeant, a Cockney, and proud of it; his wife, and a little niece they had brought out to see her father's grave. We joined up at Albert, that key to the Somme, familiar to every Scottish soldier who served in France.

It was a vastly interesting day for the sergeant, who was seeing the old battleground for the first time since the Armistice. He set out with the detached and slightly ironic manner that marks the Cockney away from home; but gradually that attitude wore off, and he became eager and excited.

As we penetrated into the Somme plain, and he began to recognise the familiar landmarks, the spirit of the old days took possession of him. Old relations were re-established. Although the captain was driving the car, and his services were at our disposal, the Londoner unconsciously dropped into the wartime habit of addressing the superior officer as, 'Sir'.

We ran out first to Mametz, where the grave to be visited was found in one of the trim British cemeteries which dot the landscape in this area. The plain of the Somme rose and fell with its gentle undulations under the sunshine, the fields brown where the ground had been ploughed, the prospect very much the same as I saw it in September 1918, when the Germans had retreated well beyond Péronne, but without the haunting aspect of desolation it wore then.

The red tiled houses of the village met the eye in every direction. The peaceful work of the fields was going forward. On rising ground a few miles away we could see Fricourt and Delville Wood serene in the clear, quiet air.

The sergeant was, at times, a little puzzled. We passed through a bright red brick village, which announced itself as Pozières. To him, and to all the Somme battalions, Pozières was a familiar name, but associated only with an area of brick dust, in the centre of which was a white board with the name 'Pozieres' for the guidance of those who passed that way. To the visitor to the old scenes, who did not realise what the passage of the years implied, the new village might well seem to have sprung up there by magic.

We swung back to Albert, and then south-east to Bray, the congested little village on the left bank of the Somme, which was an Australian divisional headquarters when the Germans were leaving the Somme in 1918. We crossed by one of the new bridges spanning this sedgy part of the river, and, turning off to Chuignes, had a look at the big gun, which the Germans placed in an excavation in a little wood to bombard Amiens and Abbeville.

There is a vacant square in Amiens, extending all the way between two streets, a little distance from the cathedral, and formerly occupied by Amiens' biggest shop. That vacant area is probably a souvenir of the big gun. The municipality of Amiens are thinking of acquiring the ground for an open space. The big gun, with its heavy and elaborate machinery, is rusting where it was left—except that a 12ft length from the end of the barrel has been cut off and erected in Sydney as a war memorial.

From Chuignes we turned north to Cappy, and crossed the Somme to Suzanne, which is practically all rebuilt. A gateway in Suzanne, however, still bears in German a direction to take cover, with a pointer indicating a cellar affording protection when an aeroplane appeared overhead.

Except for a few white and skeleton-like trunks, woods in the Somme were woods only in name in the later period of the war. A non-commissioned officer in a Border regiment was heard to express his disgust on one occasion when his company was digging in under shell fire at a place which he was told was Sanctuary Wood. He protested that there was no sanctuary and no wood.

We passed a spot known as New Wood, and had on our right Trônes Wood, familiar to men of the Somme. The undergrowth has sprung up surprisingly in these areas. There were two or three of the original trees, throwing out foliage and rising conspicuously above the new trees and bushes, which had reached a height of eight or nine feet.

The curious effect recalled a passage in Treasure Island, where a giant tree rising above the surrounding woods was noted as a pointer in the search. At Trônes Wood is the 18th Divisional Memorial. By the roadside further on we came to Gaillemont Road Cemetery, with its rows of white gravestones and its trim green turf.

Here is buried Lt Raymond Asquith, Lord Oxford's son, who fell in September 1916. The Delville Wood Cemetery, which we passed soon afterwards, has over 6,500 British graves. Here is the South African Memorial. The stonework is in position, but the sculpture group has not yet been erected. Delville Wood made heavy toll of the South Africans. As the Captain put it—'the South African Brigade went into the wood, took the wood; held the wood, but never came out of the wood.'

A month or two ago there were uncovered here two stretcher bearers, who had been carrying a wounded officer when a shell had exploded and buried them in the trench through which they were passing. In this district is the New Zealand Memorial to the men, 7,000 of them, whose graves are not identified.

A remarkably fine piece of memorial architecture is to be seen at the village of Flers. It consists of the figure of a British soldier in bronze, the right-hand carrying rifle and bayonet in horizontal position, the left hand closed and indicating tension, and the whole effect being one of vitality and naturalness.

The sculptor has seen and given permanency to the gesture and bearing of a soldier advancing in an attack, in a way that rings extraordinarily true and convincing.

We passed a spot that used to be known as 'Factory Corner'; and at the village of Velu the Londoner showed special animation. He was engaged on special work here, when a shell splinter laid him aside for a considerable period. He had been telling us about a gateway to an old *château* that used to be a familiar feature on the spot, and about two dead Germans being buried, one on either side of the avenue.

'Over there, sir,' he said, looking about him, 'there used to be a big engineering dump.' The village perplexed him, however. It was all new and strange to him. He could not get his bearings. We turned a corner, and a joyful exclamation escaped him.

Here was the old *château* gateway, with its red brickwork and ornamental wrought iron screen, left standing amongst the new village houses. The avenue sloped away down from the gateway, amongst the shrubs and young trees and old stumps that showed where the wooded policies had been.

Of the *château* itself there was no trace. Probably the dead Germans had been taken to the huge German cemetery between Bapaume and Péronne.

'Do you remember the old farm gates?' asked the Captain, as we passed through an adjacent village. 'These are the brick walls,' he said, indicating the worn gateway pillars; 'but the old farmhouse has disappeared.'

'Here was the canteen,' observed the sergeant; 'and there used to be a light railway running along here.' A little further on, and 'there's your light railway,' said the Captain.

It was now being used to bring in beet from the fields. The light railways of wartime have facilitated farming operations in the Somme. At one point we saw some old War Department wagons, with the WD letters on their sides, being hauled along with loads of roots.

'I seem to have become part of the old country again,' remarked the Londoner, as he identified himself with one point after another. 'There was a *sucrerie* there in the old days,' he said, indicating a vacant spot. 'And there is the new *sucrerie*,' answered the Captain, pointing to a building of impressive proportions further on.

A point of the landscape recalled a post-war feature to the Captain. There used to be three gnarled trees outside Bapaume, which from a certain direction, and when twilight was setting in, looked exactly like three soldiers with sloping arms and packs on their backs. 'It used to give me an eerie feeling,' he said. 'But they came along one day and cut the dear old things down.'

At Bapaume—also new and thriving looking, but with war gaps amongst its buildings—we stopped for *déjeuner*, and there by chance we met a member of a British war graves firm of contractors who came into a curious war graves story which the Captain had previously related. It is associated with the environs of Lagnicourt.

A young Australian lieutenant was killed there in the last German advance. His father, a retired colonel and a man of considerable means, came out to search for his son's body. The lad had been the only survivor of the company with the gun for which he was responsible, and defending it to the last, had been shot through the head by a German officer.

The latter took all the papers found on him, and afterwards forwarded them to the Australian Government. A sergeant with him took the dead lieutenant's boots. The father got in touch with the German officer after the war, and during the search, induced him to come through and point out the spot where his son had fallen.

He employed men to dig for two years, but the search failed. Eventually, he decided to erect a memorial to his son near the spot where he had fallen. He selected a piece of ground close to the roadway. Difficulties were put in the way, however. The farmer, amongst other things, demanded an exorbitant amount for the ground.

The colonel suddenly decided to break off negotiations, and fixed on ground on the opposite side of the roadway. The proprietrix, a French countess, sympathised with his motive, and only stipulated that he should compensate the tenant of the farm for the loss of the ground. The site was marked off, and the workmen dug the ground for the foundations.

The contractor, before these were laid, ordered the site to be deepened by another two inches. A buried body was then discovered. The colonel was present at the time, and he identified it as his son. The uniform showed the proper rankings for his son's rank and service. He was able to identify gold fillings in two of the teeth.

The boots were missing. There was, he said, no doubt of the identity; and he took off his overcoat and laid it on the body, directing that nothing should be done until he communicated with his wife who was then in London.

It was decided to form a concrete coffin for the body where it lay, and the memorial proceeded as had been planned. The contractor told me that the pole which he planted as the centre to work from when operations were begun would have passed through the lieutenant's chest.

—SOLDIER, WRITING IN OCTOBER 1925.

8

1926

When I planned to visit the Somme battlefields I pondered the map for no considerable time, debating with myself just how I should approach that once familiar zone. The ways of peace are different from the ways of war in that there are now open railways and roads which, in 1916, were tangled masses of rubble and steel, routes very different from those we followed in the old days.

Thus one might approach the zone from Arras, charming, pathetic, old world Arras. Bapaume, too, offered advantages, and even less familiar Péronne might be the ideal starting point. Ultimately practical considerations yielded to sentimental impulses, and I decided to enter the Somme as most soldiers entered it, via Albert, the battered, blasted little town which, in 1918, was just a heap of red rubble lying athwart that rivulet of evil repute, the Ancre.

Thus it was, on a recent summer morning, I heard, as in a dream, the French porters crying 'Al-bear,' and I alighted at an imposing new station of four platforms, complete with white tiled subway, buffet, and bookstall.

One did not alight at Albert station 10 years ago. It was not done. The only arrivals at Albert station were substantial shells which came from the Pozieres ridge. As a result the new station is not the old one reconstructed, for there was nothing to reconstruct, but an entirely new structure, a little to the south of the ruined station of which no trace now remains.

Albert's war story is a double tragedy. For nearly two years, prior to 1916, the enemy sat on the ridge above the little town and flung heavy projectiles into it, using as a ranging point the cathedral, whose massive walls of brick and stone, rising to a campanile, were visible to the naked eye from his observation points.

With the opening of the offensive the town came in for special concentrated 'hate,' for the enemy guessed, and rightly, that its cellars were crammed with men and that its streets at night were alive with troops and transport.

When the battles of 1916 had pushed the accursed guns far beyond the Bapaume ridge Albert enjoyed a little peace, in which men moved its tumbled houses from the roadways and tidied up the place so that it had some semblance of its former shape. Later, many civilians returned. Shops and villas were rebuilt or repaired, and it was good to come to Albert after a spell of duty before the Hindenburg Line. General Byng made his headquarters here.

Then, in 1918, the unbelievable happened, and the enemy hordes came with unbelievable speed over the hills that separated Albert from Cambrai. Péronne fell. Bapaume followed, and soon shells again came screaming over the Pozieres ridge. The new plate glass windows of Albert were shattered, its new roofs were breached. Worse followed. The town was mercilessly bombed from the air, and finally captured.

With Albert within the enemy lines, it must perforce suffer from the guns of those who for so long had defended it, and it was a sorry heap of ruins that met the eyes of the troops who recaptured the place at the bayonet's point in 1918. During the whole time that British troops held the town its distinguishing feature was the 'Leaning Virgin' on the tower of the cathedral.

High above the clustered houses the effigy had stood, in times of peace, holding aloft triumphantly the Holy Child. In early bombardments the base of the statue was hit, and the figure fell forward so that it was parallel to the street, ready at any moment it seemed to dash to death the Child on the cobbled, shell-dented square below. Instinctively one walked clear of its shadow.

Thus there grew up a legend. 'When the Virgin of Albert falls the war will end,' said the French. In April 1918, the effigy fell to British guns, obliged to bombard an obvious enemy observation post. The figure was never found, and another legend came into circulation. Prosaic people say that the mystery is no mystery to the enemy officer whose duty it was to salve metal and dispatch it to the German munition factories.

Today, on the temporary church, you may see a brightly gilded effigy of the Virgin, holding the Child heavenwards, as in the old times. But this is not the original figure. It is a replica, considerably smaller, for the little bell tower of the church would not support the great piece of statuary that crowned the old campanile.

Close by, the ruins of the old cathedral remain much as they were in 1918, and the tomb of the patron saint, near the high altar, has been railed off. The floor has been cleared of the lighter debris, revealing the fact that the only piece of its mosaic which is undamaged is a section bearing the word 'Adoremus,' a word strangely moving seen amid the broken columns and shattered altars of the cathedral.

The ruins of the cathedral are now encircled by streets of handsome shops with fine fronts and attractive displays of wares. Here and there an ugly, vacant site breaks the array of neat buildings, and even today your eye will light upon the remains of a petrol tin that may have done duty as a water container in 1916, or a piece of harness that, could it speak, might tell of a flame lit night of horror in March 1918.

Albert today claims a population larger than that which it held before the war. One reason for this increase is the establishment of an aeroplane factory employing about 1,000 men so that even now the buzz of aircraft will often be heard above the town. Moreover, the work of reconstruction, both in the town itself and in surrounding villages brings in many labourers who must have lodging.

Then there is a small colony of Britons, mostly men employed by the Imperial War Graves Commission. Further, one encounters numerous ex-servicemen who, having married French girls, have settled down in civilian occupation. So far as one can ascertain they are happy and contented. At least they are not troubled by strikes and unemployment.

One important section of these exiles is composed of drivers of motor cars who make a living by driving British visitors to war cemeteries or by running them round the battlefields. Generally they are very good fellows, and if they calculate their fares in Sterling and garner for themselves the advantage of the falling rate of exchange, they are discriminating, and temper the wind to the shorn lamb.

Sometimes a poor woman, on a pilgrimage to a distant grave, finds even the modest fare which the driver asks greater than she calculated. A British official has assured me that, in such circumstances, he had known a driver say to the old lady, 'Jump in mother, and send me the fare some day when you can spare it.'

Albert is a town of cafés. It is said to have 167, against 140 before the war. I did not count them, but certainly there appeared to be two at each corner, and several in every street. In these places you may hear a British veteran telling in the best Bill Adams manner tales of the war to some unsuspecting visitor.

'Yes,' said one in my hearing, 'my pal was wounded 33 times—aye, and he wore a wound stripe for every one, 'e did—but the 34th one did 'im in. But even so, mark you, 'e was killed by a bomb as 'e lay in the hospital at E-taps. Rotten luck!'

As one leaves the centre of Albert the continuous rows of new houses give way to a mixture of new structures and temporary huts, with an occasional ruin or partially cleared site. The roads in the town are very rough, and the principal square, the Place Faidherbe, is neglected; the old memorial to the fallen soldiers of 1870 is still scarred, and still lacks the damaged figures which the enemy removed in 1918.

Up on the Route de Bapaume the Union Jack flies on a little camp which looks much like a headquarters of the old days, a collection of huts, neatly arranged and clean, but looking distinctly worn.

This is the Somme headquarters of the Imperial War Graves Commission, the organisation charged with the sacred duty of tending for all time the graves of the fallen of the Empire. The area administered by the Albert headquarters contains no fewer than 125,000 graves, all of men of the British and Overseas forces.

Not far from the headquarters is a horticultural nursery, one of seven maintained in France by the Commission for the cultivation of flowers. Here are masses of violas, stocks, forget-me-knots, roses and a pleasing variety of other flowers essentially English. From this nursery the local cemetery wardens draw the flowers required for the graves under their care.

Talking to the official in charge of graves in this area, Major Phillips, a former Australian officer who bears scars of battle, is like talking to an enthusiastic landscape gardener, with the real gardener's gentleness and love of beauty. There is a note of pride in his description of the schemes, architectural and horticultural, employed in the cemeteries, and no two schemes are alike.

Here stone walls and rambler roses, there brick walls with aubretia and paved pathways, and the cemetery in the orchard at Warley is a perfect picture when the blossom is out. And the turf in some of his cemeteries would not shame the lawns of an English university.

The deepest impression gathered in the course of my visit to these battlefields was made by the beauty of the British War Cemeteries. No praise can be too high for the skill of the designers and the work of the gardeners. There is nothing of the soulless government department about the Imperial War Graves Commission.

It was no departmental mind that conceived the scheme of accepting from the relatives of a fallen soldier flower seeds to plant upon his grave, and then to return to the relatives for planting in their own gardens the first seeds that fall in autumn from their flowers. War graves and home gardens are thus in communion. Truly there is a heartbeat in the work of the Imperial War Graves Commission.

To tread the Bapaume Road in these days of peace is an experience fraught with new and strange sensations. This straight highway, rising sharply to the high ground near La Boisselle, was once a veritable *Via Dolorosa*, on which men, heavily laden, moved slowly at night, their faces illuminated occasionally by the bright flash of a gun as they glanced up at distant Verey light falling slowly upon the ridge ahead.

Today, starting from Albert, it is pleasant to walk out to La Boisselle, for the road is better than any in Albert, and the view away to the left, towards Aveluy and the Ancre, is rich with points of interest.

Once again, the Bapaume Road is lined with growing trees. The old, gaunt skeletons of war days, with their torn boughs and lacerated trunks, have been removed, though here and there, with a nice regard for the feelings of ex-soldiers, the French authorities have left a particularly good specimen of a tree which, though paralysed in the conflict, still stands firm, a gnarled warrior, stretching out its leafless limbs as if to protect the tender saplings, whose bright green foliage is now just thick enough to cast a shadow on the road.

Before reaching the old line one encounters, on the point we knew as Tara Hill, the first cemetery on this famous road. It is called the Bapaume Post. Here are gathered a relatively small but representative company of those who fell in the great battles hereabouts.

Enclosed by a low brick wall, and surrounded with turf as trim and as green as any in a Surrey garden, the soldierly lines of white headstones tell a moving story. Here you will find men of all sections of the Imperial Forces.

A stone records that in this cemetery are buried 78 soldiers of the Northumberland Fusiliers, 'Known For God,' while among the identified graves the eye meets with the titles of regiments from England, Scotland, Ireland, South Africa, Canada and Australia. Into this cemetery have been brought, for better care, some of those wooden regimental memorials, erected during the war, on adjacent points.

A sturdy cross which had once been blown in two by a shell, but is now repaired, records the sacrifice of officers and men of a company of Australian Field Engineers, while another, scarred by shrapnel bears the name of the 14th Canadian Battalion, Royal Montreal Regiment.

These wooden crosses have withstood the wind and rain of the Somme for 10 years, to say nothing of the hail of steel that beat about them in the battles of 1918. Weather beaten and war torn, their blackened forms stand out in striking contrast with the snow white headstones which surround them.

In this cemetery, as in every other, a story is to be read on every hand. Even as one turns to leave a stone against the way marks the resting place of an English boy of 18 years, killed within a month or two of the Armistice.

Again, as I opened the metal box by the entrance to the cemetery, wherein is kept the Roll of Honour, I saw to my surprise two or three

French coins. Their total value in British currency was not sixpence, and I was puzzled to know what they should be doing here.

One could not ask the warden, because the warden was not present. That is why the coins were here ... a widow's mite from a small purse, a thanks offering to the gardener for the care devoted to the grave of one dearly loved.

The wardens of these cemeteries are all ex-British soldiers, picked men and good fellows. You come upon them at odd times. Perchance, as you stand contemplating some once familiar stretch of country, you hear, beyond a hedge, the whirr of a lawnmower. Looking about, you find a cemetery, in which a man, sun tanned, collarless and jacketless, is pushing a mower over the green sward about the headstones. His cycle rests by the gate.

He may be the only man you will encounter in an hour's walk. Probably he lives among the French peasants in an adjacent village. He works largely without supervision. No foreman stands by to see him work. None is needed. He is doing this for his pals. That he is employed by the Imperial War Graves Commission is incidental.

The person who sets out to tour the battlefields with a timetable will destroy it after the first day. These cemeteries have a way of dissipating time. One lingers in them, and I would give little for the heart of the man who could resist their call.

Thus, traversing the Bapaume Road, one pauses at the Post, although a little further on is much of tremendous interest. At the point where the road branches off to Contalmaison stands the granite memorial to the Tyneside Scottish and Irish Brigades unveiled by Marshal Foch. It is designed in the form of a semi-circular seat, and is the first permanent regimental memorial upon a road which has many.

Its site is the entrance to La Boisselle, and today La Boisselle is a village. In 1916 it was a nullity, without form and void. Bright brick houses have been built on exactly those sites upon which houses stood before. This actual replacement is almost the general rule.

How the sites of houses were identified is a mystery to the visitor, but old communal maps rescued from *Mairie* and others stored in Amiens helped the returning refugee and the local authorities to locate the site of the old home.

In much the same way the former British soldier who served on the Somme may look about for his old home, and he will look with much less chance of success. Ovillers on the left and to Fricourt on the right are gone. Except for two sections of trench line 'preserved' as war memorials, you will find no trenches on the Somme.

Grass grows and 'reparation' cows feed where once, below ground was a battalion headquarters, complete with telephones, typewriter, maps, papers and perchance a gramophone. All gone without trace! And green grass, or beet, or corn growing on the top! Was the War, after all, only the hideous nightmare it seemed?

Nearby, a recently ploughed field gives the answer. The plough has gone deeply, and, strewn over the surface, is a miscellaneous assortment of corrugated iron (rusted, crumpled and thin), old wire and bits of shells. In a day or two all this debris will have been collected and dumped by the side of the road, and the particular metal buyer who has bought all the scrap in this area will, in due course, collect it.

This process has been going on for years, and still the plough throws up these relics of battle and camp. Sometimes an unexpected shell is found and the *Mairie* will be notified. Later, a government expert will come round and, while the farm workers are at their midday meal, he will explode the shell electrically.

But there are imported Polish labourers hereabouts, the rearguard of those civilian labour corps who filled in the trenches. These men covet the copper bands, and nose-caps to be found on unexploded shells. They will think nothing of attacking the nose-cap of a 'dud' shell with hammer and chisel! Usually the shell has so far deteriorated as to be harmless, but occasionally, their luck fails them. Casualties still occur on the Somme battlefields.

While the visitor may look in vain hereabouts for trenches, he will find the familiar features of the landscape much as they were in the war. They are the nine great craters of La Boisselle. The better known crater to the left, and in full view of the road, is much visited but away to the right is a larger cavity.

By the left crater stands a hut inhabited by vigilant young people ready, at the sound of an approaching car, to bring out postcards showing the considerable alteration made in the appearance of La Boisselle by two earthquakes invoked by the British on July 1st, 1916. On the other side of the road, the Café de la Grande Mine testifies to the pride of the inhabitants in the new possession of La Boisselle.

Away in the distance Ovillers nestles in the valley, while a bright white patch marks the British cemetery. If you are tempted down Artillery Lawn which, in the winter of 1916–17 was stiff with British guns, but it is now so peaceful that your own footfalls are the only sound, you will find Ovillers rising from its ruins. A large Nissen hut stands where once stood the notice 'This was Ovillers Church.' And the hut is now the church, complete with a respectable bell.

Farms and houses, substantial brick structures in place of the old timber and plaster buildings, now occupy the sites of such once important places as the bath house and the light railway headquarters.

The light railway is, of course, no more and Wolfe Huts, which nestled so securely with their backs to a bank below the Bapaume Road, have left no trace of their former glories, even the scars in the chalky bank having been obscured by grass.

Of all the villages hereabouts, Pozieres is the most surprising to the visitor who knew it in the war years. Of Pozieres not one brick remained. Its commanding position on the top of a ridge entitled it to special treatment by our artillery. If ever a place was actually blasted off the face of the earth, that place was Pozieres.

Today it is a presentable village of fair proportions, not a likeable village, because it is bisected by the main road and straggles its way for nearly half a mile. But it holds some substantial farms and a fine *Mairie*. Even the civilian cemetery has been rediscovered, and new monumental work of orthodox French design being erected in it.

Pozieres to the soldier has two synonyms. One is 'Australians,' and the other 'Tanks.' Hard by the village are symbols of both. The cemetery at Pozieres is an Australian cemetery beyond whose Cross of Sacrifice can be seen the memorial to the 1st Australian Division.

When the new Australian capital at Canberra is completed, it is expected that seed from flowers in its gardens will be sent to line this cemetery to the country which dispatched those bronzed giants who snatched Pozieres from a tenacious and ruthless enemy.

Soon, yet another memorial is to be erected at Pozieres. It is to be a Memorial to the Missing, on which will be inscribed the names of those men who fell in the Somme area and who have no known graves.

It is the policy of the Imperial War Graves Commission to erect one memorial to the missing in each of the six areas into which the Western Front is divided, and the name of every man who fell will be recorded—on his grave if it is known, otherwise upon a Memorial to the Missing in the area in which he made the great sacrifice.

Strategists, those 'scientific' soldiers, whose existence is more obvious after a war than during its progress, tell us that it is a mistake to speak out and write of the Battle of the Somme. They point out that this was not a battle, but a series of battles, any one of which had greater magnitude than the battles that figure so prominently in our record books.

Moreover, they exert, and rightly, that the conflict extended far beyond the Valley of the Somme. The truth of these assertions is realised when we come to consider the northern side of the Somme battlefields, for these lay about the River Ancre, a small tributary of the Somme, many miles from the larger stream.

In the old days, one went up the Ancre Valley from Aveluy, and though a more interesting impression of the battle can be gained by coming down from the high ground about Beaumont Hamel, sentimental impulse moves one to make the journey from the old starting point, for thus it is easier to recognise, if they still exist, old landmarks and 'hot corners.'

Thus, one looks, but in vain, for some remnant of the old saw mills by the railway at Aveluy, where, during 'rest periods,' battle-tired battalions whiled away the time making duckboards for the trenches, while the shells screamed their way over the valley in an effort to find one or other of the many dumps about the railway.

But the military sidings have gone, grass grows where once thousands of men lived and worked, and one's search fails, just as it failed when one looked, a little way back, for a trace of the famous Bruce Huts, near the crossroads that lead to Albert.

Authuille sleeps peacefully on the gently rising ground, as though war were a stranger to it. But it is a new Authuille, of bright red brick, like a new garden suburb. It is useless here to ask for Campbell Avenue or Black Horse Road; those names belong to a past age when another race occupied this valley.

Skirting Thiepval Wood, one passes over the invisible Old Line, close to which St Pierre Divion, tiny and obscure, is again raising its little self in the familiar red brick. Gone is the old timber and plaster farm building which was once the orthodox structure of this area.

Journeying along this valley one is struck by the fact that while the treacherous marshes have reverted to a state of peaceful pasture, the trees and bushes are very slow in recovering. On the higher ground, elsewhere on the battlefields, the woods, once blasted out of recognition, are rapidly regaining their normal appearance and dimensions. Here, in the Ancre Valley, the trees and bushes return but reluctantly.

Perhaps it is that the shells went more deeply into this marshy ground and disturbed more profoundly the tangled root growth. Perhaps, too, the gas shells, landing in water and mire, spread their evil poisons to greater effect than they could among the vegetation on the high ground. The Ancre, placid and crystal clear, gives no answer to the question.

Crossing the stream at Bridge Road, one finds a level crossing and a station. Beaucourt Hamel, they call the station, though there is no village of that name. But it is rightly named, for it serves the villages of Beaucourt, Beaumont Hamel, and Hamel. Along this line go tearing the expresses which link Lille and Paris. When, a little while ago, Death halted one of these trains, Beaucourt Hamel was, appropriately, his ambush.

In the village of Hamel is to be seen one of the few Crucifix Corners. The shell-racked cross still stands, but the figure rests propped against its base, sadly broken, while the surrounding trees seem intent upon screening from sight this eloquent symbol of war's devastation.

A little west of the railway rises a strange building which was not here before the war or during it. Built of logs, on a slight eminence, it comes as a great relief from the monotony of new red brick. This is the lodge of Newfoundland Park, and it is a replica of the log cabin of the early settlers of Britain's oldest colony.

Here one comes back to the war again for the Newfoundland Government have chosen as a memorial to its men to preserve intact the trenches at Y Ravine. The log cabin is the warden's home, and repository of numerous interesting relics. Billy Brown, the warden, is a giant of a man, a former warrant officer of the Newfoundland Contingent.

Coincidences occur in strange places. In the course of conversation it transpires that Billy Brown had been the driver of a military car which once conveyed me in a race against time on a memorable run over Vimy Ridge. The warden is proud of his charge, for here are some of the finest specimens of trenches ever dug on the Western Front.

In places the British trenches interlock with the German, and here the visitor with no first hand experience of trench warfare can acquire a fair idea of what the war on the Western Front was like. Between the trenches the ground is left just as it was in 1918 so far as Nature will permit. But Nature prefers to heal wounds. Long grass waves above the shell holes, new shrubs are springing up and Nature's hand would gently but firmly cover in the trenches were it not for the continuous efforts of the warden.

Interesting relics of battle, found hereabouts, have been brought either into the trenches or laid upon the parapet. There is something to catch the eye at almost every step. One relic, however, rests just where it landed, close to the parapet—the skeleton of an aeroplane whose crumpled wings still carry pathetic shreds of fabric.

Finger posts at the junctions of communication trenches point the way to Y Ravine where, at long last, peace reigns and the birds twitter. Within the park are three memorials. One is to the Newfoundland Contingent and represents a caribou standing on a cairn, raising its head and noble antlers proudly over the ground on which so many Newfoundlanders lost their lives.

Not less impressive is the great bronze Highlander, mounted on Aberdeen granite who commemorates the deeds and sacrifices of the gallant 51st. Hard by a smaller memorial bears the name of one of Britain's most famous 'spearhead' divisions, the 29th. The associations of the 29th with Beaumont Hamel are not very close, but the 51st and the 29th were so often united in heroic enterprise that it was thought well to commemorate them in a comrade's fashion, side-by-side, in Newfoundland Park.

'A never-to-be-forgotten day,' is the observation which Earl Haig wrote in the visitors' book at Newfoundland Park when he visited it in June

1925, and his sentiment will be re-echoed by any ex-soldier who has the privilege of visiting this unique memorial.

The attractions of Newfoundland Park trespass recklessly upon the time of the battlefield visitor, but sentiment forbids one to return without at least a passing look at Grandcourt and Miraumont. Although it is good to see these places restored, a sense of disappointment is but natural on finding in them little or nothing reminiscent of the bad old times.

The Grandcourt that was has departed together with the old Bailescourt Farm. The customary red brick village, a trifle larger and differently shaped, meets the eye, while at Miraumont, whose black and straggling ruins were once the headquarters of 50 different forms of Teutonic devilry, now boasts the largest new buildings in this area, a big dairy which, nearly completed, is to be conducted on cooperative lines.

Of the country below Thiepval Sir Philip Gibbs (the famous war reporter) said, in a dispatch written in July, 1916: 'It is historic ground. A hundred years hence men of our blood will come here with reverence as to sacred soil.'

Now, 10 years after the battle, you will find on any day that the majority of visitors to the Somme battlefields have concentrated themselves at Beaumont Hamel and Thiepval, and they come as pilgrims. Three, or even four, hundred visitors are not uncommon toll on a fine day. And it may well be that, a hundred years hence, Britons will still come here to meditate upon deeds of valour and of matchless self-sacrifice.

As if in anticipation of those days, there has been erected upon the high ground at Thiepval a magnificent tower of stone, from the top of which can be gained a view of the battlefields such as will hold the interest of any soldier for an hour or more.

The Tower was erected by the people of Ulster, and in its memorial chamber are inscribed the appropriate lines of Tennyson: 'Son's love built me, and I hold, Ulster's love in letter'd gold.'

In all its hard fighting the 36th (Ulster) Division wrote no more glorious chapter of history than it did here, at Thiepval. On the opening day of the Somme battle the Ulster battalions hurled themselves upon the Thiepval's underground fortress with such determination that all its wire and its machine guns, manned by a German regiment which had held the point for two years and boasted that it was impregnable, could not check their onward rush.

On they went for two miles into the enemy system, and though ultimately, in danger of being cut off they retired, they brought back with them over 500 prisoners. Three months elapsed before the attacking troops traversed the ground again.

The Ulster Division paid a terrible price, as the nearby cemeteries tell, and the great Tower which now throws a long shadow across the

Schwaben Redoubt is a fitting symbol of the steadfastness and strength of Ulster's men.

Here, indeed, is the heart of the Somme battlefield. Strategically, Thiepval had an enormous bearing upon our fortunes in the great battle. It is well, therefore, that this should be one of the few places on the battlefield where the trenches are preserved intact.

At the Ulster Tower you may find an able expositor of the War as it was waged about Thiepval. Mr William MacMaster, a former sergeant major in the Ulster Division, and a survivor of its great exploit hereabouts. The Tower contains living quarters in which Mr MacMaster resides with his wife and two daughters.

MacMaster is a tall, wiry man, dour of expression but kindly of heart. When I spoke to him he had not seen his native Belfast for two years, but he seemed thoroughly at home in this Somme fastness.

When he takes the visitor to his trenches (and he has conducted thousands), he does not talk the conversational 'patter' of the professional guide. When he speaks of the attack his eyes light up, and he talks with a fervour that shows clearly that he is living over again those hours of hell in the old redoubt.

Here, as in Newfoundland Park, the trenches are well preserved, with many dug-outs and bomb stores. The litter of war lies about the parapet. Close to where I saw a party of Lancashire women plucking wildflowers lay a German mess tin which, from its appearance, might well have been there since those fateful days of 1916.

As I stood chatting to one of these ladies, who was telling me that this was her second pilgrimage from Manchester in search of her brother's grave, there was a slight rustling of the long grass on the parapet, and a little brown bird darted out, disclosing to us the hiding place of four tiny eggs. Bird's nests in the parapet at Thiepval! There were times when it seemed that no self-respecting bird would ever again grace Thiepval with its song!

Indeed, so completely devastated is Thiepval that no permanent rebuilding has been attempted in its ruins. No bright new farmhouses or tilled fields are to be seen here; nothing but uneven earth, rank grass and weeds. Here and there, seeking carefully, you may find a brick or two denoting the original building line of the main street of the village but these are the only bricks to be seen.

Such structures as exist are wooden shanties and old Army huts. While Beaumont Hamel rises from its ruins, and Pozieres prospers abundantly, Thiepval remains a series of grass covered mounds. It may never be rebuilt.

Here are to be seen some of the largest dumps of old shells to be encountered anywhere on the battlefields. Ten years afterwards the stacks of shell cases stand four feet high by the roadside. The scrap metal merchant who bought the Thiepval area struck a lucky patch!

From the road that leads to the Pozieres Ridge, you pass a considerable cavity in the ground. That hole was once Mouquet Farm. For many weeks this was our only foothold on the Thiepval Ridge, and the enemy spared no effort to drive us from it.

The bricks that made Mouquet Farm were blown to powder long before the battle line moved on, and even those from the cellars were dislodged to make a semblance of a road where once a pleasant country lane wound its way down to the village.

There were many places on the battlefield which suffered elimination as complete as did Thiepval, but there were none that had a longer or more sustained bombardment. To the right the tide of battle moved slowly on, but Thiepval, with its tunnels and commodious dug-outs, defied, from the beginning of July to the end of September, the worst that our guns could do.

No ground on the Somme was cheaply gained in 1916, but Thiepval must rank among the points for which we paid the heaviest price. Driving away one instinctively looks back over this hallowed ground. As the top of the Ulster Tower disappears from view, with its wireless mast as alert to convey the news from 2LO to the exiled MacMaster, one feels that Thiepval has an invisible link with the hearts of our people, for nowhere did the qualities of our race endure a greater test or emerge more triumphantly from it.

With a mental picture of the Somme battles before your eyes, you go more gaily to the places south of the Bapaume road than to those northward, about the Ancre. Though there was little difference in the losses north and south of the road, the northern portion has a tradition of tragedy, because here, for so long, sacrifice seemed vain, progress was negligible, and the marshy ground made its own contribution to the horrors of war.

Thus one steps out more gaily along the road to Fricourt, for here were gathered the first fruits of victory. Becourt and Becordel nestle peacefully among the recovering trees away to the right, much as they did before August 1914.

But they are villages of new bricks, and, between them, is a feature which was not here in 1914—a British cemetery whose headstones, recently washed, gleam even more brightly than usual. Once a year, every stone, in every cemetery, is washed with a special solution, whose effect is not only to clean but to preserve the stone.

Around Fricourt the fields are all under cultivation, and, viewing them from high ground, one sees the same kind of chequer board design which, during the War, was so pleasing down the valley towards Amiens, because it spoke of peace.

Here, however, despite much attention, the surface of the ground is still uneven. The plough dips as it passes over a filled-in trench. It bumps across the outline of a hole made by a 'nine two,' and, maybe, drags up a piece of barbed wire. The peasant utters a strange oath. Will his holding ever be free of this accursed stuff!

Nevertheless, it is remarkable what has been achieved. During the War it was freely stated that the French Government had decided to make one huge forest of all this ground between the Somme and the Ancre, for never, surely, could the fields be reclaimed and the sites of the villages be discerned.

But the French peasant decided the issue by coming back almost upon the heels of the advancing troops, and, despite intense hardship, settled down at once to restore his lacerated fields.

Soon the story of the War on this southern side of the battlefield will be read principally in the British cemeteries and on the memorials. Only in the cemetery at Fricourt does one find a clue to the glory which the Green Howards gathered at this place at so high a price.

Here is a granite memorial to the 7th Battalion of the Princess of Wales's Own Yorkshire Regiment which revives in the minds of those who know it, the story of those Yorkshire lads who went over at Fricourt in face of murderous fire from Mametz Wood.

At Montauban, hard by, is another landmark of a notable kind, though wholly different. It is the original village crucifix, sadly damaged, but still recognisable, an eloquent witness to the devilry that went on here 10 years ago.

But this crucifix is the only piece of the original Montauban. Around it has risen the usual new village of bricks, with large barns and a comfortable *Mairie*. Many of the villages hereabouts were aided in their early struggles by the generosity of British towns and villages. Thus, Montauban owes to our Kentish town of Maidstone its water supply and lighting system, to say nothing of gifts of clothing, seeds and fruit trees.

Away back, at Fricourt too, the inhabitants have grateful recollections of gifts from Ipswich which, taking the form of harvesting implements, enabled them to win a scanty living from their first struggles with tangled, trench-scarred fields that lay between the gaunt and blackened woods.

Meantime, let us pass to Guillemont, once again a thriving village. In vain one seeks, en route, old trenches and 'hot corners.' The old direction posts are gone, the old dumps have vanished, 'hot corners' are now just prosaic crossroads, while the sunken road holds no greater terror than a shambling farm wagon, which impedes the progress of your car.

At Guillemont are to be seen two menacing nine-two shells. But they grace the front garden of a prominent villager, and about them are pretty flowerbeds and grass verges. The fine double-fronted houses behind them are places once destroyed by shells such as these.

Those who, during the War, read of the fierce fight for Guillemont station, which, changing hands many times a day, secured an evil prominence in the communiques, might have imagined it to be some extensive junction of strategic importance. Today it is possible to see it as it was, for, like most places hereabouts, it has been restored on lines no more ambitious than it possessed before the War.

It consists of a cottage with a low platform outside, bordering on a single line, narrow gauge railway, on which two trains run daily in each direction, between Albert and Péronne, taking two and a half hours to make the single journey of 20-odd miles.

I saw the little train puff its way modestly out of the station, and meander across the Longueval road past Ginchy. When its hissing was no longer to be heard, one imagined one caught again the sound of the pipes that rallied a sorely tried Irish regiment in this valley, 10 years ago, for an assault upon Ginchy.

If you walk from Guillemont towards Wedge Wood and Falfemont Farm, you will encounter a British cemetery which holds a grave of particular interest. Here is buried the brilliant son of one who was, at the time of this battle, Prime Minister of Britain.

'Equality of sacrifice requires equality of treatment,' says the Imperial War Graves Commission and thus you must seek for this grave as you seek for that of any private soldier.

At last you come upon it, one of a long line, and the stone, exactly the same as any other, records that here is buried Lieutenant Raymond Asquith, of the Grenadier Guards, who was killed on September 15, 1916, aged 37.

Then follows a remarkable inscription, the one touch of individual choice permitted to the relatives of each fallen man. The inscription reads: 'Small time but in that small time most greatly lived this star of England.'

—Raymond Bridgeway, writing in June–July 1926.

The Bridgeway name was attributed to a series of articles published around the world to mark the tenth anniversary of the Battle of the Somme. However, it is very likely the work is that of Capt. Henry Archibald Taylor, who served with 17th Bn, London Rgt, Royal Fusiliers, and on the HQ of 182nd Infantry Brigade. Passages of 'Bridgeway's' writing were reproduced in Taylor's widely regarded 1928 book *Good-bye to the Battlefields* (Stanley Paul). Taylor makes reference in the book's author's notes to writing newspaper articles in the period and the strong similarity suggests they were written by the same hand. The Bridgeway name appears on two further series of articles returning to the battlefields in 1927 and 1928 which also appear to be the work of Taylor.

*

Ypres, after eight years' absence, is so greatly changed as to be almost unrecognisable. Of the buildings in the town proper only the Cloth Hall remains a tragic ruin, a permanent memorial of the wanton, destructive cruelty of modern warfare.

The citizens, when we arrived, were still grimly smiling at the naive remark of an American tourist a few days previously, 'Waad, I do think it's the quaintest thing that the Germans destroyed just that one great building, and left all the others standing around.'

But perhaps her mistake was natural. One cannot over-praise the Belgians for the miraculous way they have tackled reconstruction. The houses they have built are far more durable and sightly than our own housing schemes; and Ypres is one of the very few places in the world today where there are too many houses, several being as yet unoccupied.

As the rents, with the franc at 186 to the pound, are absurdly low, one might do worse than emigrate to the considerable British colony of this indomitable Flemish city, awarded our Military Cross for its stubborn valour in war, and no less to be applauded for its energy in the arts of peace.

But the ex-servicemen of the Pilgrimage felt that this was not the Ypres they knew so well. Only the Cloth Hall, the shell-pocked ramparts above the moat, an odd heap of rubble here and there on the outskirts, and the battered tank flanked by German 'Hows' in the Grande Place, served to remind them of the days when gunner drivers lashed their horses to a gallop through those now crowded streets, and thought they were lucky to reach the Menin Gate unscathed.

It was at this same Menin Gate, by the irony of circumstances, that several of us were billeted, in a brand-new and most comfortable hotel. The British Government are building here a great memorial archway, shrouded at present in scaffolding, upon whose walls will appear the names of the 30,000 British dead in the Salient whose bodies have never been identified.

It was the strangest of experiences to sleep in a comfortable bed, within walls and under a roof, in peace and safety, at the Menin Gate, through which so many walked along the red road of Hooge on their way to Calvary.

One felt like a disembodied spirit in a world of ghosts, and could not fall asleep, despite fatigue, for the sheer novelty and wonder of it all. Looking through the open window upon the quiet street, I seemed to see it lit with gun-flashes and the bale-fire circle of Verey lights which ever ringed the Salient, resounding to the hollow shattering explosion of night-wandering shells, scented with gas and cordite, quicklime and mud, and blood.

A refrain from Weatherly's 'Deathless Army' came crooning into the drowsy mind:

'Twas deep black night in the city square.
Gone were the drums and the trumpets' blare,
But a gallant host were mustering there,
The men of our old brave army.

... The rain glistening on steel helmet and waterproof sheet; faces drawn with fatigue and haggard with anxiety; the rumble of guns and waggons on the broken causeway. Something in a blanket carried quietly by two weary, stumbling men....

But suddenly the morning sun was shining into the room, and we had to bestir ourselves betimes, for an early breakfast was to be followed by the service, at 8.30, in the Ypres Town Extension Cemetery.

We marched to it behind a pipe major of the Argyll, who were today in the uniform of the Edinburgh Police Pipe Band, a little procession of pilgrims headed by a minister of the Church of Scotland in black Geneva gown and bands, and by his side an Anglican in white surplice (the most delightful and brotherly of men), while the Belgian bystanders on the pavement respectfully saluted, and doubtless wondered what unknown ecclesiastical dignitary was thus arrayed in robes of sable hue!

It was a strange revenge of time which saw such a sight in the Papal stronghold of Ypres. What would his most Catholic Majesty of Spain have thought, if his spirit still broods over the fields of Flanders?

Of the service in the beautiful war cemetery, one shall say nothing here, for it was a very sacred hour, and tear-dimmed eyes could see little, when 'Lochaber no More' wailed its coronach over the silent graves. How wonderful these graves are!

If every mourner could see them, it would mean great peace and comfort. The War Graves Commission has done a noble work, and no man could ever ask, 'Why was this waste of ointment made?' if once he had felt its fragrance out there, in these quiet fields of God.

After the service many of us motored to Tyne Cot, the most easterly of our cemeteries, right on the top of Passchendaele, looking down on Ypres.

It is the second largest in France and Belgium; 11,000 lie buried there in long, unending rows, mostly unidentified.

Upon the headstones of the latter are inscribed the simple and touching words—'An Unknown British Soldier. Known to God.' Tyne Cot has the usual cross of sacrifice and stone of remembrance but is distinguished by containing within its wide and lovingly tended borders several German concrete pill-boxes, whose red harvest lies all garnered around.

Behind is a glorious sweep of double colonnades, broken at intervals by little open-air chapels for meditation, which open in turn on quiet gardens full of thyme and rosemary and simple English flowers—full also of an unseen Presence, the great cloud of witnesses encompassing the scene of their agony which is now the peaceful resting-place of their dust.

Below us stretched the great plain of Flanders, larks singing over waving cornfields 'where poppies blow,' spires of distant churches all rebuilt, the red-tiled homes of an indomitable people 'carrying on.'

If only our own nation would follow their example, and masters and men clasp hands of trust over those graves where rich and poor rest side-by-side, with no distinction of rank and class, we could truly say that our soldiers had not died in vain.

In the afternoon a private car took four of us, including a well-known Edinburgh Bailie, to see a few places that one of the party, at any rate, knew full well—Hellfire Corner, Hill 60, Messines Ridge, Neuve Eglise, Wulverghem, Locre, Kemmel.

One stood in the old familiar places, the same and yet not the same, 'fought the old battles o'er again.' Every turn of the road, every field, every ruin, had its own association. It was an unforgettable experience.

On Sunday evening a thunderstorm burst over us, and its distant rumble was like the old, unending mutter of the guns. The rain was turning the thick dust into the Salient brand of mud, the most potent in the world, as we shook it off our shoes and turned our faces homeward.

It was a quieter party tonight, though gleams of humorous relief were not wanting—the shrewd, amusing comments of Scots people setting foot for the first time on foreign soil.

At the frontier indignant passengers were bundled unceremoniously out of the train at midnight and locked into a waiting room, while stern '*douaniers*' searched the vacated carriages, and confiscated (one must regretfully add!) at least two boxes of undeclared cigars. Two Edinburgh husbands are still mourning their loss—if their wives have had sufficient courage to confess it.

And it should also be narrated that the medical officer in charge, a distinguished Edinburgh physician, had to remove cinders, during the last half dozen miles of the journey, from several eyes straining out of the window to catch a first glimpse of 'Auld Reekie.'

The Pilgrimage will be something to talk over and to think about for many a long day to come. To organisations like St Barnabas and the Edinburgh War Graves Committee we owe a deep debt of gratitude. They make it possible each year for hundreds of relatives to visit in comfort and without cost the graves of their gallant dead; 'whose name liveth for evermore.'

—Revd T. B. Stewart Thomson MC, BD, writing in July 1926.

Thomson was born in 1889 and followed his father into the Church of Scotland. After graduating from Aberdeen University, he became an assistant in Glasgow Cathedral in 1913. On the outbreak of the First World War, he enlisted as a combatant. He received a commission in 1915 and was awarded the Military Cross in 1918. After the war, Thomson became senior chaplain to the Territorial Army and was vice-president of the British Legion in Scotland.

*

Amiens! Ah! What memories. A silent but stout-hearted host we were when we arrived at this old French Cathedral town one night during the War. Up in the line things had not been exactly comforting. True, the Germans had halted before Albert, and yet another 28 kilometres separated them from old Amiens, but the war was not over! Armageddon not yet won!

Eager faces, looking out of the carriage windows, beheld Amiens in the gloom, and the strange silence that followed was only broken at times by the sudden screeching of some distant engine along the line, or by the muffled yawns of bleary-eyed Tommy Atkins, who felt the need of some diversion.

The momentary stop of the train in the midst of a network of railway lines outside the station gave us the opportunity of stretching our limbs, as we had been huddled together long enough. But alas, only a few minutes, and the hoot of the engine's whistle, a muttered 'Blimey,' a jerk of the carriage, and we were off again.

Entering Captain Oswald's Tourists' Bureau the other day at 42, Rue de Noyon, Amiens, brought me back to those times. Maps, location of cemeteries, military books, regimental histories, an old Army list, and so on, presented themselves as links with the past, with the great Battles of the Somme and 1,001 other things sacred to those who went through those crucial years.

Captain Oswald, who was in the King's Royal Rifle Corps, and won the Military Cross during the War, has at his disposal first class cars of the best makes, and it was in one of these cars that I made my visit to the Somme Battlefields and cemeteries.

The chauffeur was a British ex-serviceman, who explained everything worth knowing about the places passed on the way. The first we visited, and a town I knew in old War days, was Corbie. There are still a few battered houses, but the Church perhaps is the most outstanding ruin. As a matter of fact, I doubt whether one can still call Corbie Church a ruin; it is now a fine edifice, almost rebuilt, and a new roof added has greatly improved its once shattered appearance.

Most of the roads, especially the main roads, are good, but a few still bear traces of heavy shelling. Now and again, one comes across old trenches, barbed wire, some Nissen huts, shells and shell cases, signs on walls of divisional baths, and divisional concert parties etc., but it is remarkable how Nature has reclaimed her own.

Places which a few years ago were veritable rubbish heaps are now overgrown with grass, plants, shrubs, and the Somme can even rival Flanders for poppy fields. Looking on scenes today of peaceful villages, smiling green fields, and verdant woods, it is difficult to realise that only a few years back raged tremendous battles, terrific bombardments by shell, and these same places witnessed the lumbering of tanks in action, the traction of huge calibre guns by 'caterpillars,' the passing of Armies and the whirr of giant aeroplanes.

Then, occasionally, one passes a multitude of black wooden crosses enclosed by a wall; these are the graves of German soldiers who fell on the Somme. In fact, the Valley of the Somme seems to be a world of the dead: English, French and German.

The British military cemeteries everywhere brought into relief by the tall Cross of Remembrance, are wonderfully arranged, and models of neatness. The headstones, which in a number of cemeteries have taken the place of wooden crosses, are inscribed with the rank, name and regiment of the fallen—the regimental badge filling, more or less, the centre of the stone, with exception of the grave of an 'unknown warrior,' in which case there is simply an inscription, 'A Soldier of the Great War' followed underneath by, 'Known unto God.'

A printed Register of Graves can usually be found in each cemetery in which are set out full particulars of the fallen buried there, with exact location of each grave. Beautiful flowers adorn the graves, and in some cases I cannot conceive more peaceful surroundings.

Whilst visiting one cemetery near Corbie on the Somme, I heard sounds of weeping, and turning round caught sight of a pathetic figure prostrated before one of the graves. The old soul, who had travelled all the way from Scotland, had completely broken down, and a paroxysm of sobbing followed, which would have melted even the hardest of hearts.

All I could do was to look on in dismay, whilst the birds twittered merrily overhead in the bright sunshine wondering perhaps why all the quaint old world was not twittering as well!

After a time, the old lady recovered—a woman of sorrow, a picture of loneliness, and then stood by the headstone whilst a photograph was being taken.

As I gazed on her wrinkled yet beautiful face down which tears trickled like raindrops on her son's grave. I could not help realising how terribly the mothers of England must have suffered during the war, not only by day but in the long reaches of the night when fears and torment of mind prevented sleep.

'Your mother does not cease to think of you for a single moment,' is a pathetic message on the headstone of the grave of a 2nd Lieutenant of the 7th London Regiment. Alas, there are thousands of such inscriptions which speak for themselves.

The Scotch widow had lost two sons in the war—one killed at Arras, and the other drowned in the Somme. Her husband died last year, but despite her triple loss, she bore her burden bravely.

'I'm satisfied noo,' she said to me, with deep emotion, casting a farewell glance at her son's last resting place. 'I can go back haim ... to Bonny Scotland ... feeling different, feeling better ... they could not have done more for my wee laddie.' I shall never forget that simple, dear old Scotch widow. In the car that same day was a man who had lost his brother, a mother her son, a girl her brother, and a woman who had lost her husband.

A few days later I left Amiens, again by car, this time with Captain Oswald, and we proceeded along the very fine, wide straight road to Albert, bordered by tall, stately trees unspoiled by the vengeance of a destructive artillery. Before reaching halfway we entered first Querrien—which was the HQ of the 4th Army for some time in 1916—and then the Pont-Noyelles.

But the latter place is also famous in connection with a former war, and today a monument can be seen just outside the village commemorating the struggles of Franco-German enmity, 1870–1871.

Albert, seen from a distance, presented a picture of newly constructed buildings, works and factories, also countless bright red tiled house roofs, but a battered, ghostly cathedral ruin of brick and stone stood out in gaunt outline against the sky, as if its duty was to remind all comers that Albert was reborn out of the dust and ashes of a Great War.

Here and there, as one passed along the streets, large gaps could be seen with just a few bricks above ground level to lend one a vision of former days. In other places, fashionable, up-to-date shops have taken the place of debris, and Albert can now boast a modern station, and several comfortable hotels.

It is interesting to note that a gilt statue of the Virgin, with the infant Jesus in her outstretched arm, has been erected on the top of the new church building, and this statue is a facsimile, reduced in size, of the original statue of the Virgin of Albert which once surmounted the old cathedral belfry, and which so long remained suspended in mid-air.

Leaving Albert behind, we climbed the Albert–Bapaume road up to the village of La Boisselle—the scene of much hard fighting. Huge mine craters attest the nature of the warfare in 1916, and cemeteries in the vicinity bear witness to the appalling casualties suffered in that sector.

Although La Boisselle was entirely destroyed during the war, and a sign was found necessary to indicate the original site, today the village has recovered its former existence, and the spirited inhabitants have settled down to post war life as though nothing unusual had ever happened.

Pozieres, that straggling fortress village of 1916, is also completely rebuilt, and contains monuments to the glory of Australians, the Tank Corps and several battalions of the King's Royal Rifles. On the site of the old windmill on the ridge, there is memorial cross erected to the memory of the 3rd Australian Division.

It was thought by many, even experts, who visited the Somme battlefields soon after the war, that the ground, so completely churned and upturned, would be useless for agricultural purposes for many years to come, and a scheme, I believe, was even considered to plant the area with pine trees.

But despite these predictions and the sad upheavals left behind, Mars has 'packed' up most of the guns, shells, rifles, barbed wire entanglements, corrugated iron shelters, observation posts, etc., and only a few bare patches of chalky ground show up here and there where Death used to lurk in trench and dug-out.

For the rest the countryside is beautiful, rich and fertile; poppies flourish in waving fields of corn, and old shapeless, shell-torn trees lie at the foot of young, slender trees—especially is this noticeable along the Albert–Bapaume Road.

The plough having become master, a few bones are unearthed now and again, but the ghastly instruments of war are thrown aside and lie there rotting or rusting, beside the hedges and paths awaiting removal to a destination other than the fair fields of Picardy.

Five hundred yards or so north of the village of Le Sars, and a little distance on the right of the road to Bapaume, there is a primeval burial ground famous now as the Butte de Warlencourt, rising to about 50ft.

Three large crosses are outlined on the crest, one of which—British—was erected in memory of the gallant officers, NCOs and men of the 6th, 8th and 9th Battalions, Durham Light Infantry, who fell in an attack on the Butte and surrounding trenches on November 5 and 6, 1916. Nearby, another cross—German—stands out in memory of the Sachs, Infantry Regiment 179, who also fell on the same date.

As we gazed in silence at the surrounding country from the summit of this famous spot (a panorama which the Germans evidently valued in the Somme battles), the sound of the bells of the new Le Sars Church floated across the intervening space—a pleasant contrast to echoes of 10 years previous.

Then, winding our way to the base of the Butte de Warlencourt, we followed a little track for some distance, with Eaucourt l'Abbaye on our right. The route was evidently used at one time by a light railway, but the tree trunks now lining it, all shattered and torn, stood out strikingly pitiful against the blue sky and the green foliage beyond.

I doubt whether anything echoed so much of the old War days as an incident which occurred whilst we were extracting a shrapnel ball which was embedded in one of these splintered tree trunks.

Away on the crest, suddenly loomed a cloud of black smoke, followed by a loud explosion. Shells, collected on the battlefields, were being blown up, and so familiar were these sounds of war, amidst War's devastation, that it was hard to believe we were not actually on our way to the line.

As time was passing, alas only too quickly, it was not long before we were on the road again, this time direct for Bapaume. I recollect viewing Bapaume through field glasses in October 1916, whilst under fire in a shell hole, after we had come down from that infernal Ypres Salient.

We had already had our baptism of Somme warfare in July, but three months later we found ourselves again trudging the Somme valleys. Even before we left Montauban behind, one of our number 'fell out'—curiously, he shot himself dead in Happy Valley, not 20 yards from where I lay asleep in a dug-out!

After that we 'went on,' past Bernafay and Trônes Woods, Guillemont, Ginchy, to Lesboeufs and Morval. At that time, Bapaume was in German hands, and seemed a long way off to us in muddy trenches below the ridge.

In fact, the British did not occupy Bapaume until five months later, and on withdrawing the Germans systematically and totally destroyed the town—all the houses were then standing like skeletons in a maze of ruins.

Today, Bapaume is again Bapaume, but not so the Hotel de Ville, which used to stand in the Place Faidherbe. War can erase a town, and Peace can restore it, but reconstruction cannot bring back to ravaged Bapaume the atmosphere of its old 15th, 16th and 17th century buildings.

For all that, it has much to be proud of; whereas in 1918 it was entirely in ruins, today it is taking a worthy place among other reconstructed villages and towns of France—and that is saying much.

On our way back along the Bapaume–Albert Road, we branched off in the direction of the village of Martinpuich, and then along the fringe of High Wood, which still bears a haunted appearance in parts.

Several memorials can be seen commemorating the gallantry of troops who were engaged in those actions. I think I am correct in stating that such woods as High, Bernafay, Trônes, and Leuze, have not yet been thoroughly explored or searched.

One only has to try to penetrate into one of these dense labyrinths today to realise what a formidable task it would be. The clearing up of the wreckage of war in such thick undergrowth and utter desolation would, without doubt, add to the already distressing total of graves of unknown warriors.

To write of the other villages we passed or noticed in the distance, such as Contalmaison, Bazentin-le-Grand, Bazentin-le-Petit, Fricourt, is but to repeat what I have already said: that these former death-traps and fortresses, one and all, are almost back to normal existence, and reconstruction is proceeding rapidly on sound modern lines.

On another day, we visited the scene of the fierce fighting on the Ancre of 10 years ago. The road from Bertrancourt is as peaceful as ever, and Mailly-Maillet is now practically whole. Even the iron monger at the end of the village, whose shop received a supplementary load of metal from the German guns, is smiling again. I caught a glimpse of the house, now rebuilt, in the cellar of which I spent a few anxious nights during those early days of July 1916.

The road beyond Mailly-Maillet, where the light railway crosses, brought back poignant memories of 'going up to the line' in the Beaumont Hamel sector. The old silent windmill on the left of the road I recognised, also further on the military cemetery just below Colincamps, where many of our brave fellows found their last resting place in those days.

The remains of the *sucrerie*, that unhealthy spot, sent thrills through me as I recollected the number of shells that went screaming overhead by our reserve lines, depositing themselves with a deadly thud on or near the British gun positions in the rear.

The battlefield on each side of the bleak Serre road is a wild tangle of every conceivable relic of war days, and the severity of the fighting is well illustrated left and right by broken rusty rifles; hand grenades; leather equipment; German and British tin helmets, peppered with shrapnel marks; and so on.

The Newfoundland Memorial Park, enclosed within the triangle formed by Auchonvillers, Hamel and Beaumont Hamel, presents a grim picture of the actual battleground, seaming with deep trenches, guns, dug-outs, big shell holes, a network of treacherous barbed wire, etc.

Excepting the fact that Nature these past few years has asserted herself freely over Mother Earth by profuse growth of grass and shrub, the whole track, from beginning to end, could not convey a more accurate impression of what the Western Front really looked like at the close of the War.

True, the trenches today instead of being of that familiar earthy colour, are shaded by delicate green and yellow through plant and flower; nevertheless, it is a source of satisfaction that some part of the old trenchline in France is being preserved as far as possible in the sad condition of eight years ago. It will serve as a memorial far more vivid than any group of monuments or statues.

As to other things of special interest in the devastated area, now and again one comes across a shapeless tree, fixed to which, on one side, is a ladder, and needless to say these observation posts in trees served the Armies well during war. In parts, some old road signs are still standing, very much the worse for the bitter shelling of war days.

In a civilian cemetery, below a crucifix utterly desecrated, I noticed a machine gun emplacement. And so on. One could write forever on the tragedy of the battlefields, but the scars of the old days are gradually healing up and a few years hence the valleys and hills of the Somme will betray little, excepting for the War Cemeteries, of those mad years 1914–18. As well, perhaps!

—Lt Ernest Matthews Channing-Renton, 5th Bn, Duke of Cornwall's Light Infantry writing in September 1926.

Channing-Renton was special commissioner for the Ypres League after the war and returned to the battlefields several times, living for a spell in the early 1920s in Wiesbaden, Germany. He was wounded in May 1918 in Foret de Nieppe. After the war, he worked as an artist and author, writing several books about the war.

*

We found Albert struggling to rehabilitate itself—a fairly large inn of corrugated iron had been erected and the streets cleared, while the famous Virgin no longer hangs dependent from the church; the inhabitants are rather incensed because they are not getting all the compensation from Government to which they feel they are entitled.

Amiens was very largely normal; the Cathedral and famous Spanish buildings still showed their scars, but the station has been entirely rebuilt. At the time of our visit it was still impossible to get across the Somme battlefield by rail so we hired a car (driven by an English ex-soldier), which took us through what is still a scene of the utmost desolation, and deposited us eventually at Hébuterne.

Delville and Oppy Woods were still mere shell and gas blasted skeletons, and the whole scene was pitted with craters and shell holes, littered with rifles, small arms ammunition, unexploded shells and bombs. It is worthy of note that the latter are best left untouched, because as the hair-spring rusts they are liable to explode when disturbed.

We heard of a little girl who had been killed in Oppy Wood a few days earlier by the explosion of a shell, and as it was still full of mantraps, we passed it by—no need to storm it now. Here and there were the remains of a body which we tried to notify to the Graves Commission, and there were literally hundreds of boots enclosing skeleton feet—less gruesome but no less strange was it to find a German field gun, with its breech block carefully removed, still in position and directed at the British lines.

From Hébuterne we walked to Gommecourt, the spot which possibly carries more sinister memories for the Staffords than any other spot in France. Here the German trenches were still standing, as were many of those very deep dug-outs we found when the enemy retired in March 1917.

Gommecourt Wood was a mere spectre, little attempt had been made at rebuilding, though many inhabitants had returned and erected wooden or iron 'cabines'. As a strange contrast with the war we gathered luscious raspberries on the edge of the wood and found strawberries in Rossignol Wood as we went towards Bucquoy.

There was a lot of building activity at Foncquevillers, where (doubtless in memory of the men of Burton) the brewery was the first large building to be re-erected. The church was a mere ruin, but we still found traces of our light railway while, wonder of wonders, there were two *estaminets*.

It is true that one of them was little more than a hovel, but, as we had decided to remain as near the line as possible, we tried to get accommodation in the larger of the two. This was a difficult matter, since there was only one bed for visitors and that was occupied by the manager of the workmen employed at the brewery.

However, with true French courtesy he vacated it, so that my wife and I could get a good night's sleep while Monsieur made the best of things on the floor. We stayed two days in the Gommecourt district and were much touched by the familiar names in the war cemetery there and by the (then) wooden Memorial Cross erected, near the corner of Gommecourt Wood to the memory of the dead of the 46th Division.

The next day we went on to Bienvillers in order that we might examine the trenches in front of Monchy and Adinfer Wood. Alas there were none to examine, for the soil was valuable here and had been less tortured by the war years.

Cornfields smiled where once our trenches lay, though Monchy on one side of the line, and Bienvillars, Hannescamps and Berles-au-Bois on the other, were still very much under the weather. The people of Bienvillars and Berles-au-Bois remembered the Staffords, nor would they let us go even so far as Pommier without loading my wife with food and flowers, such miracles do friendship and a good reputation work.

Traveling further southward we visited Loos and the Brickfields. Little sign of cultivation here, just the scarred chalk and hard dug trenches which we had once occupied. The positions were most interesting in this locality for our (and the German) three lines of trenches, with wire entanglements in front of each, remained much as they were during war time.

It was strange to walk erect by Harrison's Crater and up the main street of Loos, and we visited particularly that old enemy Nash Alley, before taking which, and in reply to Battalion Orders, Captain McGowan sent back to the Colonel the following message, 'No orders from you are needed to tell the men of my company that they will not leave the German trench while they can walk.'

Lens was entirely rebuilt and the mines in working order. The Staffords well remember its approach through the long street of Liévin which used to receive rather more than their share of gas shells. We walked along the road to Bully Grenay, reminiscent of many a night march and the shells which followed us as we passed our gun positions or picked our way through the scattered ruins of Maroc.

The French are noted for two main characteristics, their courtesy and their practicality. We had many evidences of the former, and the latter was shown by the fact that they had concentrated their main efforts on restarting their mines, factories and agriculture.

Nowhere was this more plainly seen than in the district around Lens and Loos; wherever a mine could be reopened it had been done, wherever a factory could be rebuilt the work had been completed, wherever land was not too badly scarred for recultivation the labourers were at work.

Only apparently as quite a secondary matter had the Frenchman considered his own comfort, he was content to live in any sort of a hovel and to work any hours if only he could wring a living for his family from his desolate surroundings.

One could not help wondering how near to the scene of the war those men have studied the conditions who preach to a smug England that she has suffered equally or more hardly than her late ally.

But sentiment was not entirely lacking. To the south of the Vimy Ridge a portion of the battlefield had been enclosed in memory and as a lasting proof of the valour of those who stormed in and held it. Still further on we reached Béthune, which evacuated in 1918 after three and a half years of shelling, was now once more almost normal.

The buildings round the clock tower were rising again, but the Cathedral seemed beyond repair, while we looked regretfully and in vain for such landmarks as the shell holed embankment which an unconquerable optimist once dubbed, 'The hole in the wall.'

In front of this town the old trench system remained untouched, and here and there were to be found the old trench signs, 'Boyau 15,' etc., while occasionally a bone protruding from the wall of a trench served as a grisly memento of things as they once were.

Perhaps the Givenchy Redoubt looked as realistic as anything remaining on the battle front. A really majestic memorial stands nearby, but the redoubt itself and mine craters as frequent as holes on a solitaire board bore witness to some of the hardest fighting of the war.

As we stood by the old redoubt memory conjured up a picture from the past—one was back in 1915. French bands and English had marched gaily along when that memorial was unveiled, but we saw only the smoke of battle and a mournful procession of stretchers running blood, while shell and bomb and bursts of rifle fire provided the only march we heard.

We were tired and lay down to sleep near Windy Corner but again we remembered the days when men stood not there on the order of their going, but went, and as the sergeant major would doubtless have had it, 'went — quick.'

At Festubert there was little to be found. There never was much, but now those waterlogged trenches had caved in finally and no blasphemous digging party sought in vain to reinstate them. They had gone utterly, never, we hope, to return. Frenchmen scarcely remember Festubert, and if you ask for it they first of all look slightly puzzled and then reply, 'Ah! *monsieur, c'est un marais*.'

They are right, it is and always was. Le Plantin still stands, and in the *estaminet* which once served as our billet we found French youths playing darts—we joined in, drank some of their wine, ate some '*ouefs avec pommes de terre frites*' and went our way.

Unfortunately, we could not spare the time for Belgium and the salient. Hazebrouck was as far as we got, and then, free agents at last, free to go or free to come, we went regretfully as we had come joyously. Truly '*Tempora mutantur, nos et mutamur in illis*.'

—Former officer, 6th Bn, North Staffordshire Rgt writing in December 1926.

9

1927

That a visit to the old battlefields is likely to breed chiefly disillusionment has become a commonplace. What have these wide, smiling lands, with their mellowing crops and clean, new homesteads to do with the regions of horror which once we knew so well?

It is impossible even to go and look for traces of our old frontline, for one cannot trample the hip high corn. And where the German line ran lie cows, tethered at punctual intervals, chewing meditatively in the thick lucerne. Or have we got it wrong?

Ought we be farther to the right? With the disappearance of the old landmarks, the whole country, as we stand full height and without fear in the sunlight, has changed in all dimensions. It has grown out of drawing. It was never as level as this, and the ridge there was ever so much higher. But without the hummock that we knew as the brick heap, how is anyone to get his bearings?

True, there are areas which still, we are told, remain 'in their original condition,' as on the Vimy Ridge, in the Railway Triangle behind Arras, and that dreadful stretch by Thiepval to Beaumont Hamel, past Newfoundland Park to Auchonvillers, and other places. On the ridge the ground is purposely left untouched to the glory of the Canadians and the Highlanders who went with them up the slope from Roclincourt 10 years ago.

In the Triangle, where, perhaps, more Germans met their death in 1917 than at almost any other place within an equally narrow area, there is no purpose to which the land can profitably be put. On the high ground above the Ancre the soil was so thin over the chalk that when it was ploughed deep by the shells it was rendered useless for agriculture.

These areas, indeed, remain waste; but 'in their original condition' they are not. Nature sees to that. Slowly, year-by-year, trenches fall in, parapet and parados are washed away, dug-outs collapse or are choked and disappear, the shell holes slowly fill, and over all the dense growth of grass and flowers, bushes and young trees, masks all the inequalities of the torn earth below.

You push your way stumblingly among the young poplars, sallows and buckthorn, through the tangle of lesser growth ragwort and ox-eye daisies, wormwood, vetches and, above all, nettles (and such stout fighters are these last that in the vegetable warfare that now rages here it looks as if in a few years the whole Thiepval region would be one vast nettle patch) and your feet trip on hidden strands of barbed wire, ragged sheets of corrugated iron, heavier fragments of limbers or tanks.

And everywhere the scavengers of the battlefields, in gangs of two or three, are still at work. They have a long rod sharpened at the end and with a T-shaped handle, like the handle of a garden roller, with which, leaning on it with all their weight, they probe into the loose earth.

Experience has taught them to know when the probe comes in contact with metal, and then they attack the spot with the great hoe-like spades of the French worker. But it is dangerous digging. Continually there are accidents still from unexploded shells or hand grenades; but the rewards are enough to justify the risks.

The driving bands and cases of shells, parts of the mechanism, the bullets in shrapnel duds, even the shells themselves—all have some value; and the man who comes upon one of the innumerable minor dumps which, in the ebb and flow of war, were left all over this country, has earned good pay for a month.

If human bones are found a fixed fee is paid, whether the remains are those of a British soldier, a Frenchman, or a German. The ground must be left religiously alone and the Imperial War Graves Commission notified, so that every care may be taken to identify, if possible, the dead.

At central points you may see the heaped harvestings of recent work—shells and bits of shells of every sort and size, bases of trench mortars, fragments of gun carriages, all rust covered, rifles from which the wood has mostly rotted away, and saddest of all, trench helmets. British or German; and not seldom they are found side-by-side.

Everywhere throughout the battle areas the fences of farm and garden are of barbed wire, sometimes of the old wire, rusted, twisted, only half-straightened out, sometimes of new wire strung on the old uprights, whether of the British or of the enemy type.

Ragged sheets of corrugated iron are put to a thousand uses, and among the spick-and-span new buildings—so vastly more commodious than the old cottages that they replace—are Nissen huts, still seemingly sound and weather tight.

They are used as *estaminets* and chicken houses, as homes where children play about the doors, as stables and garages. To some, porches of the corrugated iron have been added. Some are wreathed in rambler roses.

These things still remain; but they will soon pass—except, probably, the uprights of the barbed wire—and the only vestiges of the war will be the wastes which are still in 'their original condition,' the monuments and the cemeteries, so admirable in their peacefulness and beauty. Already the Great War is fading into ancient history; the battlefields of the Arras and of the Somme becoming one with Malplaquet and with Blenheim.

—SOLDIER, WRITING IN JULY 1927.

*

'Won't it be amazing coming here after the Show!' How many times one used to hear that, in Flanders and Artois, in the days when few men could stand up in either; when at their breasts towered a barrier more final than unending Everest—the Line—on the other side of which lay a world as apart and forbidden as the Moon.

To stroll about that mythical, barred world in after years … to *stand* on Thiepval; to *motor* up Vimy or Passchendaele way! I wish I could convey one tenth the geographical wonder such thoughts inflamed 10, 11, 12 years ago. Nor, now that the miracle has been fulfilled, do I think that probable future emotions were overestimated in those days.

Provided you still had the war 'within you,' that you were able again to live precise, appalling happenings at precise, tremendous places, it *was* amazing to stand on Thiepval, it was staggering to drive to Passchendaele behind a white horse, it *was* … but let me on with my tale, such as it may be.

There are ways and ways of seeing the Old Line. Private car. Rubberneck. Train and taxi. Some may be able to recapture the past while lolling in a limousine or being bawled at by a guide. Not other people—so we walked, with an occasional lorry hop, and two memorable drives in ordinary fiacres along the Vimy and Passchendaele Ridges.

On the eve of the 11th anniversary of the Battle of the Somme, we set off from Albert, and on the eve of the 10th anniversary of Passchendaele we arrived at Ypres—three of the most thought compelling days it has ever been my lot to spend. Albert today is a trying red agglomeration (adopted by Birmingham) with savage splashes of architectural jazz here and there, causing the wayfarer to wince.

One small, peppered house alone stands of long ago—the Café de la Musique, by the station. The cathedral, with its new golden Virgin, will be ready next year, completing the place, a reflection concerning which was this; that should ever again Albert be visited by another war, there should be no lack of '*bon* for the troops'—cafés, bars, and kindred expanding places.

After counting 56, we chucked it—and that monstrosity 'Yessir, you're my Baby' emanating from almost every one, Sunday evening in the Cemetery City of the Somme, and the eight-year-olds of that past epoch beginning to shake a leg. Though perhaps more interesting than they were the boys and girls of 10 and 11—the war babies. A Cockney touch? The *soupçon* of a lassie? (No bon, promenade!).

Albert is down to 6,000 population today, its chief sources of income being an aircraft factory employing 800 at Méaulte, and the forging of tools and implements from battlefield leavings. Surprisingly few old inhabitants have returned, this secession being a marked affair all the way up the Old Line.

Reparations have permitted many to seek healthier and sunnier climes, so that should you ask for so-and-so—even though that person may have been a famous civilian 'map reference'—don't expect to meet with much more than polite apathy from substitutes for whom the War was a financial affair now filed with Waterloo.

In the English stillness of dinner time at the hotel at Albert—following a banquet attended by 110 South African farmers—charming feminine prattle aided the proper atmosphere: 'I hope you had a nice day. I have had such a nice day—that is, I mean a long day. A long day is always a nice day to me.' A nice, long day on the Somme.

But there were others—women—who kept very much to themselves in that room. For battlefield visitors may be grouped—those who come to sightsee generally, patriotic parties visiting certain memorials, and those who come to visit certain graves. Another solo type is the ex-officer, drawn unto himself and tramping to places once held by the battalion.

At Albert station one such turned to me after booking for Contalmaison on the Petite Vitesse. 'Too damn extraordinary for words,' was what he said, 'saying, "third class return Contalmaison." Sounds as if one were tight!?' And then, of course, there are old comrades looking up old friends and *estaminets* and pals living on in France, besides visiting graves. A certain joyful latitude is allowed these.

Our trek took us due north through Aveluy Wood; a lovely summer's morning, complete stillness save for triumphant bird life, but not much doing in the fields on either side ... those fields whence so many never even got started one July 1.

Now red cottages and Nissen cafés dot the Authuille Valley, scarred and smashed to this day. As guide I had a map of the Imperial War Graves Commission displaying about 400 little black squares—military cemeteries—on this front.

'There's Blighty Valley over there,' we would say, indicating a white patch (tombstones) nestling across the Ancre. So we found our way all up the Old Line, by white patches—over 1,000 of them on either side. And what these gardeners have done!

Take Aveluy Wood. A repulsive green freak of strangled vegetation stabbed by skeleton trunks. Yet suddenly one comes upon an acre of sheer loveliness, upon a corner of England beautifully mown and sown, verdant and fragrant, lavender and roses on every grave, the whole so peaceful on the little hillside, so certainly forever England. Within we read the messages relatives write, 'Till next year, Jackie.' And turning over a 12 month, 'Till next year, Jackie,' again.

Thinking to cut across the Ancre marshland and so up to Thiepval, whose 36th Divisional Tower dominates the entire battlefield, we became bogged down in untouched shell holes and had to turn back; though not before sighting a fisherman ensconced by a huge rush grown crater. 'What are you fishing for?' I asked. 'Frogs.'

From Hamel we branched off up to the Newfoundland National Park—a telling memorial representing a caribou perched high over the exact, still wrecked trench area whence the Newfoundlanders attacked one famous November day in '16.

Monumentally speaking, I fear the Old Country has a poor showing in France and Flanders, the Dominions having everywhere not only availed themselves of the proudest sites, but also put twice the imagination and taste into their memorials.

And yet ... and yet ... well, if you want to see the worst, indeed the only undoctored battlefields that survive along the Old Line today go to Beaucourt Hamel, and think of the Naval Division, and thence stump up to Thiepval and think of some Irishmen.

Viewed from Thiepval Tower, this area of the Somme is desolate, maimed, horrible still, a long way the saddest natural survival, besides which the Ypres Salient is a smiling, Flemish countryside (of course I make no comparison of deeds done in either).

While Poles and Portuguese still hacked up the hillside beneath for copper, and a sudden wind moaned, and the very air seemed to nauseate as long ago, the caretaker of Ulster Tower, Sergeant MacMaster shouted: 'It's rather bleak and lonely living up here, five years come this summer—with the missus. Especially now that people aren't coming any more like they used to. Used to have as many as 400 a week. Now it's nearer 100.'

At Beaucourt the countryside changes entirely—fertile fields of corn and beet, and all sign of the Old Line obliterated. So we got on the train and zig-zagged up No Man's Land, past Serre, where our tanks crushed our own troops one misty morning, past Hébuterne and Blairville into Arras.

Such a journey, meaning nothing to the natives seated opposite, is a kind of unreal, unfolding dream to you. 'Miraumont.' Germans had a big aerodrome here. 'Monchy-le-Preux.' Allenby's cavalry were supposed to fetch up here on April 9. And so on.

Led on by the immense white Souchez lighthouse, the French monument commanding this sector, we erred into Canada's National Park, 250 acres of shell torn, earthquaked Vimy Ridge which France has presented to the Dominion, and which is to be reconstructed as a battle zone with concrete trenches and sandbags and duckboards, just as it was on April 9, 1917.

At present there are notices stuck everywhere to the effect that it is a *chasse guardée*, and that one must beware of wolf traps. And then, coming to the crest of the Ridge, we saw a wonderful thing—the whole of industrial northern France spread out far away below—a great red city, newly sprung up, and with Lens as a centre. What a victory sight for the Canadians that must have been, and how right they are to erect their giant memorial on this spot.

While surveyors shouted the odds at one another, we picnicked ... on Vimy Ridge ... and tried to pick out Loos (hopeless, lost in the red sea) and were hardly surprised that Lord Horne never made much progress in the First Army area.

And so up the Salient which, I suppose, begins at Armentières (nothing to be seen in the Neuve Chapelle–Laventie area where the British Army stood with its back to the wall one April 12, not even a minor obelisk to commemorate obedience to Haig's order, as far as I could see, how modest we are compared to others!).

Armentières has risen from its ashes *à la* rose and rather formidable, style *très nouveau*, and with the square removed a few hundred yards, which completely baffles the returned wanderer. What to say of the old Ypres Salient today?

We walked all round it in a semi-circle from Messines to Passchendaele, and sometimes when it poured and blew a gale and no-one was a-sightseeing, it was sacred, but at other times when cheap Ostend was let loose in rubbernecks (cameras, giggles, guides, and all), well, we slid into wayside *estaminets* to wait until things grew quieter.

In a Christmas Number which I got out in 1915—*The Salient*—a poet contributor foresaw all this, though only this doggerel returns as I write:

And when o'er ruins we know so well,
Night in Flanders has come to dwell,
The Ypres Asteria will ring,
With furores from the Ragtime King.

It may not be quite like that, but anyway be it said that the Salient has become a tourist centre today. In fact it has got to be or else Ypres could not exist in its new-fangled form. Gone the Belgian garrison, gone half Ypres' best off, pre-war residents, gone such weaving and jewel cutting industry as the city once possessed.

Another grim joke of Wipers concerns the recent sale to an American of the battered Cross of St Pierre's—perhaps the first sacred relic of the town. '*Les Américains ont acheté le bon Dieu*,' it is whispered.

Again, on June 6 last, General von Hügel, who let loose the first gas attack on Ypres on April 22, 1915, turned up on a visit to the town, in the course of which he sought out his old billet people near Zonnebeke.

'And have you still your wife and charming daughter?' inquired the General on the doorstep.

'Yes, and I have also my gun!' rapped out the brave Belge, making as if to get same.

Down by the Canal bank, one night in '15, I recollect a brigade major, a very fine fellow killed a week later, holding forth with regard to the future in this style: 'They should keep this ruddy place as it is. Teach 'em what it was like and stop 'em joy riding!'

They should have. For us, sentiment, historic sense, remembrance should have dictated so. For the Flemish inhabitants of Ypres, common or garden financial acumen if nothing else. Today Ypres is neither one thing nor the other. You cannot erect a brand new, spick and span city and expect people visiting it to imagine it is, or was, Wipers.

The magic of that name perished with the removal of the ruins it stood for. Yet what a perennial monument was here—primarily to the armies of the United Kingdom and Ireland, for of all who fought here—particularly the Canadians—it was the old BEF which immortalised the Salient in which, moreover, three quarters of the 250,000 graves being tended today indicate English, Scottish, Irish or Welsh regiments, and this not counting the further 58,000 who lie dead with no known resting place, and the vast majority of whom must also have been home troops.

To this whole army corps of unknown soldiers Lord Plumer is tomorrow chiefly dedicating the new Menin Gate; yet how much more fitting, more wonderful, would have been a simple cenotaph rising in the centre of the ruins of Ypres, in the Grande Place, by the skeleton Cloth Hall.

I was told at Ypres the other day that a certain British officer, holding an important post there when the War ended, had almost to be removed from the scene by force because his exhortations that the ruins be preserved were not listened to.

How the good Flems—though perhaps not their ancient mayor—must bitterly regret their unimaginative obstinacy today ... when they are seeking to keep every upset stone in position in order to attract tourists, the pre-war industry of the city having languished.

For this British officer's plan was simplicity itself; draw a cordon round the principal ruins in the centre of the city, and then build a new city next door with all the hotels and fine buildings one cared for.

Geographically there was nothing to stop this being done, while both sides would have been appeased. Wipers would have remained as a warning and a token. And tourists would have flocked thither from the ends of the earth as to a new Pompeii. And the good Flems would have benefited accordingly, as they probably deserved to, instead of being in the rather pathetic 'Queer Street' they are today.

But there ... they preferred to draw the seven and a half times the pre-war figure of their properties, as offered them by the Belgian Government if they came back within a given period, and so we have the New Ypres of the present.

In the gay and unchecked columns of the daily press I have seen this rebuilt city referred to as 'thriving.' Unless my information be all wrong such is far from being the case. In effect I was asked by a local official to do everything I could, with a typewriter, to induce English capital across, so that industry might be set a little on its feet again.

'What kind of industry?' 'Any kind,' was the eloquent reply and my good burgher proceeded: 'Tell them you can get Belgian labour extraordinarily cheap—about the equivalent of three pence an hour. And female labour for even less. Most of our weaving has gone to England. And a jewel cutting factory we started has failed. Beer and butter are now almost all we've got.'

'You see, in the old days Ypres was mainly a residential city with a garrison of over 4,000. Well, because of our new arrangements with France, all these troops have gone to the Liège–Namur area. And a large number of our former residents in easy circumstances have never returned. Just sold their properties and settled where they drifted to during the War. "Ypres," they said, "had always been right in the centre of every war, and probably would be again."'

'Now we are mostly taking in each other's washing—about 14,000 of us against 19,000 in 1914. And yet you English could acquire a house and garden freehold in the centre of the city for about £300! And there's Ostend and...'

'But surely you appreciate that English people would scarcely like to make their homes in a city around which something like 300,000 of their kith and kin lie buried in 360 separate cemeteries?'

A shrug of the shoulders, and silence. Such was my exchange with one good burgher of Ypres, 1927. On the other hand there is no intention whatever of conveying a picture of an under nourished, listless population.

The farming folk round about are going strong—in the fertile fields of Passchendaele and Wyteschaete and Gheluvelt—and the city folk, besides having 'put something by,' are amazingly frugal and non-spending.

There they stand at their shop doors (almost every householder of Ypres seems to run a shop or *estaminet* of some description) pastorally contented as ever in the first all new city to be erected in the history of the world.

For if the old architecture has been religiously and felicitously copied, the bricks are new, and red and cheap viewed from behind. Unlike some others, these Flemish War victims are very, very friendly to the British, very remembering.

And you only wish that they could have had a happier rejuvenation. But what will you? The Belgian prohibition law has killed café life, with all the animation that such entailed, thereby adding to the dominant impression borne upon one at Ypres; namely, that you are walking abroad in a strangely silent, depopulated town which, while possessing all the prerequisites in the form of sumptuous hotels and restaurants and *estaminets* and *tinkhauser* (all terribly new and shining) has nevertheless only half returned to life.

If it were not for the small British colony, principally engaged in tourist business, even this *va-et-vient* would not prevail. Although there are also about 60 overseers, gardeners, etc., resident round Ypres, and working on the cemeteries at £3 10*s* a week, who also come into the hub of things occasionally.

The idiotic 'axe,' wielded so formidably and blindly by the 'popular' press, has cut the War Graves Commission down to this (of course this Press never meant to—nor did the donkey mean to kick its dish of oats over), but let us hope that the Commission, whose work has been perfectly splendid, may be able to carry on all the same.

However, for two hours each lunchtime in the Ypres season (June–September), it is different: when the motor coaching tourists arrive from Ostend to 'do' the Salient.

Lunch in the trenches (vin compris)
Five bob a head, and then to tea,
Over the way in the White Château,
Graves guaranteed—row upon row.

Well, no—it hasn't worked out like that. Not one bit ... and yet how much better things would have been if, the ruins remaining, all visitors had been invited to descend and walk where the old frontline of the Salient ran by Wieltje Hooge–St Eloi.

Now they go flying round the place, past Shrapnel and Hellfire Corners, through Polygon and Sanctuary Woods and Railway Cutting, and so on, because, of course, they have to get back to Ostend by teatime.

The demeanour of these day trippers, preponderantly British-on-holiday-in-Belgium, as far as I could see, left nothing to be desired save in the case of the usual flappers giggling over Kodaks and snapping each other up against the ruins of the Cloth Hall.

The bearing of other visitors, however, is different. Many Germans come to Ypres. Almost incomprehensible! But never think the Germans will alter because they can't. They are all down the valley of the Meuse as well—where they massacred nearly 2,000 civilians at the outstart, and burnt whole towns.

In Ypres one afternoon I overheard one bull-necked Teuton airily observe to his *Frau*, as the twain surveyed the new Grande Place: 'I don't see what these people have against us. We gave them a fine new city!' (*Eine hubsche neue Stadt*).

Rather a remarkable character in the New Ypres, Mr L. N. Murphy, relates further, concerning the late enemy, that Germans freely visit his local War Museum, in which are set out all the weapons and curios of the trenches and battlefield, the finest collection in existence I believe.

'They even try and engage me in conversation about the rights and wrongs of the War. Old General von Hügel, who loosed off the first gas attack against Ypres, was down here for quite an hour the other day blathering away.'

'Then he sailed off to attend the unveiling of our 20th Division Memorial near Langemark. Utterly impenitent, the whole bunch of them sign the visitors' book with a flourish. But now I've got a special one for them.'

Mr Murphy (by the way he holds the French equivalent to the VC, the *Medaille Militaire* for spy services of a very special nature) is, *inter alia*, clerk to the borough council of Ypres, participates in the official welcoming of illustrious visitors, runs a souvenir shop, tourist agency, and War Museum, and in the wintertime—the close season—turns town electrician!

A kind of glorified town-major of peace. And he would like more units and individuals to send out relics for the Museum, which may soon be located beneath the ruins of the Cloth Hall. In passing, quite a squabble continues to hinge on this historic remnant.

The mayor, M. Colaert, is said to desire that it be rebuilt, as the adjacent cathedral is being, to please him, but powerful natives have put down their foot … and M. Colaert is an old, old man.

Apart from the shell-torn ramparts by the Lille Gate, I saw only one other ruin remaining in Ypres—the old prison as you turn down towards the canal bank. How strange it was to cross this latter and stroll over lush meadows where Skipton Road, one vast communication slush, used to lead up to the alleged frontline!

Out beyond, too. I tried to locate where Hindenburg Farm once lay, for there one of the jobs of those knowing German used to be to lie out all night up against the German wire trying to overhear what they said in their trenches (usually one's report next morning took the form of a series of curses ejaculated by *feldwebels* or *wachtmeisters* bossing working parties!).

Memories, memories! Was ever square mileage so teeming with them? A bock in Essex Farm—served in a real *estaminet* by a fine-looking, English talking 'Promenade Mademoiselle!' Another opposite Hooge Château where Haig made his *beau geste* one critical afternoon, riding along, perfectly uniformed and mounted, at the head of his Staff!

And by the way, a little later, along the same road (I should not have noticed it had I not been afoot), a small slab set into the side of a house. Just a small stone slab—yet what did it commemorate? The stand of the Worcesters at Gheluvelt in November 1914, which saved Ypres and probably the Channel Ports.

A trio of monuments round Ypres that I liked best were the Guynemer stork, the huge Canadian soldier near Langemark, and the beautiful Canadian rose terraces, rising one above the other at Zillebeke. Always the Dominions!

Wandering about the Salient, this reflection occurred: that if Ypres itself has rejoined normality—a finely-built, decorative, brand new Flemish town—the Salient never will, not at least for centuries of time.

If knowledge obliteration should occur again, as it seems to have done some time or another since the megalithic menhirs and dolmens of southern Brittany, excavators of the future should have a wonderful time in the Salient, with its pill-boxes and concrete dug-outs, tumble-down monuments, and buried cemeteries, trying to work out what the whole collection meant.

Think of it—the dug-outs along the canal bank all face the setting sun!... Thus the Wipers of 12 years after. Tomorrow 'Old Plum' will inaugurate Its new historic passageway. Does he remember the wag who, during a weary march in file from the ramparts to the trenches, passed back the message: 'Last man shut the Menin Gate!'?

—Capt. Ferdinand Tuohy writing on the eve of the inauguration of the Menin Gate Memorial to the Missing on 24 July 1927 by Field Marshal Lord Plumer.

Tuohy served in the Intelligence Corps during the First World War. After the war, he worked as a journalist and author. Leo Norbury Murphy served with The Queen's (Royal West Surrey Regt) and the Royal Fusiliers during the First World War. He settled in France after the war and established the British Touring and Information Bureau to help people on battlefield tours. In the 1920s, Murphy created the Ypres Salient War Museum.

10

1928

My recent visit to the battlefields of Flanders left one outstanding impression on my mind. Not only has this little country buried the hatchet, but she has set the world an example in the way of getting back to peace.

In short, she has cleaned up the hideous mess of the war and, in the small space of 10 years, rebuilt her towns and villages and made the countryside fit to look upon. Like many other fellows who were out there in the war, I felt when peace was declared that if I never saw this then desolate country again, I should miss nothing, but curiosity led me to make the trip.

Traveling along what was the British frontline from Nieuport to Dixmude and thence to Poelcapelle, Langemark and Ypres, I found little to remind me of what I saw there in the days of 1915–18. Everywhere devastation seemed to have given place to nature's peaceful pursuit, and with the exception of an occasional pill-box along the roadside with its great ugly 'eyes' glaring in the direction of Passchendaele, the outward visible signs of war were few.

It was difficult to realise that 10 years ago on this very ground British Tommies sacrificed their lives in thousands, but an elegant reminder of this, however, is to be found in the many little cemeteries scattered here and there by the roadside all so prim and proper.

These, together with the Menin Gate Memorial with its 56,000 names carved in granite, will stand for all time as a reminder of the grim years when the Almighty seemed to have wearied of human life and given the devil a free hand to destroy it.

One of the Belgian acquaintances I made on the trip was a youth of about 16 years, whose perfect Scottish accent made me curious. It turned out that at the outbreak of war he was transported to Glasgow as a babe in the arms of his mother, a Belgian refugee.

His father was one of the gallant little Belgian Army which went 'West' at Liège before most realised 'there was a war on'. This little fellow is now boots at the Exelsis Hotel, Ostend. He has had his schooling in Scotland, which explains the fact that he told me he was saving up to return to Glasgow, and in aid of the event sold me a packet of postcards. He's a lad who'll get on.

Langemarck was a village that interested me much, for it was there I saw a party of 33 men of the 1st Border Regiment on the night of August 3, 1917, crawl from the British lines and cross the Steenbeek stream—then the dividing line of No Man's Land—to raid a pill-box, which at that time represented Langemarck on the landscape. Only three of the gallant little party returned, and there were no prisoners. The pill-box and its occupants remained intact.

I suppose the official communique issued at home at that time read: 'British raid at Langemarck repulsed with slight losses,' or perhaps it was not mentioned at all, for I suppose in the big scheme of things it would be regarded as a very small 'affair.'

It seemed incredible that this now picturesque little village and the charming freshwater stream running alongside could ever have been the scene of such happenings. Incidentally, what remains of the pill-box has been utilised as a hen roost.

One had to search closely to find any disfigurements of war in Ypres. Houses, shops, hotels, churches and schools are all rebuilt. Even the ramparts flanking the Memorial—once a network of dug-outs—bear little sign of their wartime occupation. All I could find there were a few workshops and a generating station.

There is no more interesting spot in the whole of Belgium than the famous Hill 60, which was the scene of the most fierce fighting on the sector. One might truly say of it: 'And every mark beneath your feet will be a soldier's sepulchre.'

Close by is a wooden hut sporting the sign 'No Man's Land Hotel.' This is a welcome place of refreshment and very appropriately the proprietor is an ex-member of the famous Seventh Division—'The Contemptible Little Army.'

Looking down towards Ypres one sees Zillebeke with its beautiful lake glistening like silver against the sky a striking contrast from the days when Jerry had knocked the bottom out and blown the sides away, causing it to spread all over the landscape and trickle into the boots of the British Army as they slept in their dug-outs round about.

At St Julien, where in the Second Battle of Ypres the Canadians fell in thousands under the first German gas attack, peace and tranquillity now reigns. In the centre of the village has been erected a monument to the memory of the fallen Canadians.

As one sees the country today it speaks volumes for the industrious manner in which the Belgians have tackled the task of reconstruction. Belgium seems to cry out to the world, 'The war is over, let us get on with peace,' although she suffered the hardest of all in so far as her homes and country were devastated, she fosters no hate, but asks; 'Have we in our time not civilisation rot with hate, why poison the hearts of our children?'

Those who utter empty phrases of the inevitability, who sit at home, but are ever ready to shed other men's blood, would do well to visit the battlefields and linger long in those military cemeteries until the real meaning of war strikes home.

—PTE PERCY WADDINGTON, WRITING IN AUGUST 1928.

*

Fourteen years ago today we were in a state of innocence. I don't know what else to call it. We knew that we were at war. We did not know what war was. A few individual Frenchmen or Germans may have had memories of 1870.

Some of the British Expeditionary Force had been under fire in the Soudan, South Africa or remote India. It is doubtful whether those who had seen fighting were not the most astonished. In a few weeks they were learning something new. In a few months, not only they, but entire nations were involved.

Now, on the Continent there had been at least some formal training and legal obligation to be so involved. In Great Britain none. And to emphasise the fact came the revelation that, without compulsion and constraint, men were coming from overseas, finally from wherever English is spoken, and even beyond.

That is why the British Legion is unique. The British Army, in France and elsewhere, had the furthest to go, mentally as well as physically to get to the Front, and can never altogether go back. Some of its members will never leave the place where they laid down their lives. The others will revisit it, from time-to-time, in person or in memory.

Forget! Who can possibly forget? Not I—a mere platoon commander of what used to be called the 'PBI'—'pore bloomin' infantry.' Nor yet any gunner, without whom we should all have been killed, nor yet any of the skilled services, without whom we should have starved, drowned, and have died all sorts of deaths that some of us, at least, escaped.

Forget the feeling of finding oneself left, with a handshake and some laconic orders, responsible for so many yards length of a ditch half full of water, bordered by dissolving sandbags and broken wire, which was yet the edge of England?

Nothing was visible, but there were uncouth noises and smells, and the sudden realisation that such an experience was what is called in books 'baptism of fire.' Then the dismal superhuman task of clearing the first casualties, the hopeless attempts at rebuilding and draining that line, at last the beatitude of the first relief, of marching somewhere and lying down to sleep in the rain. That was the character of the Ypres sector, well chosen for this day's gesture of memory.

The terrific artillery protection, the great battles, the decisions were later on and farther off. But at Ypres, in the early days, the war was at its grimmest, most helpless, costliest.

If it were only for us, who remember so well, there would be little need of that great arch that spans the Menin Gate that is the main passage to those fields of memory.

The battered old 18th century portal, belonging to the time when armies solemnly shut each other up in towns the size of Ypres, would do well enough. As for the new road and the houses that line it, for some of us, they are not there. We have but to turn our heads and we forget them.

In our minds, whatever the day, it is always raining, always dusk, always lighted by a greenish flicker, deafening with hideous noise, on that road. But we must remember that we are a dwindling number. Who will march through that gate 10 and 20 years hence, and with what knowledge?

No, the names are well graven up there, on so solid a structure. For the day will come when they will be but names and the arch will be their only memorial. It is a strange place to go to, the new Ypres of post-war, and the very way there is strange. The road from Lille was hardly one for motoring when I last saw it, nor did one linger in the square by the Cloth Hall.

An extraordinary resurrection has rebuilt halls and houses, and brought back a population to streets where danger stalked alone, years ago and men made haste to get out into the open fields, where, at least, the rich soil of Flanders smothered some of the shrapnel and there were no walls to fall on them. I remember the canal too, where pontoon and other extemporary bridges made a dangerous alternative to the town, until the causeway was built in 1917.

That is why the great stone arch, for all its solidity, makes little impression on my habit of mind. Here today are such crowds as I never saw, seemingly more than half women, some no longer young and bearing on their breasts the medals of men whose heads will never rest there again.

Here are standards, British, from Legion branches, or bearing the signs of the old infantry divisions. Allied standards, some I cannot recognise, a sight such as I never saw here before.

And here are two princes, more generals than I can count, dignitaries of the Church and State, and, as column after column moves into position, a sea of upturned faces and waving flags.

Queer, queerer sight than I ever thought to see. So queer, so unusual that, as I look, it fades and disperses. The bright weather, the great stone arch, the scores of notabilities, the 20,000 common folk, the standards and bands all disappear.

To me, once again it is night and raining, and the shrapnel blasts the place, minute after minute, and some Jim or Jock of a transport driver lies there alone, but for the mule beside him, all dismembered. Now, on that very spot, an Archbishop prays, and princes uncover, generals salute, the great crowd is hushed.

And if wishing were any good, no doubt that great unified wave of feeling might reach him, that man of the unknown grave, wherever he is, now. Can he hear us singing: 'Oh Valiant Hearts, who to your glory came,' or feel that we mean it?

Here now are the Guards' bugles, they should know the road to Ypres. And now, above lowered standards ring out the Last Post and Reveille, and then the bands play the 'Brabanconne,' the 'Marseillaise,' and 'God Save The King.' The solemnity lifts the crowd—the most orderly crowd imaginable—marches off, party by party.

A long column winds down the rebuilt street. I feel as though it passed more than a saluting point. I feel as though there stood watching that procession a dim exorable figure; Destiny perhaps. We all march on, and the past recedes, and the long agony of the Salient becomes every year an actual experience to fewer and fewer of us. At last it will be mere history. This is the best that we can wish for it.

Today's ceremony will be a mockery indeed if, instead of marching past, we are merely marching towards some other world catastrophe, with means of destruction 10,000 times more deadly. I, for one, will not yet give up hope that we may be better advised. Not until the actual fact forces me to such a conclusion, will I believe that a ceremony so heartfelt, reverent and attended by the great and the holy, as that I have witnessed today, is a mere piece of sentiment and vainglory.

'Still through the veil, the visitors' pitying eyes
'Look down to bless our lower Cavalries,' we sang today.

The echo of the footsteps dies, the last reverberation of the drums become inaudible, the cheering has ceased. But still up the Menin Road they come, the long procession of spirits of those whose very graves could not be found. I cannot see them, but I can feel that they are there.

We say that dead men tell no tales. Neither do they own any nationality. That long invisible column seems to me to contain even more than the tens of thousands of our own.

I hope it is so, I hope I shall live to see a celebration at the Menin Gate, or elsewhere, that may embrace all who have lost and suffered. For are we not all mortal? That is the last and strongest impression the March Past leaves on me.

—Lt Ralph Hale Mottram, Norfolk Regiment, writing in August 1928 from the British Legion's Grand Pilgrimage to the Menin Gate.

After the war, Mottram forged a successful career as a writer and author. He was sent by the *Daily Mirror* to report from the remembrance event, which saw 11,000 men and women travel from across Britain to Belgium and France to visit the battlefields and take part in the commemoration service.

*

The eyes of the people are at present fixed upon the battlefields of Flanders where the pilgrims of the British Legion are at present, some renewing acquaintance with spots where they spent unpleasant hours in other days, others on a sadder mission, a visit to the grave of a loved one, and in spirit the great body of ex-servicemen who are unable to make the journey in person marches behind them.

Along roads bearing familiar names these people will go, and we, who have passed this way before, follow and are puzzled. This is not the land we knew. We are astonished at the changes that have been wrought in 10 short years, and our astonishment changes into wonder and admiration for the nation that has brought about this marvellous transformation.

As we reach Poperinghe strange feelings fill our breasts as we recognise, or rather fail to recognise our old camping grounds, for a rich harvest awaits the gathering where once camouflaged huts stood in profusion.

Even the town itself seems strange and unreal, and a vision rises before our eyes in the evening twilight. We see soldiers entraining, and we accompany them, and after a short run through some hop fields we enter the plain of desolation.

There are no signs of life anywhere, and each side of the railway track is as full of holes, shell holes, as ever. All is quiet save for the shrieking of shells. Our train glides noiselessly forward to the outskirts of Ypres. Silently we detrain and company by company the soldiers move off at intervals through a town of ghosts over which the angel of death hovers continually.

The broken walls cast weird shadows as we pick our way amid the debris of what were once the homes of prosperous citizens and hurry across the square once the show place of the town, which with its renowned architectural treasures, has shared a common fate. A huge shell hole the size of an ornamental lake, has a place under the shadows of the Cloth Hall. On all sides destruction and desolation.

And the vision fades and we stand in the same square once more after a lapse of 12 years and again we are puzzled by what we see. The square is palpitating with life, the houses glaringly new meet the eye on every side, only the roofless walls of the Cloth Hall tell of the cataclysm but even it is different—it has been tidied up.

If one should search for some part of the line, the excursion will most probably be fruitless. A smiling country bearing in bounteous measure the fruits of the earth has hidden the dreadful scars. Hellfire Corner is a jolly place, and one may be held up here while a tram crosses the roadway, and from the doorway of the little *estaminet* Madame will smile her thanks for what we did.

At different places one comes across little stones which mark the farthest limits of the Germans' advance, and by the canal some dug-out which recalls days in reserve, but the trenches—well, they are napoo.

But we forget. One glimpse of what the whole countryside was really like can still be obtained, and that at Hill 60. Here the ground is still in its war state, and an overturned concrete pill-box testifies the fierceness of the fighting.

One will feel annoyed, too, at being asked to buy souvenir bayonets and the like after gazing at the three little crosses that stand near the crest of the hill, two British graves and one German—three little crosses, surely symbolical.

To stand on the top of this insignificant height is to realise its strategic importance. But today, instead of a country seared with trenches and ploughed with shellfire, we see the waving crops and Ypres, the new Ypres that has risen out of the ruins of war. Houthulst Forest, you will be told, is still being cleared, and the canal too, has not yet given up all its dead. Truly the Belgians have beaten their swords into ploughshares.

But a visit to the Ypres Salient will teach anyone a great lesson, that of the futility of war. Well-known names are to be forever preserved, but instead of indicating places of bloody fighting they mark the last resting place of heroes, men who died for country and freedom.

What a poignant sight these beautiful places make, and how many lying there are 'known unto God' alone. Here is the strongest argument against war, stronger than any League of Nations—teach the young the meaning of these little white stones under which lie the flower of

Right: Leyland Motors workers on a pilgrimage to the battlefields explore the trenches on Hill 62 in June 1929. (*Photo: Stuart Clewlow*)

Below: Members of a 3,000-strong party of Leyland Motors workers on the ruins of an old mill on the Hindenberg Line at the Yser Canal in June 1929. (*Photo: Stuart Clewlow*)

Leyland Motors workers gather on the German frontline in June 1929. (*Photo: Stuart Clewlow*)

A war invalid sells souvenirs in the ruins of the Cloth Hall, in Ypres, in 1921.

Above left: Tourist bus outside the ruins of the Cloth Hall, in Ypres, in 1919.

Above right: Visitors pay their respects at the English cemetery on the ramparts of the Lille Gate in 1919.

Abandoned tanks became a popular stop on tours of the battlefields, this photograph was taken on 28 June 1921 at Zillebeke.

Notice on the ruins of St Martin's Cathedral, Ypres, in 1919: 'This is holy ground. No stone of this fabric may be taken away. It is a heritage for all civilised peoples. By order, Town Mayor, Ypres'. (*Photo: Australian War Memorial/Mr Alfred Sharp Collection*)

A group of civilian men, women, and officers visiting the battlefields of France in 1919 stand in front of a German short-barrel 21-cm Morser 10 howitzer. (*Photo: Australian War Memorial*)

An abandoned German pillbox on the Messines Road. The signboard reads: 'Ploegsteert Wytschaete'. (*Photo: Australian War Memorial/Mr Alfred Sharp Collection*)

Mr Alfred Sharp examines a howitzer outside the Cloth Hall and St Martin's Cathedral at Ypres, Belgium, in August 1920. (*Photo: Australian War Memorial/Mr Alfred Sharp Collection*)

Trench on top of Hill 63, Messines, Belgium, December 1919. (*Photo: Australian War Memorial*)

Chinese worker selling discarded shells as battlefield souvenirs to a group of tourists. (*Photo: Philip Woets*)

Abandoned tanks on Poelcapelle Road, Ypres. (*Photo: CWGC/Goodland Collection*)

Tending to graves at Arras. (*Photo: CWGC/Goodland Collection*)

Recovering shells close to a wartime cemetery. (*Photo: CWGC/Goodland Collection*)

Grisly photo of human remains and war detritus on Mount Kemmel sold as a souvenir to visitors. (*Photo: CWGC/Goodland Collection*)

Above left: Gardener tending to Hooge Crater Cemetery in 1920. (*Photo:* CWGC)

Above right: Battlefield debris piled up on the roadside for collection at Thiepval.

Girls attending to the grave of Lt Walter Evelyn Parke, 2nd Bn, Durham Light Infantry. (*Photo:* CWGC)

Left: Demarcation stone at Hellfire Corner outside Ypres marking the limit of the German advance.

Below: Albert Cathedral pictured in April 1917 with the famous leaning statue of the Golden Virgin.

Skindle's Hotel, in the former officers' club, in Poperinghe, was a popular haunt for officers during the First World War and in the post-war years. (*Photo: Chantal Callens*)

Above left: Preserved trenches at Hill 60 in the 1930s. (*Photo: Philip Woets*)

Above right: Ruins of the Church of Notre Dame, Armentières. (*Photo: from the Jordan/ Ference Collection, courtesy of greatwarin3d.org*)

Above left: Searching for the dead at Nieuport. Zig-zag trenches from 6–7 feet are dug, and the intervening earth carefully levelled. (*Photo: Jordan/Ference Collection, courtesy of greatwarin3d.org*)

Above right: Guns and wire entanglements on the battlefield at Langemarck. (*Photo: Jordan/Ference Collection, courtesy of greatwarin3d.org*)

Above left: An old battlefield trackway at Mametz Wood on the Somme. (*Photo: Jordan/Ference Collection, courtesy of greatwarin3d.org*)

Above right: Ruined interior of Albert Cathedral after the war. (*Photo: Jordan/Ference Collection, courtesy of greatwarin3d.org*)

Above left: Ruins of St Martin's Cathedral, Ypres. (*Photo: Jordan/Ference Collection, courtesy of greatwarin3d.org*)

Above right: Shattered Bapaume Road, Albert, after the war. (*Photo: Jordan/Ference Collection, courtesy of greatwarin3d.org*)

Above left: Military cemetery at St Jean, Armentières. (*Photo: Jordan/Ference Collection, courtesy of greatwarin3d.org*)

Above right: Curious visitors climb on the Big Gun at Chiugnes. (*Photo: Jordan/Ference Collection, courtesy of greatwarin3d.org*)

Above: Farmer guides his plough around a headstone in a field near Ypres in the shadow of a derelict tank. (*Photo: Jordan/Ference Collection, courtesy of greatwarin3d.org*)

Below left: Celebrated wartime cartoonist Capt. Bruce Bairnsfather returned to the Western Front in 1921 and in this image captured a Belgian family living in a former Nissen hut on the battlefield. (*Image published courtesy of the estate of Barbara Bruce Littlejohn*)

Below right: This cartoon by Capt. Bruce Bairnsfather features one of his famous wartime drawings inset into the same scene he discovered returning in 1921. (*Image published courtesy of the estate of Barbara Bruce Littlejohn*)

Wartime tunnels open to visitors at Hill 60 in the 1930s. (*Photo: David Blanchard*)

Entrance to the Hill 60 Museum in the 1930s. (*Photo: David Blanchard*)

Wartime exhibits on display in the Hill 60 Museum in the 1930s. (*Photo: David Blanchard*)

Grand Café, Zandberg, made from a converted Nissen hut to cater for tourists on the Menin Road.

our Empire who died for a peace that was to make war in the future impossible.

There is the ever-present challenge of the dead to the living. See to it that they have not died in vain. To see such places should fill each one with fresh resolve to preserve peace, to assist the maimed who, unlike those who passed out the Menin Gate and returned not, came back broken and shattered. See that they did not die in vain. Keep faith with them.

To you from falling hands we throw
The torch; be yours to hold it high,
If ye break faith with us who die,
We shall not sleep...

—ANONYMOUS, WRITING IN AUGUST 1928.

11

1929

On the 15th anniversary of the outbreak of war between Great Britain and Germany, here we are again in Northern France; but in what different circumstances. The shadow of the invader no longer hovers over this pleasant land; on the contrary there are signs of prosperity on every side which are evidence of a wonderful recuperative power.

Not all of our party have been on this side of the Channel before, and there are many women amongst us, so that we did not recapture on the crossing quite the old spirit or the old sensations; but ghosts of almost forgotten days did walk amongst us.

It was good to see the gendarmes and other functionaries at Dunkerque as excitable and voluble as ever; but many of us would have preferred the old trucks for '*huit chevaux*' or '*quarante hommes*' to the execrable third-class carriages in which we made the journey here.

What a journey of memories! Hazebrouck, Strazeele, Bailleul, Nieppe, Armentières; with Mont Cassel and the Mont des Cats dominating the Flanders plain on our left. Little sign can be seen from the train that this was ever a devastated area, except for the number of new buildings, occasionally a concrete pill-box, more frequently old corrugated iron and barbed wire put to good use by a thrifty people; otherwise nothing. Every inch of ground is utilised, and the crops appear to be splendid.

Lille itself is a flourishing and prosperous city, but one can detect signs of the four years of hardship during the German occupation in the appearance of those who were children at that time.

This morning we spent marching round the city behind a band who set a step about twice as fast as that of a light infantry regiment, quite impossible to keep up; attending an official welcome at the Hotel de Ville, where we were entertained to '*vin d'honneur*'—a very popular part of the proceedings; and placing wreaths on the city's war memorial and the memorial to five citizens who were shot by the Germans for acting as spies for our own Army.

There has been a blazing sun all the morning, but one can get most attractively cool glasses of lager or bock at equally attractive prices. Naturally, one does. Tomorrow we go to Béthune, Neuve Chapelle, and the Aubers Ridge.

Today has been somewhat disappointing. The train journey to Béthune running alongside the La Bassée Canal for a considerable distance, past historic spots like Givenchy, Cambrin and Cuinchy, had its interest; but much time was spent at Béthune itself, waiting for lunch time, lunching, and waiting for buses, which might have been better employed. We had to wait interminably in the Army, but it is a pity to do it now.

The bus journey back, on the other hand, through Festubert, Neuve Chapelle and Aubers, was far too rapid. The only halt was at the Indian memorial at Neuve Chapelle, an extraordinarily beautiful and appropriate monument, but I personally, and probably many others, would rather have stopped in the village itself and looked for old spots.

Is that old house, for instance, heavily reinforced with concrete, in which my gun team spent an exciting week, still standing? Where is that old position by the church?—the church, of course, is rebuilt, but one would like to stand on the spot again. But we go through so fast that we can hardly identify anything.

Only the Bois du Biez, that wood of mystery, grave of many a thousand good men and true, but thick and green again now, stands quiet and lonely and, one can almost imagine, menacing as of old, on the other side of the road.

Going back over Aubers Ridge, we can see how well the German lines were sited and understand the accuracy of their fire. No wonder they had the range of Windy Corner to a nicety, and knew what was likely to be there, and when.

Profiting by yesterday's experience, we have made today a memorable one. Travelling by train to Arras with the rest of the party we left them there, and four of us chartered a taxi to visit some of the places in the semi-circle cast of Arras which became historic in April and May, 1917.

Expresses run into Arras now; but they are not the 'Arras expresses' that we used to hear lumbering over our heads when we were in the Wancourt line. There are still a few houses that have not been restored, but all the principal buildings are rebuilt or rebuilding.

Leaving Arras by the main road to Lens, we stopped at Vimy Ridge to see the famous mine craters and the 'show' trenches. Both the old German and Canadian frontline trenches have been restored, the sandbags are filled with concrete, concrete duckboards are substituted for the original wooden ones, and as far as possible a sector of the line has been made permanent so that future generations can get some idea of what trench warfare was like.

It is all very true, but far too good to be true. Life in those trenches would have been luxury compared with the real thing. The most interesting part of the restoration is the dug-out in which the Canadians gathered for the attack.

Here can be seen, on the soft chalk walls, names and dates cut by those men during the weary hours of waiting—one has written 'Goodbye, Canada,' another has carved an excellent head of a soldier in full relief—and at one point, where a shaft was being driven upward, a 5.9 shell remains embedded in the roof where it had come through and failed to explode.

All that is lacking is the press of tired men, the murky glimmer of candles, the thick and foetid air, the general mess, mud and confusion, and the everlasting rumble of the bombardment overhead.

The view from the summit of the ridge is marvellous, and the Canadian memorial, when it is completed, will be a massive and wonderful landmark for miles around, more impressive even than the French lighthouse at Notre Dame de Lorette.

From Vimy the car took us through Thélus, Bailleul—the lesser known Bailleul—past Oppy with its wood of unpleasant memory, Gavrelle, Fampoux, and Roeux to Monchy-le-Preux. It was easier hereabouts to recognise old features. The superficial traces of warfare have gone here as completely as elsewhere, but the configuration of the land, more varied than in the northern plains, remains, so that old spots can be more readily identified.

It is not hard to see where our dug-outs were in the railway embankment behind Bailleul, and now that we can stand up in the open it is possible to appreciate why Ouse Alley and those other interminable trenches that led down the long slope towards Oppy were of such ghastly length—what was it, two kilometres? Something like that, but it used to seem like ten miles.

Oppy Wood looks no more attractive in the distance than it ever did; but the quiet waters and ponds of the River Cojeul make a peaceful and beautiful scene now. Monchy-le-Preux, best known of all those villages, on the hill by the side of the once dreaded Arras-Cambrai Road, is largely rebuilt, but there is not a great deal of it now.

In the centre stand the ruins of the old *Mairie*, bought by the Newfoundland Government as a war memorial and surmounted by their impressive figure of a moose. Here we found an English gardener who has charge of the three British cemeteries. The previous Friday, he told us, two Frenchmen were killed here by a shell which they treated without sufficient respect, and bodies are continually being dug up.

Many a thousand in the ground in front will never be disturbed. The Bois du Vert and the Bois du Sart are full of them—who forgets the attack of the early morning of May 3, 1917, which in effect marked the limits of the advance in the Arras offensive? Here at Monchy—think of it!—we enjoyed a most excellent lunch at a ridiculously low price.

Leaving Monchy, the route lay through Guémappe, Wancourt—scene of many battles for the old water tower now replaced by a new one—Heninel, St Martin-sur-Cojeul and Henin-sur-Cojeul then back to Arras through Neuville Vitasse and Beaurains. To me, at least, this part of the journey was particularly interesting, because it was on this front that we 'kicked off' on Easter Monday, April 9, 1917, when, as old soldiers will remember, instead of the rain which usually accompanied our attacks, we had a day of snow.

Up this road from Beaurains galloped the field-guns—with what high hopes we saw them go—and here German snipers, over-run in the first advance, carried on throughout the day until they were rooted out. Automatic revolvers, field-glasses and souvenirs of all sorts were cheap that night.

Down the hill from Beaurains are still traces of the old trench that used to run along the roadside, but the trench itself has been filled in. Nor can the old Hindenberg Line, with its deep concrete dug-outs, be seen from the road, though probably there may be traces of it in the fields.

But there is the hill behind which we watched a mass of cavalry, under cover from observation as they thought, blown to bits with five-nines, and there is the skyline over which riderless horses came galloping back the same day—ill omen of worse to come. Neuville Vitasse and Beaurains are both rebuilt, but, Beaurains looks different; there is more brick and less of the white stone of the country used in its construction.

And so to Arras, leaving unvisited even now so many of those places we should like to see—Cherisy of unholy memory, Mercatel, and, farther back, Agny, Achicourt, where the square, packed full of lorries loaded with shells, went up in one glorious holocaust one day, while we stood at Beaurains and watched; Dainville, Simencourt, and many another.

From 1914 to 1918 the Ypres Salient—'The' Salient—was always the most dreadful part of the British front, and even now it keeps something of that horror. A quarter of a million British soldiers fell in those few miles of ground and today we are sick and depressed from seeing cemeteries—cemetery after cemetery, cemetery after cemetery.

There has been an official ceremony at the Menin Gate, but our party—kindred spirits have gathered together—have again been covering old ground in cars, and so missed the official 'stent'.

Our first visit was to Tyne Cot Cemetery, on the summit of Passchendaele Ridge, passing through Potizje and Zonnebeke on the way up. It is almost impossible to believe that all this smiling countryside was once the impassable quagmire of mud and water that we knew in the autumn of 1917.

Even here, apart from many concrete emplacements, the traces of war have almost all been swept away. Pill-boxes and cemeteries—always cemeteries. Passing one of these someone asks the driver how many graves there are there. 'Oh, only about a thousand,' he replies, 'that's a small one.' To think that one should be able to say that so casually, and with so much truth!

Tyne Cot is the resting place and memorial of 55,000 men—too many of them unknown. One finds a headstone 'Five unknown soldiers,' or 'An unknown sergeant' of such and such a regiment. It is hard to think of a regiment that is not represented here. Like all the other British cemeteries, it is beautifully designed and beautifully kept, a worthy resting place—if any place can be worthy—for these men.

Around the walls, as at the Menin Gate, are the names of those 'to whom the fortune of war denied the known and honoured burial of their comrades in death.' The immensity of the place makes it heart-breaking, just as those little cemeteries, containing only a few graves, that one finds in unexpected places are heart-breaking in their peace and loneliness.

Hill 60 is still worth visiting, though it has become too much of a show place and there are too many people selling souvenirs. The ground is still yielding up its dead—whilst we were there a boot was dug up, containing the foot, and an identity disc of a soldier in the Devons.

But the most interesting place of all is at Hill 62 in Sanctuary Wood, where a private proprietor has dug out the old frontline and maintains it exactly as it used to be. Here is the real thing; the water is as deep as ever, the duckboards have the old trick of getting up and hitting you in the face when you tread on them and the whittled stumps of the old wood still stand in front.

Here, rather than at Vimy Ridge, is the place to get some idea of trench life. The ground is still so deeply poisoned with gas that no crops will grow. Ypres itself is unrecognisable—a completely new city. Even the ruins of the Cloth Hall appear to be in the process of reconstruction.

It is extraordinarily difficult to identify any of the places that we knew when the town was level with the ground—one cannot be certain, even, exactly where the switch road at the back of the Cloth Hall ran. It is not the old Wipers at all, one can hardly believe that the old Wipers ever existed; it seems such stuff as dreams are made of.

Fancy arranging to meet at the east end of the Cloth Hall when Ypres was Wipers! Yet that is what we did this evening. Wipers is Ypres again, and although no one who has seen what we have seen today would hesitate to give all that he had to prevent another war, some of us will go home a little sad tonight knowing that those things that meant so much to us, that were so much part of that other, deeper, more elemental life that we lived when death waited for us every inch of our way, are now no more.

—Soldier H. C. P., writing in August 1929.

12

1930

The Cathedral reopening last weekend gave me excuse to see Ypres for the first time since the War. I came back strangely depressed. A garish and shoddy post-War city stands on the shell-riven ashes of immortal Wipers, and lacks the august allure of the old spectral ruins.

The Cloth Hall, even in its pre-War perfection, never loomed with quite such majesty as those ghostly silhouettes left by the German guns. St Martin's Cathedral is said to be rebuilt of its original materials. But even my own bit of lead-lined stained glass cannot be the only treasured souvenir scattered about the homes of this country and the Empire.

Nobody will see Ypres again as we saw it on Christmas Eve, 1916, its mighty ruins shrouded in snow, and blood red with the glow of German incendiary shells. In those days the Cathedral was almost as familiar a landmark for troops in the Salient as the neighbouring Cloth Hall itself.

But under the German batteries its frozen beauty avalanched into debris. Built in the 18th century, on the site of a church two centuries older, it became a Cathedral in 1559, and two paintings adorned its walls, which have now vanished, illustrating the siege of Ypres in 1383 and 1645.

So persistently did the German gunners range on St Martin's and the Cloth Hall that the Square wherein they stood was out of bounds. But it was a short cut, and many khaki figures 'risked it' in two senses. I liked to think my Army boots were waking echoes that linked up with Cromwell's Ironsides who knew the scenery of Wipers well in their day, too.

—SOLDIER, WRITING IN APRIL 1930.

*

It is a curious experience to stand in the middle of a field of young wheat and remember that it was at this spot, as nearly as one can tell, but ten feet underground, that one spent, nearly 13 years ago, two or three most cold, most weary, most uncomfortable nights, in a narrow tunnel lined with railway sleepers, infested with lice and plastered with mud and candle grease.

There one slept intermittently from sheer exhaustion and woke at intervals to scratch, to drag more empty sandbags over one's frozen feet, to listen to the drip of water from the roof, and to hollow whistlings and muffled concussions in the night.

It is odd to look at a sunlit landscape, in a deep silence broken only by the twitter of larks and the faint hue of a distant ploughman, and to think that when one last saw that scene the air was shaken by the barrage, and the smiling slopes opposite, whose crown of gaunt and splintered trees is already half hidden by new growth, were slashed with trenches, girdled with rusty belts of wire, littered with the shells of broken tanks.

On that day a black smudge in the sky showed where Marcoing was burning, and the bare ridge, from which grey and white mushrooms of earth and smoke spouted and spread, suggested rather the unnatural desolation of a frozen ocean rather than the rich soil from which a new harvest is now springing.

Over the hill, today, the new church tower of Flesquières shines above the trees; the red and grey and brown roofs of Ribécourt are trim and warm under the sun on the skyline, the raw concrete water tower of Havricourt stands solitary, like the abandoned Martian war machine in Mr Wells' story—a silent sentinel in an empty countryside.

Beyond the Flesquières ridge the gilded weathercock of a new steeple marks the village of Cantaing, of grim memory, whose very name is like the double cough of an 18-pounder in a hollow; and by climbing the hill to Graincourt one can see the dark mass of the terrible Bourlon Wood—a black pall thrown over a grave.

I came to Marcoing prosaically, from the east this time, in a bumping little tram that runs from Cambrai to Bapaume; and before starting to tramp the five odd miles to our old frontline at Trescault—the frontline of 1917—I made a lunch of bread and cheese and thin French beer in a resurrected *estaminet*. What a haven it would have been at the end of a long march in other days; how difficult it was to relish its rather unclean provision now!

But Madame was a friendly soul, she had lived on at Marcoing until the Battle of the Somme and the German retirement, when she was sent with the other civils to Valenciennes. She had 12 German soldiers and a corporal in her attic; they behaved well—'*au moins ils ne mont jamais provoquée.*' It was a pity, she said, that we could not take Cambrai once and for all in 1915.

Like the rest of them, too, she had an unobtrusive indulgence for the stray Englishman which one does not find everywhere, but which is common still in the North; for these people have not forgotten.

With those many little cemeteries close by nearly all their villages—with the endless rows of plain white stones, bearing the names of soldiers from Great Britain, from Canada, from Australia, from New Zealand, even of able seamen of the Royal Naval Division—they do not forget.

The 'addition,' so to speak, came to one franc—this particular battlefield has escaped the tourist—and I set out along the high road to Ribécourt and beyond. The fascination of the Cambrai battlefield, in the 12th year after the Armistice, is that there is so little for the stranger to see, but so many small reminders to reward the keener search of the initiated.

Of all that formidable system of defences which constituted the Hindenburg Line—the treble and quadruple lines of trenches from Mœuvres through Havrincourt to Banteux, with their wide belts of wire; the innumerable saps and strong points and cunningly-sited machine gun posts which covered the whole area—hardly a trace remains.

But here and there a white smudge on the brown face of the hillside marks the emplacement of a trench; a chalky patch shows where a deep crater has been filled. And if you look, you will see little eloquent things mixed with the white stones among the shoots of wheat; a cartridge case, a button, a bone.

Where all the deep scars of battle, which once seemed so permanent, have disappeared, scattered trifles, not worth collecting, still tell their tale; an old boot, of War Office pattern, by the roadside; a mouldy bayonet-frog in the ditch, the head of a German stick bomb.

All along the embankment by the road are grass-grown depressions, from which bits of rusty corrugated iron, or tangled swathes of netting, project; they show where the dug-outs have fallen in.

And suddenly, where the Bibecourt road crosses the ravine, halfway to Trescault, you come upon a hollow, once the emplacement of a heavy gun, which yields a rich harvest of memories.

The peasants of the war zone have no use for 'souvenirs'; the poor wreckage stays where it fell. German and British tin hats lie together among the brambles; one British helmet hideously pierced, from within, by a long shell-splinter whose work, at least, was swift. There are the usual boots and bottles; a broken rum jar; the bleached rags of a haversack and a British soldier's water bottle, still tightly corked.

On the summit of the ridge at Trescault there used to be a country house, the Château de Bilhem, with a walled garden and an orchard. In

November 1917, the shell of the house was standing; one went to it for shutters, doors to improve the lining of a dug-out; its garden, though partly overgrown and broken up by shell craters, still had neat paths with box-wood borders, neglected flowers and fruit trees.

It was a sunny, quiet place; it seemed to keep war at arm's length, to thrust it outside its broken walls. Today, all this has disappeared. Thick new willow shoots and saplings have covered it, but among them the green, rotten trunks of the old trees can be seen lying on the ground, and here and there a moss-covered remnant of a wall remains.

Fifty yards down the road is a British cemetery; opposite the forgotten garden a new farm has sprung up, and in the shadow of the barn stands the memorial to the 42nd Division, which stormed the Hindenburg Line at Trescault in September 1918, an ugly monument, but solid and durable.

From that vantage point the Havrincourt Wood appears on one hand, with something of its old grimness; on the other, the sunny downs roll away to Cambrai. Over them in the silence, cloud shadows sweep like ghostly cavalry—the ghosts of the British horsemen who galloped eastwards in 1917.

The new stone steeple of Villers-Plouich peeps over the skyline on the right; and from the valley of Gouzeaucourt, where at the end of a grim day the sound of machine guns and the first flares of evening rose in the very rear of our thin defence, there come now only the faint crowing of cocks and the blue smoke of wood fires.

But a breeze stirs in the thickets of Bilhelm, and the whisper of machine gun bullets seems to sweep faintly once more over those who sleep in the cemetery. There we must leave them, with the twittering larks for company; and the wind, the clean wind of the uplands.

—Officer DS, writing in May 1930.

*

Eleven years have fled since the ceasefire sounded and the Great War ended, but through the years that followed there remained in the minds of those who served memories of those never-to-be-forgotten days.

To the ex-soldier those epic days seem as yesterday, and he thinks of the Somme, Ypres, Messines, Passchendaele, and all those 'billet' villages and towns as they were in '15, '16, '17, and '18. To go back now, 11 years after, and revisit the battlefields is only to be disillusioned. Many ex-soldiers have made the pilgrimage, but a greater number have not. To those who haven't I would say—keep your memories.

For years I resisted the call of the battlefields, that yearning to get back to those unhappy far off things and battles long ago, then one May morn the pull became irresistible, and packing a rucksack I set sail in the SS *Grania* from Eden Quay, Dublin, and landed at Dunkirk on the first stage of my pilgrimage. From Dunkirk I motored to Armentières along the treeless roads once lined with poplars and arrived at Half-Past Eleven Square.

Everything was changed—the buildings and the people. The Town Hall with its lofty clock spire had disappeared. So, too, had the quaint cafés and shops with their higgledy-piggledy architecture, their picturesque green, white and yellow fronts.

In their place stood new shops and offices, blue slated with glaring brick walls, stereotyped and symmetrical—ugly in the extreme. In the centre of the Grand Place or Square, a large and very ornate war memorial stood, while the pavé, over which once echoed the swish-swish of marching feet and the rumble of transport, was replaced by gravel.

I looked for a familiar face among the passers-by, but in vain. Wandering disconsolate along a new Rue de Messines, a new Rue de Dunkirque, I dropped into what was known as Suzette's Café. Suzette was there, but what a different Suzette. I scarcely recognised the buxom mother-of-five as the petite, vivacious brunette of war days.

In the Rue de la Gare I espied a notice '*Le Cheval Blanc*.' Ah, here was one of my old billets. I entered full of anticipation and, seating myself at a little round table, ordered a vin rouge. The room was little changed. It had been remodelled and repaired.

In that corner once stood a dingy piano on which Sgt ___, long since 'gone west,' rattled out 'Pack up your troubles,' 'Tipperary,' and 'Who's your lady friend.' The room became crowded with memories. I used to sleep upstairs. Calling over the corpulent proprietor I explained matters to him.

'Could I see the room upstairs?'

'*Mais non*!'

He waddled off to the table where his large family was seated and for the few remaining moments of my stay, judging from the scowls in my direction, I was the subject of very uncomplimentary remarks.

Le Bizet, a suburb of Armentières, was my next objective. Suicide Post, once my observation post, a tall brick kiln chimney 800 yards from the German lines, had vanished. In place of the old kiln two new kilns with two new chimneys were going full steam ahead supplying bricks for the reconstruction of the devastated areas. I wandered in and out among the sheds. Somewhere about here so-and-so was killed. The old cookhouse used to stand over there.

'What do you want here?' I was confronted by a large expanse of blue smock, and looking up into a scowling face I meekly explained that I was an ex-soldier and that I used to observe from the old brick kiln chimney.

Muttering, my interrogator re-joined his workmates, and after a momentary regard of me they stolidly resumed their work. I felt that I was not welcome and wandered off past a new Le Bizet Church, a replica of the old, but glaringly new, to the Belgian frontier.

At the pillars crossing the road a Belgian sentry halted me and asked me to declare any '*tabac*' I had. I did so, while a party of schoolchildren made remarks about '*le soldat Anglaise*,' for I wore a pair of khaki breeches.

I thought of the old days when this road was pock-marked with shell holes and strewn with charred debris; when a New Zealand Tommy lay dead propped against this very pillar, a handkerchief over his face. Here, too, a team of horses lay in their tracks, gassed, a feast for innumerable flies.

Having satisfied the sentry I walked along the Armentières–Messines Road, trying to locate old battery positions; recalling a dug-out here, a shell dump there. A lofty stone cross stood silhouetted against the sky. The Cross of Sacrifice. Behind, in serried rows, stood the little white headstones. One bore the inscription: 'Private Patrick ___, Royal Irish Fusiliers, Killed in Action, Messines, 1917.'

How peacefully they slept, those comrades of mine. How lonely I felt standing among strangers of little understanding. I wandered to and fro between the rows of headstones, reluctant to leave. A country cart bumping over the road, where once heavy limbers rumbled up the line, was the only sound that broke the stillness.

Softly I closed the gate of this city of my dead comrades and paused beneath the shadow of the cross of sacrifice with its Crusaders' Sword and the inscription—'Their names liveth forever more.' I wandered further along this once well-known road.

Turning a bend, I saw a large signpost fixed at an angle to the road. On it was inscribed in one foot letters—'Ploegsteert.' What magic was in that name 'Plug Street.' Alas the name was the only familiar thing about the place. A long standardised row of ugly red walled, blue slated houses replaced the quaint houses of war days, picturesque even in ruins.

Plug Street Wood had also vanished. All those torn toothpick-like trees had been dug out by the roots, and in their place rows of straight limbed saplings whispered in the breeze. Not a trench, not a dug-out remained, not even one of the countless shell holes.

As I approached Hill 63 I noticed that the fence along the road was made from old British barbed wire and corkscrew stanchions. A farm with an 'elephant shelter' outhouse and a duckboard path seemed like an oasis in a desert of lost memories.

On the hill itself little was changed. The old shell holes were still there, half concealed in the grass. A dug-out was still intact, and among the debris at the bottom of the rotting steps lay a rusted steel helmet and several empty bully beef tins. As I stood, a fat rat scuttled away into the darkness. At last I had found something I knew.

Kemmel Hill and Messines Ridge smiled in the summer's sun. I was happy again. But this was the only familiar spot in the district. A new pavé road, down which a shepherd drove a flock of sheep, led to Messines.

The tall column of the Australian War Memorial silhouetted against the sky stood on the ridge crest sharply. Petite Douvre Farm, once a heap of bricks in No Man's Land, had been resurrected and was now a pretty farmhouse with barns painted in broad stripes of blue and white.

Up the long white road to Messines I climbed, past ploughed fields which once was 'No Man's Land'. On the left of the ridge a new Messines stood on the site of the old. Neat gardens with well-ordered paths replaced the barbed wire and the cordite stinking rubble of the German trenches.

A little weary from my climb up the hill, I sat down at a table in a neat little café and called for a '*petite verre*.' As the old lady attended to me I remarked casually that everything was changed.

'*Monsieur* is a soldier. I know the *Soldat Anglaise* well. I lived in Bailleul during 1916–1917.'

'It must be very strange to you now, *madame*, when there are no British soldiers in France?' I remarked.

'Ah, yes, *monsieur*,' she replied. 'But we get so many tourists, English officers. Sometimes one like you will say: "*Madame*, you remember me, do you not?" and me, I often think do the English forget so soon when they can be bon comrades with the Sales Boches. The English now hate the French. Is it not so? The poor beautiful France that has suffered so much.'

I tried hard to explain matters to her, and asked could England ever forget with those green acres filled with thousands of the flower of her manhood who died on Flanders fields. 'But, *monsieur*, that is forgotten now. Money and trade count with England most.'

I gave up trying to persuade the old lady, and lighting my pipe, I sauntered out into the garden. A round rustic summerhouse stood in the corner, the concrete floor of which was the floor of a German pill-box. I sat down and thought of what the old woman had said: 'England hates France. Money and trade to us was everything.'

Sadly, I got up and walked along the new road to Wytschaete, and thought of June 1917, when the men of Ulster and the men of the South carried this crest while gallant Captain Redmond died cheering them to victory. He lies asleep in Locre, over there not far from that red pile of new brick, the newer Neuve Eglise.

Below me stretched a once well-known countryside—then a network of trenches and barbed wire, a honeycomb of shell holes, now a series of well ordered, furrowed fields and new farmhouses. Over there was 'Hell

Farm'. About there was 'Four Huns Farm'. 'Daylight Corner' would be down there in that little hollow. 'The Bird Cage,' 'Ulster Avenue,' 'Watling Street,' and 'Happy Moments' trenches I was utterly unable to place.

Dranoutre, Locre, Neuve Eglise, Westoutre, and all the old villages were there, yet not there. Ugly groups of red walled, blue slated houses clustered all over the plain—a contrast to the picturesque farms and quaintly formed houses and time-tinted churches of war days.

Slowly I sauntered along the road, and marched in the silence, step-by-step with the ghosts of my dead comrades. A whispering breeze springs up, darkness closes in, and the lights of the farmsteads, so like battery lights, twinkle here and there all over the plain.

'*Bon soir, monsieur*,' a farmer trudged home, a fork over his soldier, a shaggy dog at his heels. A door of a cottage opened, and I heard the wheeze of a gramophone playing the latest foxtrot. I was back from the land of memories to the land of realities.

Taking a shortcut across a field, I stepped off the Wytschaete–Messines road. Then I noticed that the foundation of the new road was composed of the debris of the old Ville de Messines.

Next day I travelled to the Somme country and alighted at a new Albert station. A new cathedral has been built on the site of the old—less ornate and less pretentious. In the Café de la Gare artisans and railway porters were playing cards and drinking café cognac, where once a concrete dug-out, amid ruined walls, sheltered signal headquarters.

I walked down the 'Signal Road'—a refuge in days gone by for raiding parties, and on occasions a veritable shambles for the dead—past new villages, with an elaborate War Memorial in each; past little hills where the blood of thousands of British soldiers had been shed, and up the well-kept avenue to Thiepval Tower, the memorial to Ulster's glorious dead.

On these slopes the men of Ulster, 14 years ago (how time flies!), had advanced on the first day of July, and with both flanks in the air, unsupported in the rear, had swept over five lines of German trenches, carrying the 'impregnable' Schwaben Redoubt and suffering heavy losses, where this memorial to their valour now stands. Over on the left, where flows the River Ancre, many gallant Irishmen of the 29th Division had perished on that July morn in the Ancre swamp.

I tried to reconstruct the lines of the attack, but failed. All was strange to me. Everything was changed from the days when I made my way through this country along twisting communication trenches, making strange detours over camouflaged roads. In those days I had a totally different conception of distance. Looked at from ground level from off angles the perspective was entirely different.

Now roads which were obliterated were reconstructed. New roads had been made in different directions. Woods and even hills had vanished, and the country of the Somme, once so familiar, was to me now an entirely foreign land. All the trenches were gone. Thiepval Village was gone and was now a plantation of young trees.

All the old shrapnel torn, blackened trees had gone, dug out by the roots. Elgin Avenue, Lancashire Post, Gordon Castle—all these trenches had been filled in while a train rumbled over the lines which once ran though No Man's Land. A woman with a red flag was in charge of a railway crossing near what once was 'Stone Bridge Post'.

I treaded my way through the young trees of Thiepval Wood. All the old familiar things had gone. No, not all. There, amongst the green foliage of the saplings, stood a gaunt, toothpick like stump. Here at last was an old comrade. With what friendly feelings I lingered beside that war worn veteran.

How much more beautiful to me it seemed than those fresh young saplings swaying gracefully in the breeze. As I fondly ran my fingers over the shrapnel seared trunk the young trees vanished 'neath memory's magic wand. Elgin Avenue, Gordon Castle—all the old trenches and dug-outs and duckboards reappeared. I was no longer alone—I was marching step-by-step in the ranks of the Deathless Legion in company with my comrades long since gone west.

Over toppling duckboards we splashed through a nightmare wood of grotesque trees to relieve the ___ Division in the line. To memory time is but a breath. Eight days of privation and death; nights of nerve-wracking excursions into No Man's Land, had passed. I was marching 'out,' down the dark, muddy trench through the ruins of Hamel, where fitful gleams of candlelight filtered from out damp, straw littered cellars. The reflection of the gun flashes in the sky, flickering like summer lightening, and a rumble like distant thunder bespoke a 'big do' up Arras way.

The rumble of the guns became the rumble of a train, and as the brightly lit carriages streaked by the blackened stumps disappeared. The young trees nodded and whispered to each other again. I heard, ever so far away, the lilt of a marching song '... to Tipperary, but my heart's right there.' The marching song of the Deathless Legion as they march through the portals of Valhalla. And I—I was alone with my comrade, the blackened stump.

Turning my back on the new roads, the fresh red bricks, blue slates, and white mortar, I left this land of many memories and sailed back to Blighty, the greatest memory of my pilgrimage—a blackened stump in Thiepval Wood.

—Soldier J. B. M., writing in August 1930.

He served from 1914–1919 first as a private during the Battle of the Somme and later as an officer.

13

1931

Thirteen days before this article was written, I was walking in perfect security along a road which, to say the least of it, was decidedly unsafe for pedestrians 13 years ago.

No one would now imagine that this ordinary country road meandering through the unenclosed French fields to the village on the skyline was a road with a history; but to me it was a '*Via Dolorosa*'. For this unpretentious country lane had also been a victim of the world war.

It had acquired an unenviable distinction; it was 'taped' because it happened to lead up to the battalion headquarters of the First Gordons, and although it never knew its own importance, the Germans did and tried to wipe it off the map with all the artillery tricks they knew.

The road has sunk into rural obscurity again and is now known simply as the road to Hinges, the Gordons who gave it its reputation having departed, except for a number who remain—sleeping in the little cemetery at the end of the road. Heavy was the toll the Gordons had to pay on the road to Hinges!

The village is now completely rebuilt, and the desert left by the war has blossomed again, but I had no difficulty in locating the exact places where my own lot was cast, 13 years ago. Wheat now grows on the ridge above the Aire canal where 'Gordon Line' and 'Aberdeen Trench' were meant to protect the reserve companies, and you may now cross the canal in perfect safety, by means of a bascule bridge, the unpleasant occasion having passed which necessitated a narrow and half-submerged pontoon to serve the unfortunates who had to cross the canal on their 'unfriendly road' to the frontline.

Having crossed the canal, I discovered the path that led to our old frontline posts and taking my direction from 'lone tree'—a surviving landmark—I soon found myself in No Man's Land. What memories crowded into my mind, and what emotions stirred me as I stood there—actually on the terrain where I had first gone over the top!

'*Nunquam minus solus quam cum solus*'—I was alone, yet conscious of the presence of others. I stood immobile, but my mind was active, coping with the swift succession of memories and impressions which the scene before me stimulated.

The sighing of the wind in the Bois de Pacaut was answered by the sadness of my own spirit, and I thought I heard other cries, but it was only my fancy that deceived me, for those cries were stilled in deathly silence 13 years ago.

Impressions and experiences registered and preserved in some hidden recess of memory came out of their obscurity into my present consciousness, and I lived again through the tension and terror and bloody strife of that first assault. You too, my comrades, tasted again your bitter experience! I saw you fall, I heard your cries, even your last low whimperings!

That hedge still there!—where I fired and the grey, steel-hooded figure writhed!—where, frenzied, the sergeant shouted, 'Bayonet! Bayonet!'—a steam tram went lumbering along somewhere on the Merville Road, and I was jolted out of my dreaming. Hastily I retraced my steps. I for one will never visit that place again. Thirteen years ago we came to this place and conquered; 13 days ago I came alone, and saw, and was overcome.

From Béthune I proceeded by train through the Lens coalfields, an unattractive country from the point of view of natural beauty, but full of interest to the ex-combatant. The whole district has undergone an unrecognisable transformation, and mining operations are now in full swing.

At Bully-Grenay a number of miners boarded the train, and I have seldom seen such a variety of headgear, ranging from red 'tammies' to British 'tin hats,' as that which adorned the heads of these '*mineurs*.'

The train skirted slowly along the foot of Vimy Ridge, and I reflected that many a Canuck in Montreal or Quebec would have gladly exchanged places with me to obtain even a passing view of the place where their nation made history.

Neat little chalets now adorn the 'abomination of desolation,' and there are new plantations on Vimy Ridge, but here and there a tell-tale stump obtrudes its charred and mis-shapen arms above the unspoiled green foliage.

I arrived at Arras on the morning of the French national fête, an occasion when the perfervid Gallic patriotism of the French nation is gallantly and always picturesquely expressed.

The Café des Officiers was crowded with immaculately groomed officers from the garrison, and the less exclusive cafés and boulevards were thronged with the merry 'bourgeois' of Arras, and everywhere I met priests and '*poilus*.' I thought of another occasion when men of a different race crowded into the capacious cellars of Arras, intent on sterner business than merrymaking.

At the Hotel de L'Universe, where I put up for the night, I met fellow a clansman, Colonel William Robertson VC. He spotted my tartan necktie and, of course, that was a sufficient introduction.

Through him I had the honour of being presented to Lady Haig, and, in the course of a few minutes' conversation with that gracious lady, I was informed that the late Earl Haig had a near ancestor who bore the name of Robertson, a fact which I record with not a little pleasure.

From Achiet-le-Grand I hiked to Gommecourt, where I found a neat little village in place of the shattered ruins which were the objective of the attack in which I was wounded 13 years ago. The long undulating plains of the Somme country of infamous memory, are no longer a shell-torn, gas drenched waste of mud, but have been transformed by the magic of peasant industry into a richly cultivated champaign.

The crops reached normal quality, I was told, about six years after the war. Courcelles was easily picked out on the far side of the Arras-Albert railway, and I soon found the railway cutting midway between the two villages—the actual place where I was hit on August 23, 1918.

The dug-outs have disappeared, and I saw no machine guns or trench mortars, but one or two familiar landmarks reminded me of my first and fateful acquaintance with that country 13 years ago.

In my retrospective fancy I saw again the protruding muzzle of a Mauser rifle—I heard the ominous staccato crack—I felt the stinging sensation in my right forearm. A bayonet gleamed before my eyes, and a menacing figure lurched and fell at my feet, and I knew that a timely intervention had saved my life. I saw a blood-stained but smiling comrade standing over me.

After a visit to the little cemetery on the outskirts of Gommecourt, where my deliverer sleeps, I set out for Ervillers, where I had the good fortune to jump a motor lorry back to Arras. It was one of the tricks we learned 13 years ago.

From Arras I made, in one day, the long journey by train to Ypres, via Lens, Armentières and Comines. In a siding at the second of these places, I saw several wagons with the familiar device: '*Hommes* 36-40, *Chevaux*, 8,' which reminded me of the prolonged journeys we used to make in these 'Pullmans' bound for an unknown destination, which rumour always insisted was Egypt, Ireland, or India, but which experience proved to be St Pol, Pop or Abbeville.

At Armentières we experienced all the lively sensations of shunting operations, and for some 15 minutes our carriage was a mere counter in a game of 'railway ludo.' The boredom and discomfort were somehow relieved, however, by the burlesque antics of the director of shunting operations, who also periodically entertained us to bugle blasts so realistically executed that I expected to hear once familiar slogan: 'Balloons, balloons, bottles, and jeely-jars!'

A new Ypres has arisen on the ruins of the old, and all that remains of the latter is the skeleton of the Cloth Hall, which stands as a grim testimony to the precision of the German bombardment, and to the ruthless vandalism of modern warfare.

The Menin Gate memorial is a beautiful and impressive tribute to the memory of the British Forces who defended Ypres, and to their dead—57,000 of them!—who lie in unknown graves in the Salient.

Last Post is sounded by three Belgium buglers at the Menin Gate every evening at nine o'clock, and during my visit to Ypres I had the privilege of attending a service at the Gate, held under the auspices of the British Legion (Edinburgh Area). It was a moving experience to hear the familiar words of the 23rd Psalm sung to the tune 'Wiltshire' in a place hallowed by the sacrifice of thousands of our compatriots.

The following day, I walked out along the famous Menin Road as far as Sanctuary Wood and Hooge passing on the way 'Hellfire Corner,' with its monument marking the limit of the German advance.

In Sanctuary Wood, the Canadian frontline trenches are left exactly as they were during the war—complete with dug-outs, duckboards, and barbed wire—and littered all over the ground you can see the whole paraphernalia and impediments of trench warfare, from broken rum jars to trench mortars.

The Canadian monument in Sanctuary Wood is built on a commanding site, with a maple-lined avenue leading up to it from the Menin Road. From the terrace of the monument, a magnificent view of the strategic natural defences on the right of Ypres may be obtained, from Zillebeke and Hill 60 to Kemmel and the far Mont des Cats, with its conspicuous monastery and chapel.

My next itinerary took me to the ever memorable Passchendaele Ridge via Zonnebeke and Broodseinde. At the latter place, I visited a German cemetery, whose plain black crosses mark the resting places of many of those cadets who 'came over' in 1914 from Langemarck to Polygon Wood, singing their college songs, and determined at all costs to break their way through to Ypres under the eyes of the Kaiser.

Their gallant but costly attack broke down before the stubborn defence of the immortal 7th Division, and hundreds of these fearless 'Junkers' sleep within two miles of the prize which neither they nor their successors ever attained.

A Belgium workman to whom I spoke, told me that some of the fiercest hand-to-hand fighting of the whole war took place on the spot where we stood conversing, on the Passchendaele Road. When alone again I paid a silent tribute to the brave men of both nations who fell in that bloody duel for Ypres.

Near the village of Passchendaele, and situated near the brow of the Ridge, stands the most beautiful cemetery I have ever seen Tyne Cot Military Cemetery—containing the graves of over 20,000 British and Colonial dead. The central monument is built on the ruins of the Tyne Cot 'pill-box' captured by the Australians in October, 1917. They rest in peace now in this beautiful necropolis, who came out of great tribulation on that field of death.

The strategic importance attached to Passchendaele Ridge is at once realised when you climb the steps of the Tyne Cot monument and survey the surrounding country. The Ridge dominates the whole Salient up to Ypres itself, and an investing force entrenched on the heights could, without difficulty, observe practically every movement of the defenders in the plain below.

The evidence of the Germans' determination to maintain their advantage is still seen in the chain of 'pill-boxes' along the brow of the Ridge. Built of reinforced concrete, these former machine gun redoubts betray evidence of the terrific intensity, concentration, and destructive power of the British bombardment.

I again had the good fortune to jump a lorry from Broodseinde to Ypres, and, on route, the chirpy Belgian driver showed me a field where he himself had found, the day before, the remains of six German soldiers.

I may mention that, nearly every week, bodies are found in the Salient, and indeed all along the battle front, and there are special exhumation parties at various centres whose business it is to remove the corpses to a military cemetery, where they are reverently and decently re-interred.

The military cemeteries in France and Belgium are hallowed shrines, and are visited by thousands of pilgrims every year. The ground on which they are situated has been gifted in perpetuum to the British nation by our former allies. The smaller of these cemeteries is kept as carefully as the largest by an efficient staff, whose work is a labour of love, and a tribute of respect to the memory of their former comrades.

I too made a pilgrimage, one morning, to Lijssenthoek Military Cemetery, near Poperinghe, where my brother lies. There was yellow broom and white roses on the sacred spot where he sleeps. Sad and burdened was I with the pathos and tragedy of it all; but a voice—was it his?—admonished me: 'Why seek ye the living among the Dead? He is not here!'

And I realised that not in a foreign soil, lonely and cold, are our loved ones, but here in our midst they live, serving still, and watching. 'Wherefore seeing we also are compassed about with so great a cloud of witnesses...'

—REVD C. P. ROBERTSON MA, WRITING IN AUGUST 1931.

*

On Monday, at 9.15, our long train of 11 charabancs and attendant taxis left Lille for the South. Soon, over the flat country, appeared the pitheads of the Lens coalfield; that Lens on which so many fruitless hopes fastened in the fatal fighting at Loos in 1915.

Presently we came to Vimy Ridge; and here I understood in half an hour, more of the fighting in this sector than in all the months I spent in France during the War. And the same is true of all the places we visited. These, then, were the slopes where uncounted thousands fell.

There, still wreathing its coils through the coarse grass, is our old frontline. A few paces away is the German line. And between the two are the craters of those carefully prepared mines that, in one second, blotted out interminable hours of brave and weary tenacity.

We descend a steep dug-out. Here are the original tunnels cut out by 10 months of patient toil, mostly by the Canadians; as complete and eerie and full of ghosts as the Catacombs of the Campagna.

Here is a rusty bed; mouldering gum boots; the old water and air pipes; the gas door; notices painted on boards; emblems and initials cut in the chalk by unknown soldiers; blackened candle sockets.

Here, especially, is a German 5.9 shell that penetrated 20 feet and failed to explode. Else, it is likely, the secret of the tunnels had been discovered. Here, finally, is the detonator that sent so many German lives, so many hopes, to their doom. A little later, and the enemy, working 20ft below (as we now know) would have done the same for us.

The surface is thronged with ex-servicemen from Wessex, from the West Midlands, from the Metropolitan area—old soldiers renew their acquaintance with the most glorious episodes of their career.

We await our stragglers and the silence of the battlefields almost hurts. We feel we need clamour—or the dead will pluck our garments and ask if we remember, and are loyal.

We pass down the misty hillside. There, close at hand, is a huge French cemetery, partly filled by the black crosses of the German dead. On the stricken field they lie together. Further off are the ruined towers of St Eloi, where in 1917 I obtained my first view of Vimy.

Now we are entering Arras. This is the suburb of St Catherine. There stood our billet, taken over from the Naval Division, till the Cambrai anti-climax called us hurrying south, six Divisions at once on the Arras–Bapaume road. It was this same route we took, and a friendly cookhouse made us early tea in the early morning.

Past this square we went, and in that park the officers' club then stood, where a hot bath and haircut were always available. And here is Arras; the Town Hall rebuilt in the Petite Place, but the grand cathedral (connected with St Gregory's at Downside through its XVII century Abbot Caverel) only slowly resuming its noble proportions.

We sat down to an excellent lunch, efficiently served. On re-assembling we found a wedding party arriving at the Place, and pleased and embarrassed them by hearty cheers.

At 2.15 we were off again. Oh those old scenes! Arras station, not grass-grown now; the railway bridge, that somehow always escaped destruction; the smooth Bapaume road, part of which was once No Man's Land.

Then to the right, through Boiry, where I enlisted a Labour Company to build a plank church; through the other Boiry, its neighbour, and our summer camp of 1917; up the hill to Ayette where I used to cycle and visit my brother a few weeks before he was killed. His CO was General Freyberg, who comes sometimes to Mells.

Now we are entering the bleak Somme area, grave of the bravest and most gallant Citizen Army this country ever sent overseas. In the driving rain we halt at Newfoundland Park, opposite Beaumont Hamel, where the old trenches still wind forlorn, but grimly eloquent.

There is Y Ravine where our Area Organising Secretary was wounded; and others too, who are of our party. There, down the hill, was the German line. And far away in the misty distance lie the objectives that never seemed to get nearer, yet were in our hands by Spring.

On we go through the desolate country passing ever and anon the beautifully kept cemeteries 'that are forever England.' Leaving behind Aveluy Wood we reach Albert of the hanging Virgin, and pass, wondering, round the magnificent church that we knew only in decay.

A fete was in progress, and the band hurried across to the Square to play 'God Save the King' in our honour. I have never heard it sound so much like music! We went to Bapaume. This was the part I knew so well. Only now the villages are re-built, every stick and stone; church towers spring to view on every side; corn waves golden over the fields.

There is the notorious Butte de Warlencourt, still grimly aloof. Here is Ervillers. Last time I passed there was a small heap of stones and two notice boards, 'This was Ervillers' and 'Ervillers church.' A huge dud shell also stood at the crossroads, and some humorist had carved a tiny one out of wood and set it up alongside.

Beyond is Mory, where the 58 and 21 Divisions first drew near enough together to enable me to cycle over from Boyelles and visit two of my brothers in the London Fusiliers. One of them had just been missed by a dud 'Archie' shell.

There to the right is St Leger where the 12-inch railway guns were; and Croiseilles, scene of heavy fighting, where I watched three English and four German aeroplanes destroy one another. Here is the cart track across the main road where I used to cycle up to the gun positions from Division HQ.

Moyenneville (where someone stole my new trench coat); and here Boyelles itself and my first taste of the line (and that, the Hindenburg line) and Boiry Becquerelle, where we raised a fallen Crucifix, and Mercatel where another brother was wounded; and Beaurains now reaching right into Arras.

Then Vimy again, past the German support line, and Lens, and Lille, the German 'back areas.' What a day of memories! And of them all, perhaps the most vivid is the low, sun-lit crest of hill, where, for the first time in my life, I saw men who had died violent deaths.

On Tuesday we went North. Concrete pill-boxes still lurk amid the cultivated fields, After Quesmoy we come to the Comines canal, the frontier between France and Belgium. The name figured largely in the early phases of the war. It was easy now to see the strategic importance of this natural barrier reinforced by the hill of Warneton rising up behind and dominating the plain.

Warneton, like so many towns hereabouts, was rebuilt with reparations money, and its striking War Memorial and lovely, lofty church occupied my attention whilst our drivers were arguing with the customs officials over an international passport. The Belgians used to smuggle tobacco over the border by means of their dogs, but now after dusk any stray dog is shot at sight, and the traffic has ceased.

My heart beats more quickly at the first view of these low hills that commanded the Ypres Salient, Mont des Cats, Mont Rouge, Kemmel, and suddenly I look up at a crossroads, dividing prosperous farms and there is Shrapnel Corner.

Why, then, Hill 60 (where I was wounded) and Verbrandenmolen must be away yonder. Yes, there they are, and the Molen (mill) has been re-built, and whirls its sails above the restored railway.

I arrived once in that cutting just after a shell had ripped open the bank and demolished the servants of a battery HQ, and by the mill I saw a dump of duckboards go up like giant matches, and a deserted battery of our Brigade on fire, and RFA drivers bringing up ammunition at the gallop.

On a Thursday, September 20th, from that ridge I saw, in answer to an SOS, every one of the thousands of guns of every calibre leap into flame against the evening sky.

We enter Ypres, an unbelievable city, alive and teeming with traffic. I have a strange sense of walking in a dream, struggling with an obsession of being in two places at once—this busy Ypres, and that ghost city that still clings to the imagination, burnt into it by the fiery stress of past endurance.

We disembark by the Cathedral—rebuilt! It took nearly 50 years to build (like Solomon's Temple), but was replaced, after destruction, in five. We form up in fours. Waves of emotion beat across the Square like gusts of wind.

Slowly, and in silence, we set out for the Guild Hall. Ah! Here is the Cloth Hall, still mostly a tumbled ruin. This is more familiar. The sense of double existence is re-lived a little by the well-known disorder.

Presently we mount stone stairs and shake hands with the venerable, silver-haired, courteous Burgomaster that saw his city perish and rise Phoenix-like from its ashes. In halting English, but with great dignity, he gives us greeting.

The splendour of British Arms is now forever part of the tradition of the City. Our Chairman replies. Our own pent-up feelings are let loose in three mighty cheers. The book is signed. Friendship is deeper rooted.

We pass, silent as in the war years, but for different reasons, towards the Menin Gate. Then, it was the gate of Death. Now, it enshrines the Dead. The English Chaplin conducts a service. There is a brief speech. A bugle rings out. Silence again and almost endurable tension.

From far away thunder rumbles, as if the guns spoke again. The eye travels up and down, up and down, that endless list of those who perished and were never found. Immortal Dead!

We have one more wreath to lay, where the Belgian Memorial faces the Cloth Hall. Dr Spencer Palmer advances. Silence again. Then, after this last gesture of national friendship, we relax a little. Madame of Skindles (who did not know Skindles at Poperinghe?) has transferred to Ypres, and her energetic staff soon satisfy our needs.

I wandered away after that, glad to be alone. In the Cathedral are Belgian Girl Guides, and English Boy Scouts and Church Lads' Brigade. It is well. Let them see and realise a little the valour of their race.

I linger a while. Fourteen years ago I sat here on a heap of stones and brooded over the utterly ruined Cathedral. Now it towers over me, resplendent and shining. If we had known, in those dark days, of the coming resurrection, with what good heart would we have endured. Yet, we did endure.

I returned to the ramparts. In the Grande Place a fair is in progress. So much the better. Let the centuries' old life flow strong again. I climb the steps. There is the Mill again, and Hill 60 and the ghastly Salient, and the Canal and Zillebeke; and away to the right Dickebusch and our old camp near Reningelst, misty and wet now, as so often then.

I come back to our party, brushing through memories that flowed strong and swift as running water. Our long convoy gets into motion and drives (imagine it!) straight from Ypres to Passchendaele. Past concrete emplacements still commanding every approach, we ascend the grim slope.

At the crest Tyne Cot Cemetery dominates the battlefield. We enter. Thousands of trim stones to the right, thousands to the left, thousands in front. Between them pink roses growing and blue lavender, and everywhere the smooth green turf.

Some strange cloud of emotion falls suddenly upon the whole party. We move silently; speak, if at all, in whispers. Above, in the lonely sky, a lark rises, like a spirit, joyously, to Heaven.

On the wide encircling wall I find my brother's name. Away to the right is the tower of St Julien, near where he died. To capture this crest, obedient to duty, he led his men out in the cold and mud. A forlorn hope. Now, with his companions, he reigns upon the crest for evermore. It is well. Let us return.

We traverse the battlefield again, taking the course thousands of German soldiers took, for their last time. Then we wheel on to the Menin Road, unrecognisable save that the rise of the hill leads unmistakably to Hooge.

Now we branch off to Maple Copse Cemetery where every stick and stone has come from Canada. Here the Canadians caught the first gas attack and perished where they stood. Here, later, we had our battery positions.

Just under that crest an infantry officer called in for a chat on the way down from the line. As he left the dug-out with his servant a shell found them. Here, brave genial Captain Maxwell was struck down by shrapnel. And there in the valley, is Zillebeke Lake, and church, and their own flood of memories. We return by Messines Ridge and the glorious Berkshire Cemetery at Ploegsteert Wood.

One boy of 17 lies here, and one of 16, and some names are those of men three times as old. Spent with a strange emotion, but grateful and reverent, we leave the Battlefields behind.

—Revd Tancred Ambrose Agius, Roman Catholic chaplain to the forces (4th Class), 21st Artillery, writing in September 1931.

Agius arrived on the Western Front in April 1917, one of five brothers to serve in the First World War. He was wounded during the Battle of Polygon Wood in September 1917, and during his twelve months on the frontline, he was mentioned in despatches. In the Second World War, his church in Liverpool was destroyed during the May 1941 Blitz.

*

During the war Hénin-Liétard had been occupied by the Germans. When we were there, the corner house of the market still had painted upon it the German directional sign, '*Nach Letis*.' A heap of masonry in the market square was the remnants of the village church, that, one day, it was hoped to rebuild upon its original site.

That little mining village of Hénin gave our pilgrims a wonderful reception. As many of the population as could be accommodated, congregated outside the station. When our lads and lasses appeared the cheering with which the French greeted them showed that time had not diminished the affectionate regard the people of France had for our Army.

Along the route to the Town Hall Venetian masts had been erected, from which were strung lines of flags. Foraging parties must have been out to Arras and other neighbouring towns to have procured such a lavish display of bunting and Union Jacks. The tiny shops of Hénin never had such stocks.

Our first tour was to Beaumont Hamel. We left the car at Beaucourt and started to walk up the road: it was unfamiliar, not the road we used to take. To help me find my bearings I asked two Frenchmen (acting as guides) where was the *Sucrerie*?

'Back in Mailly-Maillet over there,' one of them said, pointing across country. From that direction (the old one) I wanted to start, so leaving the road, went across country, still uncultivated and rough, although the trenches had been filled in and the barbed wire removed.

As we approached Beaumont Hamel, that in 1916 had so long defied us, a road running out from it and up the ridge at its back puzzled me. Then I remembered that in the time I was again living, artillery had obliterated it.

Still, I was not satisfied. It couldn't have been where I was that we had crossed No Man's Land, because we were to have entered the village at its northern end. With my compass that was still set as it had been for the attack, I was able to locate our old position.

Slowly I moved forward and as I moved the past reappeared before my eyes. Again and yet again would I hear the roar of the cannon, the rapid 'phut, phut, phut' of the machine guns assailed my ears, and automatically I looked round to see how the men were moving forward to their first attack, but they were not there.

In their place stood a solitary Highlander. What was he doing so far behind? The Highland Light Infantry were attacking on our left! Why didn't he move? It wasn't like my friends, the Jocks, to stand and look on.

A voice saying, '*Que regardez vous*?' recalled me from the past. It was Jean, my host at Hénin, who had accompanied me. I told him that I was admiring the memorial erected to the memory of the men of the 51st (Highland) Division. Where we were standing, the pedestal was hidden, giving the impression of a Highlander standing on the ground.

We clambered down the banks of the road into Beaumont Hamel, but I was sorry for doing so, because when I saw its size, the stupid thought came into my mind, My God! This tiny little hamlet wasn't worth all the valuable lives lost in the taking of it.

Sanity, however, returned, and before quitting I realised those lives gladly had been given, so that England should be spared the devastation that France had endured, and that the taking of Beaumont Hamel was only one move of many that were to culminate in driving the invader back to his own country.

Whilst Jean wandered back to the car, I went over to have a look at the trenches in Newfoundland Park, still preserved by the Newfoundland Government in the condition that they were when occupied by troops.

At first it was rather a treat to find one's self again walking beneath the surface of the earth, but after passing a machine gun emplacement, a gas alarm post, a bombing post, tin helmets, old rifles and other familiar sights, the atmosphere of the past reasserted itself, and around each traverse I expected to meet old friends, and because I didn't, I hurried thinking they must be in the next bay, and when they were not, I ran to meet them in the next, and kept on running, because always ahead of me I could hear their laughter.

Breathless I came to the end of the trench and sadly mounted the steps that were to take me back to earth whereon I was to continue my lonely path through life, because those that really knew me are spirits haunting so many fair fields of France.

From Beaucourt we drove to Longueval. There I got out, telling the others, who were going to Delville Wood, that I would join them later. I wanted to be alone. With the atmosphere of the trenches still clinging, I walked up the Longueval Road towards Bernafay Wood.

Looking towards the wood, great was my surprise to see, at the entrance where our communication trench had been, two British sentinels on guard! A closer inspection showed my sentinels to be a couple of steel helmets on posts each side of a gate.

On the side of the road opposite the wood was a cemetery. It didn't surprise me, but what did, was the thought that so many dead could have been accommodated in such a limited enclosure.

From the cemetery I retraced my steps, following the route we had taken that afternoon of July 1916. Again, did I see those boys lined up beside the wood, struggling into their gas masks? Then I followed the line of the old trench, now a ditch, up to Trônes Wood.

Between Bernafay and Trônes Wood the going was not too easy, as whilst the trenches had been filled in, shell holes were still to be met with all over the place; likewise rusty barbed wire and old rifles; even a piece of puttee caught my eye, also a dud shell.

Arrived at Trônes Wood, the healing power of nature was incredible. Gone was the blackness, the odour and all the other uglinesses of which man had shown himself capable. Instead, a young, beautiful, refreshing green wood!

Where we had cut communication trenches through it, the foliage had regrown on either side, and meeting at the top, formed natural, shady arched pathways. I could not enter. Think me a coward if you will, but I had known that wood in its extremity: friends of mine had found their last resting places in its heart, and their spirits were hovering around.

As it was not my fate to be of them, I could not disturb them. Wishing, however, to see once again our old frontline, I walked round the wood. What had been a lovely green slope leading down into Guillemont, was a field of waving corn.

I stood on its edge and gazed long and earnestly into Guillemont; then, as of yore, turning half left I looked across to Delville Wood. Its blackened skeletons of trees had gone, in their place appeared a lovely example of nature's handicraft.

Everything was so quiet, the familiar sounds of shells were but memories, their absence was uncanny. And as I stood looking, and looking, for I know not what, again did I see those men of Manchester disappearing from view on their way to where in time we must all go.

Before leaving, from the southern corner of the wood I plucked a tiny piece of honeysuckle, its fragrance was irresistible. Was it wrong of me, old pals, to steal from the garden of your spirits?

You were all watching when I did so, and whilst thief like I stretched forth my arm, when the blossom was in my hand, contentment floated around. I think you all realised, in spite of my sadness, I was relieved at finding that you had such a lovely resting place and were pleased that I took a tiny souvenir.

Trônes and the adjoining woods belong to your spirits. I hope that never again will they be disturbed by man. What wastes be made of them! How beautifully nature has reclaimed them.

I saw a French peasant slowly climbing the road from Guillemont and feeling the want of human intercourse, I waited for him. To start the conversation I said, 'Can you tell me the name of this wood?'

'Sorry,' he replied, 'but I've only been in these parts for four years and don't know the names of the places roundabout.' What was there to say to that but, 'thank you, and good day!'

Returning, I stumbled into one or two shell holes; once I trod on soft ground and for a moment thought it was a corpse. To the others awaiting me in the car I explained away my long absence by pretending that I lost my way. They might not have understood had I told them that the time had been spent with old friends.

—INFANTRYMAN HENRY V, WRITING IN SEPTEMBER 1931.

*

Thousands of men whose paths have been paths of peace these dozen years and more have now and then a wish to revisit those places which are inseparably associated with their memories of the War.

Perhaps it is that in the post-war hurly burly they sometimes miss the camaraderie and mutual understanding of their more spacious, though uncertain, existence at the front.

Whatever the reason, you will each summer find parties of Britons—and Germans—on foot or awheel, straggling along that belt of country stretching from Ypres to Switzerland through which the trenches ran; but principally at Ypres, for, I should think, every British regiment knew it and the desolation which lay to the east of it.

There is now, however, barely a trace of that desolation, for an industrious peasantry have returned to till and build (with German money), laying out their fields and planting their marches exactly (or so it seems) as they were when I first knew them in 1915.

From the Menin Gate to Hellfire Corner is not more than 3,000 yards but when on a recent visit I traversed it for the first time in broad daylight it seemed surprisingly shorter than in the days when to show your nose in daylight was to court immediate annihilation.

Arrived at Hellfire Corner, I paused to reflect with satisfaction upon an occasion when my youthful self and my companion, a Deeside stalker, narrowly escaped extinction at this same corner: and all because of a bag of coke and the 'Hill 60 gun'.

The coke was wanted at the Ecole de Bienfaisance (of which not a vestige now remains), and upon us the lot fell to carry it. The 'Hill 60 gun' was a field howitzer which at short regular intervals dropped a shell on the crossroads; shrapnel usually, and containing, they said, such diverse missiles as horseshoes, gramophone needles, and pukka shrapnel bullets. For the truth of it I cannot vouch. It seems a queer assortment.

Standing at Hellfire Corner I could identify the site of the trenches which my battalion of Gordons held in the early summer of 1915. Behind that hedge was our support trench; through those two fields of wheat run

Union Street, the communicator, leading to the frontline; there to the left of the road in the cottage garden was our advanced post, where No 13 Platoon suffered heavily.

From this position we launched our first attack, and somewhat, I think, to our own surprise found it successful and excitingly tolerable. Those, however, were the early days. If anyone had told me in 1915 or 1916, or, for that matter, at any time during the war, that I should one day pay to get into Sanctuary Wood, I should most likely have replied, with that greater vigour of speech which marked the place and period, that I should be glad to pay anything to get out of it then and there for good.

Nevertheless here I was in this year of grace 1931 meekly paying my threepence to be admitted to the farther side of a fence of rusty barbed wire and screw pickets which enclosed an acre or two of land unreclaimed from the devastation of war.

Here remain several of the old British trenches much dilapidated and muddy, but not more dilapidated nor muddier than neighbouring earthworks were when, manned by a company or two, they constituted the sole barrier between the enemy and Ypres.

To this noxious spot one raw October morning the battalion came badly blown and staggering, each man under a burden of bombs and ammunition, having played a deadly game of hop, skip and jump with a diabolically accurate concentration of whizzbangs which sought us out all the way from Kruisstraat to Maple Copse. From this higher ground I could still trace the route we took then, and in fancy relive that exciting day and many more that we passed in this the bloodiest angle of the Salient.

Where once was a nightmare forest of black, splintered trees and everywhere the acrid odour of high explosive and the sickly smell of corruption is now a shady growth of chestnut, plane, and hazel shooting up from the parent stumps, amid a litter of rifles, mortars, bombs, machine guns, and such other debris, to remind you, if reminder were needed, of the time when man's chief end was to be a killer.

There is now in Sanctuary Wood an inn, and as I quitted the place I saw the keeper's daughter, aged five, playing with great content among the discarded relics of war. 'There is,' I thought, 'something instructive in that; some visible sign of the peace for which men laboured in sweat and blood on this very spot. It is good to see the engines of war become the playthings of little children.'

To walk round the Salient during the war would have been impossible for even if you had escaped being blown sky high you had surely perished in a morass of mud; but now an able-bodied man can circumambulate the Ypres front comfortably in a day with time to tarry where he will.

From Sanctuary Wood to Hill 60 you can roughly follow, by road and footpath, the old frontline whose zig-zag course is approximately marked by those pill-boxes which the Belgian farmers have not yet been able to remove.

Some of the pill-boxes which used to harbour armed men and machine guns are now devoted to the more constructive purposes of sheltering chickens and goats; some have been broken up and used as road metal.

Much of the ravaged land here still remains to be restored to agriculture, and much of it has been planted, with fir mostly. Hill 60, crowned with a regimental memorial, remains derelict, and standing on its summit you at once realise its importance as a tactical point which commands both sides of the ridge.

A little to the south runs the railway to Comines, in whose embankments we burrowed our temporary homes in a short period during which we were hewers of wood and carriers of very heavy material for the somewhat less fortunate holders of a precarious frontline.

At one of its culverts, I vividly remember, a distinguished Aberdeen colonel and a stiff-stick English officer with whom he was talking narrowly, missed obliteration by the agency of a 'rubber-heeled' German shell. It did, however, play old Harry with the cookhouse.

My next objective was the Bluff, for which, when for a lengthy term it was practically our permanent abode, I had conceived almost an affection, principally, I suppose; because it interposed its bulk between us and the enemy, cramping his style in gunnery, but adding considerably to our security.

The Bluff is still there, and recognisable, with a small cemetery where we used to unload those light railway trucks that always creaked. La Chapelle Farm adjoining, where a strong point was held by one of our platoons, seems now to be remarkable for the ferocity of its dogs.

Entering the cornyard, I was about to examine the familiar place with a pardonable feeling of part-ownership (who of the battalion would not have felt the same?) when three enormous dogs rushed out with fearsome, raucous howls.

I hastily withdrew, for I had no wish to share the traditional fate of the Donside gamekeeper who vanished in his own kennels, leaving only the heel rings of his boots to tell the tale. Or so it is said.

From the Bluff it is an easy walk to Ypres, by the ruins of Lock No. 8, where the Messines Road crosses the now disused Comines Canal, and by Lankhof Château, or rather the site of it, for all that remains is a few stones and a cluster of concrete dug-outs. The moat is filled with debris and overgrown with rushes.

Not so the moat at Ypres, however, which I crossed at the Lille Gate, it is a lovely stretch of water fringed with sedges and overhung with willow and alders. On it swans floated, preening themselves, and from the drawbridge several fishermen plied their rods with bread for bait. After the fashion of their kind, they seemed well pleased although they were getting no bites.

One half of the Lille Gate, the left as you enter, has been repaired in harmony with the architecture of the ancient fortifications. The other half and the adjacent curtain wall remain battered and ruinous as the German shellfire left them.

—2Lt Andrew Lawson Ingram, Gordon Highlanders, writing in November 1931.

14

1932

Arras this weekend has many British visitors who are making their first return after 14 years, or more. For them it is all so familiar—and all so strange. When they were here last it was a city of eerie quiet by day: a place of bustling activity in the hours of darkness. It was almost in the frontline.

The grand old Hotel de Ville, with its famous carillon—a priceless relic of the days when Arras was one of the richest centres of Spanish Flanders—was in ruins. The quaintly gabled houses round the great square were sadly battered. The cathedral was an unsightly wreck. On the eastern side of the city, out from the railway station, scarcely a building remained with a roof: mostly, the houses were mere rubble.

Today, to the untutored eye, there is no mark of war on Arras. A new cathedral has arisen; an Impressive Hotel de Ville, crowned by an imposing carillon tower dominates the great square. The old Flemish gables of the surrounding houses have been restored, 'so as you'd hardly notice,' commented one veteran of the 7th East Yorkshires, who, 15 years ago this very weekend, took part in a raid on the Douai railway cutting just to the east of Arras and helped to bring in a machine gun and 14 prisoners. There are very few traces today of those old German dug-outs in the railway banking.

Recollections are stirred again in this new, yet familiar, Arras. There are men here who know the 'underground city' with a thoroughness which no native can challenge—men who spent long days in its labyrinthine galleries while a storm of shellfire swept the streets above.

Before the Battle of Arras, which began at Easter in 1917 and more or less continued until the autumn, our troops came to know this subterranean maze in every detail. Its great storehouses and tunnels provided not only secure shelter, but a safe way through from the rear into the very frontline.

Some of the storehouses are in commercial use again, but the tunnels and galleries of the old quarries have not been maintained, and their exploration, even in part, is not an easy feat.

In the days when the German menace was greatest, and life above ground very precarious, there were cafés and shops still carrying on; and Arras had its evenings of gaiety while the guns boomed all round. Some of these old resorts remain to this day.

How they escaped the successive bombardments is a mystery; but there they are, just as they were in '15, '16, '17, '18. The same old dingy curtains obscuring the vision of the curious passer-by, but giving to those inside a clear view of the street and the approach—shall we say?—of an unwanted APM. In this post-war Arras there are new, more flamboyant resorts; but the old haunts, dim and unobtrusive as of yore, still cast their spell.

There is a very full day ahead of us tomorrow. In the morning, we of the Leeds Pals party are to pay homage to our old comrades in the British cemetery at Serre, on the very ground over which the first waves of the Battle of the Somme surged on the fateful July 1st, 16 years ago.

Our act of remembrance—the third we shall have performed there since the war—will be to place a wreath on the Memorial Cross which stands guard in this beautiful sanctuary.

Thereafter we are to visit Auchonvillers, through whose blackened ruins we filed on our first introduction to the frontline. The village now is entirely rebuilt, the new church having been completed since our last visit....

The Prince of Wales led us in our homage to the Somme dead when he unveiled the great memorial here today. Over 10,000 people, French and English, heard his stirring speech. Just as the Prince went to unveil the monument the sun burst through, illuminating the beautiful memorial arch. It was an unforgettable moment.

The scene here today has changed much since some of us were last here. Looking south from the Thiepval Ridge, not two miles away and almost in the shadow of the great Memorial, lies Fricourt now rebuilt, the scene on July 1st, 16 years ago, of a fight to the death in which the 10th West Yorkshire, a battalion which came very largely from Leeds and district, played an heroic but tragic part.

The village seems strangely remote now from drama so vast and terrible. The place has been reconstructed on its original foundations, and the old vaulted cellars of its houses restored to domestic uses bear few traces of the days when they were German dug-outs and gun-pits.

Even today, when its main street has seen again many visitors from the stirring days of other years, it seems impossible that Fricourt, in its rich summer setting, should ever have been shattered and rent and become for a time the very pit of hell.

Yet there are men here who can tell you of that shell and bullet swept advance towards the village, when the 10th West Yorkshires almost ceased to exist. On that July morning in 1916 the unit had 733 casualties, of whom well over half were killed or missing.

Like so many other happenings on that fateful day, the advance started well. Two companies passed through the German line with comparative ease; but the other two were caught in a rain of machine gun fire from the ruins of Fricourt and almost wiped out.

The advanced company, cut off, isolated and without any support, pushed forward gallantly to their objective, only to be overwhelmed by smashing massed counter attacks.

Broken up into detached groups they fought on—a magnificent but hopeless effort—until they were all but obliterated. Just one of the small groups contrived to carve its way out.

There are men in Fricourt today who played their part on that agonising morning. They find it difficult to believe that their memories ever had any foundation of reality. Yet here are familiar landmarks in plenty: but where a German machine gun nest made life unpleasant and precarious, the vintages of France are on offer today—and in such circumstances, who cares if you can't get a hundred francs to the pound?

Before the Thiepval ceremony the Leeds Pals' contingent laid a wreath on the memorial at Serre, in memory of comrades killed on the Somme battlefield. Away on the crest of the slope—a stone's throw, no more—is the new hamlet of Serre. Just a small group of red-brick dwellings and a squat little memorial stone which commemorates the men who fell on the very threshold.

The old village was never taken by storm: it became untenable when the Thiepval ridge, to the south, fell into our hands. But as you view today the serried lines of headstones in the British and French cemeteries, which lie at its very gates, you may conjure up some idea of the awful price of modern war.

To those of us who spent long days in and out of the lines here, and survived to face the ordeal of the first onslaught in the great battle, it seems little short of incredible that anybody could have lived. Seen from the Serre slopes, our old positions lie before us like an open book. It would appear that the enemy must have been aware of all our movements. He held the crest: we were at his feet.

There, just across the gentle dale, is La Signy Farm. We knew it as a tottering shell in the heart of our trench system. Today it is the centre of a community busy with the harvest, which ripples in waves of gold almost to the walls of the sanctuary where we make our pilgrimage.

We are only a small company who have come again to be for a while with our old comrades. As we gather round the white memorial cross the memory of them becomes so real that it is not difficult to believe they are with us again. We leave our wreath of remembrance, and we find it hard to speak as we turn away to tread the pilgrims' path to the great commemorative symbol which towers over the ridge of Thiepval.

But these are not unhappy moments if we cannot put it into words, we know that this is a great and happy reunion. The Pals' party today bade farewell to the distinguished company who have taken part in the Somme ceremonies. Air Marshal Lord Trenchard came to us specially to say goodbye.

The Pals and the contingent from the Leeds Rifles spent today visiting familiar areas. The weather was beautiful after early rain. An essential part of any pilgrimage of the Leeds Pals is a return to Bus-lès-Artois, the village which in the earlier months of 1916 was largely our 'home.' From its comparative security a few miles behind the line, we first entered the trenches opposite Serre.

To it we returned, and up to the Battle of the Somme it was the centre of our corporate life. In those few months we came to know the people so well that to this day we have many friends there. Some of the older generation have passed on, though a few remain to give us cordial greeting.

The tiny tots and schoolchildren of the war years are the adult citizens of today; but they have not forgotten '*les anciens soldats de* Leeds *et* Bradford,' and everywhere it is open house for us. Even the young children who play about on the little stretch of grass which fronts the church and the *Mairie* have a shy welcome for us.

They bring little bunches of wild flowers which they have collected in and about Bus Wood of unforgettable memory. In externals the village has changed but little, for it escaped the full blast of the storm, and there has been small need to rebuild.

Most of our old billets remain intact—though one or two of the decrepit sheds which perforce we had to use have collapsed at last. How they contrived to stand up at all, even when we were there 16 years ago, is one of the insoluble puzzles of the war.

We could linger on in this unpicturesque, though to us attractive village, but there are other places we must visit. Along the lane and round the corner by the old cemetery, with the Calvary still standing on the green verge, we come to Courcelles.

Here there is more change, for the German artillery did considerable damage. Nevertheless, there are many familiar landmarks. In the centre of the village is the little *estaminet* where the alluring but very aloof *Mademoiselle* used to condescend to serve us with atrocious *vin blanc* when we were in funds.

Alas, the place is as dingy as ever, *les vins* have not improved, and the personnel of the establishment has not the decorative qualities of yesteryear. The old church remains and nearby is the enclosed yard where many tasks had to be performed which, at the time, we thought properly attached to the duties of the Royal Engineers. But today we can forget those irritating little differences of the past.

And so, along the familiar road to one street Colincamps. When last I passed through in wartime it was lashed by German shells. Its buildings were collapsing like houses of cards.

Today it slumbers peacefully again; its orchards are laden with fruit. The church has no gaping shell-hole through its clock tower. And in the Café de la Jeunesse Dorée—the only gilt is in the name—we can rest luxuriously and recall the old *Via Dolorosa* through the *Sucrerie* and into the trenches.

It is not easy, from now on, to locate exact spots in what was our trench system. All the land is under cultivation again; but helped by a trench map, miraculously preserved through the years, we find our way and in the very heart of the harvest trace out the historic line. Across the way the roofs of Serre peep over the ridge, and in the still uncleared scrub on the slope ahead of us we can see the old German front.

Somewhere about where we stand, with all the hum of high summer about our ears, we recall one of our old pals who fell. It was within a few yards of this very place. He was little more than a boy, who came to us with a draft, and was thrown straight into the thick of it. After a day or two in 'rest' billets, he was up in the frontline with us, out into that fearful strip, No Man's Land, putting wire up.

It was all so wonderful to him. He marvelled at the complexity of the zig-zag trenchworks through which we groped our way in the darkness. A sudden burst of Verey lights reminded him—a homely touch—of Roundhay Park on a Gala night! A sharp rattle of machine gunfire suggested to him the work of some hidden trap drummer, and he started to beat out the steps of a dance on the duckboards.

The front trench impressed him by its silence. The sharp injunction to 'shut up' as he began to talk in his rather high-pitched voice moved him to a giggle. 'You blasted fool! Don't you know Fritz is only a few yards away?' That quietened him for the moment.

'Spread out to the left,' was the whispered order as we clambered out on to the top, and soon we were busy on the job. It was a still, black night. Not a sound except the muffled tap of mallets as stakes were driven in. Things were going nicely. Another half hour and the task would be finished. Then back to Courcelles and a long night's sleep.

Suddenly a great burst of rocket signals illuminated the sky behind the German lines: and in a moment Hell was let loose. Their guns whipped our reserve trenches and set down a flaming barrage through which nothing could penetrate. Their heavy guns pounded away at our frontline. And there we were, crouched low in the shell holes in No Man's Land, waiting for our cue. If this was the prelude to a raid, we might play an important part.

Almost as suddenly as it started the storm of fire ceased. There was no German raid on our part of the line. In silence we pulled ourselves together to get back to the trenches. But our light-hearted young pal did not move. A ricocheting nose cap of a German shell had killed him where he lay. Memories! The ground exhales them at every step. We drag ourselves reluctantly away: but this soil will call to us as long as we live.

—Pte Lance Grocock, West Yorkshire Rgt, writing over three days at the unveiling of the Arras and Thiepval Memorials in August 1932.

Grocock worked as a journalist before the war, and on the outbreak of hostilities, he enlisted with the Leeds Pals. He was wounded on the first morning of the Battle of the Somme in July 1916 and lay in a shell-hole on the battlefield until nightfall when he crawled to safety using the stars as his guide. On discharge from service in 1917, he returned to journalism, working for newspapers across the north of England. He was a frequent visitor to the battlefields.

15

1933

It was a hot July day, but I almost shivered as I found the shelter of the great Memorial Arch at Thiepval. It was not only that the cool breeze was such a contrast to the heat outside, but more the sense of isolation one felt beneath this huge monument.

I had found my way up the slopes from the station at Beaucourt Hamel, a not difficult walk, but one on which, owing to the entire absence of directing notices, one might easily add a mile to the journey.

I had seen no Englishman since leaving Amiens, so it was with a feeling of relief as I emerged at the other side of the arch that I found the stone mason there at work was a Briton.

No, he was not repairing the memorial, but adding still more names to the enormous total of 73,000 already inscribed as having no known graves on the Somme. Here, if anywhere, there is a sermon written in stone—73,000 names of brave men whom war does not even allow a named grave.

There is a chapter here too for every ex-serviceman, for as he looks down his regimental roll—nearly 3,000 of the Northumberland Fusiliers with whom I served after the City Battalion—he finds the names of a multitude of pals and they bring back the memories of Contalmaison, Pozieres, High Wood, Scots Redoubt and so many others.

There is the same quiet in the cemeteries—those charming little gardens of love, tended and cared for by men of understanding, no less attentive even in the absence of visitors. For the battlefields today are deserted.

It was the same at Thiepval. I asked a gardener if there were many visitors? 'Very few,' he replied, 'except natives,' and as if to prove his word, half a hundred French people, complete with priest and children, emptied themselves from a huge motor-coach and scrambled up the steps to the memorial.

I glanced at the visitors' book in the various cemeteries. In some of them there was only a handful of names this year, mostly inscribed at Whitsuntide.

The keeper of the Ulster Tower, at Thiepval, was only too glad of a chat with an Englishman. As we ran over old times together, his daughter played with the dogs and addressed them in perfect French.

'Don't they understand English?' I asked, amazed. 'Oh, yes,' replied Paddy, 'I talk to them in English,' but he admitted that he had only been out of France once since he became keeper many years ago.

'And what about visitors?' I asked. 'Oh, we only get an occasional one from home,' was the reply, 'most of them go to Sheffield park.'

In Paris I had asked about the battlefields tour. It does not often go nowadays, I was told, there is no demand.

In Amiens I looked for the office of a famous tourist agency, but was told it was closed down. Yet the pretty grounds of the Ulster Tower, with their memorial trees, are kept as charmingly as ever, and the cemeteries themselves are multi-coloured pictures.

Outside one I noticed a shoe-scraper, and though in this weather there was no need to use it, one felt indeed that here was holy ground. The roses of various colours were in full bloom and mingled with them were the blue of the delphiniums and the Canterbury bells, the red geum and the yellow and red gaillardia.

At the Sucrerie Cemetery, the first used by the Sheffield and Barnsley Battalions, I saw the grave of A. McKenzie (April 4, 1916), the first man of the Sheffield Battalion to be killed in action, and as I read other names in the different cemeteries and noted the dates I was reminded of various episodes. Here a bombardment, there a raid, and more than all, of course, of that sunny July morning 17 years ago.

In the French Cemetery down the Serre road every grave was gay and with a tiny tricolour placed there by *Les Camarades des Croix de Bois*, Lille, but the painted wooden crosses remain.

In the Allied Cemetery before the Thiepval Memorial the French crosses are all concrete. At Thiepval the church is almost finished. Ex-servicemen of the Somme—imagine a church at Thiepval!

The only Englishman I saw during my day in the Serre district was a YMCA assistant, who had come by motorcycle from Boulogne to place a July 1st wreath on a West Yorkshire grave in the Serre No. 3 Cemetery.

But our old companions of the trenches, the blithe swallows, have not deserted the battlefields. They soar continuously overhead singing their bright songs. I could find no other explanation of the deserted battlefields than the franc.

It is dear to live in France. Two shillings for 20 cigarettes, 4*d* or 5*d*, for an apple, while in the matter of motor-coach trips, one thinks in pounds.

But if a walk has no fears for one, it is possible to get from Amiens either to the Serre district or to Thiepval for an outlay of less than 20 francs (5*s*) second class return.

Both in city and country one is assured that Germany is preparing for war, so great is the fear, and the same man will tell you that war is no good. An Englishman living over there assured me, on what authority I know not, that the French steel works were full of material in case it should be needed. How much reliance one can place on statements made in such an excitable country, one does not know, but it is disheartening talk after a visit to the peaceful cemeteries.

—Sgt Arthur Wilson, Northumberland Fusiliers, writing in July 1933.

Wilson was twenty-two years old when he put his job as a junior reporter with the *Sheffield Independent* on hold to join the Sheffield City Pals Battalion. He was shot in the left leg on the first day of the Battle of the Somme and later transferred to the Northumberland Fusiliers. After the war, he returned to Sheffield and joined the *Northampton Chronicle* as news editor in 1938. He died in 1964.

16

1934

Towns and villages that were no more than heaps of debris when we left have been so rebuilt that they look as though a shot had never been fired in them. It is indicative, perhaps, of the sentimentality in the French race that instead of replanning the ruined towns, they have rebuilt them just as they were.

Some of the smaller villages have, of course, disappeared altogether. The houses had been blown down by shellfire and the debris used for filling sandbags. Every stick and stone has been removed, and their sites indicated by a simple signboard inscribed 'Here stood "A" Ville' or 'Here stood "B"s Ville'.

The most wonderful reconstruction has, however, taken place in Ypres. I stood on those famous ramparts and talked far into the night with old comrades about the nights of horror we had spent there.

Twenty years ago all was mud and destruction. Incessant shellfire had churned the ground over and over. Canals were blown in, drains were smashed. It seemed impossible that anything could ever be done with the area again. But it has all been levelled out, farmhouses have been built, and agriculture flourishes.

I found my old landlady with whom I was billeted, and looked again into the room where I slept and into the cellar where I sometimes had to take shelter. I noticed she had made a fine screen out of the old linen war maps we had left behind, but she refused all temptation to sell it.

I went down also to an old sunken road and lived over again the movements of that led to my falling into the hands of the enemy as a prisoner. I came across an interesting incident at one of the cemeteries a few miles from Arras.

Entered in the visitors' book on August 1st this year was the signature of a German, who had appended a drawing of the Nazi badge with the inscription '*Heil* Hitler.' Following it was the signature of a Frenchman who had blacked out the badge and written '*Vive la France, Viva l'Angleterre.*'

We attended a service at the Menin Gate and were there in company with a party of German tourists. At 'Last Post,' which is sounded every evening, they stood rigidly to attention. It was a trip of exceptional interest, and I was particularly glad that relatives of the fallen who were making their first visit to France had an opportunity of seeing how well the graves of their loved ones are cared for.

—OFFICER, SPEAKING IN AUGUST 1934.

*

Amiens feels just the same outwardly, but to us the atmosphere is totally different. We realise now that we are living in the past and that it is useless trying to imagine ourselves back in the old days when everything was activity, when we all had a job to do, and when our comrades were with us. Returning to the battlefields is like returning to an empty theatre the morning after a successful show, when everything is dull and lifeless, and one feels hopelessly alone. This is the best analogy we can find if multiplied a thousandfold.

We have now finished our tour and proceed back to Ypres. All along the road places of famous battles are pointed out, but we seem to have lost interest. We have seen enough, and as we pass cemetery after cemetery our minds travel back, and we think of those four years of war, which seem to us so near and yet so far away.

We think of the state of the world today and as all these memories come surging up in our minds it is with great difficulty that we can control our emotions. What was the good of it all? Why cannot we settle our international disputes in a more reasonable way? Could we not have an international rugby match to settle such matters? No, of course; that would be hopeless, as no one would abide by the result.

Hullo! Here is Neuve Chapelle. We must have a look at Croix Rouge, where we first went up digging trenches with the Indians in November '14. We recognise this village and the old road down to Les Lobes, along which we marched day after day. Rations were short in those days, and we knew what it was like to feel hungry.

But let us get on—Armentières—through the *Douane*—Plug Street. Here the wood looks a little patchy, while the *château* is still in ruins; and finally along the old cobbled roads back again into Ypres.

Feeling a bit lonely and depressed, we seek the company of some of the inhabitants. We tell them of our experiences, and how the atmosphere seems to weigh down upon us. They are sympathetic, and say that we are not exceptional, and that it affects everybody the same. And as we talk to these simple people who have really seen war at its worst, who have been driven from their homes, and with whom we have a natural bond of sympathy, we wonder how many millions of ordinary people in the world today are of the same opinion as ourselves on the question of war.

Next morning we leave Ypres, passing through Vlamertinghe, Poperinghe, to Hazebrouck. Hazebrouck to Calais, and then on the boat. We feel that we have been away for months instead of only for a few days, and as the white cliffs of Dover loom up in the distance we experience the same sensations as we used to experience in the old days.

Dear old England again. At any rate, she was spared the horrors of invasion. It was not for nothing that all those splendid fellows went under. Supposing they had not fought, where would England be now? The whole business is so confusing.

Rotten business, war. Nobody gains anything, and afterwards everybody is broke. Worst of all—all the best chaps get killed. Millions of widows, orphans, sorrowing parents—rotten business. Suppose we'd join up again if they wanted us, just the same as before, although, ironically, we always say we wouldn't. We try to stop thinking about war, but our short visit has set our memories going, which we cannot somehow stop.

Victoria—home again—back to earth again. Rotten business, war. Glad we got through. Didn't deserve to. Are we better men for it? In the next war, what about the boys? Yes, they would go, of course. Let's hope they won't be asked. But what's the use of speculating: it won't make the slightest difference. 'Evening paper'—good idea, let's read the football results. And so we pass down the line again.

—Corporal 1435, writing in November 1934.

The anonymous corporal was on the Western Front from early in the war serving at Neuve Eglise in 1914. He appeared in the documentary film *The Battle of the Somme* in 1916 and was at St Quentin for the launch of the German Spring Offensive in March 1918. During his 1934 pilgrimage to the battlefields, the corporal spent several days touring dozens of towns, villages, and key wartime landmarks across France and Belgium he had known during his four years of service. Once back home, he wrote a five-part report of his experiences, and these are his concluding thoughts.

17

1935

Round about Serre, where the battalion as we first knew it ceased to exist, there is little likeness today to the deep-scarred, war-scorched terrain that was the grave, almost 19 years ago, of our closest comrades.

As I stood yesterday on the land where our trenches were battered into chaos on July 1st, 1916, it was with difficulty that I recalled the wartime scene. Here on my left, now, are the trim new buildings of La Signy Farm, of famous memory. My last view of it on the opening day of the Battle of the Somme was of roofless walls and a crazy chimney stack which reeled drunkenly in the deafening concussion, but refused to fall.

Stretching before me now are well cultivated fields, bearing early promise of a bountiful harvest. A deep hollow nearby, with young trees striking up about its rim, does not, at first glance, look anything like Basin Wood.

But if you take the precarious path to its depths you will find evidence still that it sheltered many stricken men in days of great hazard and trial. Here are traces of funk holes where men tended their wounded pals after the big attack.

Just a little further down a gentle slope to the east it is not easy to find Matthew and Mark, two of the copses which figured so prominently in battle orders. They are there, if you search thoroughly—but tread carefully; you may endanger growing crops.

Hereabouts, too, there is the little cemetery and memorial to the Sheffield Pals, valiant comrades of ours on a fateful day. We pay homage as we move along towards Serre, the village that was never taken by assault in the war, though many men died in more than one attempt.

And now, up another gentle slope, we approach the old German line. To the right, as we move slowly, thoughtfully, over land which it seemed no man ever could cross and live, the memorial cross in Serre No. 1 Cemetery—our cemetery—stands sentinel. Here, where they fell, our men sleep.

Strangely enough, only a few yards away, there is still a portion of the German line uncleared. Its trenches have collapsed, but the scars are there and, in the dank undergrowth, an obscene tangle of rusted wire, shattered gunstocks, broken stakes. You walk with care here; it is dangerous ground.

It was here at Easter 1916, that we manned the line up to our knees in water. Some of us have recalled this weekend how, with a wheezy, antiquated pump, we tried to make things a little more tolerable, only to bring over our heads a shower of whizzbangs and such like—so that we decided to bear the ills we had.

Serre itself, an entirely new village, is a much smaller place now. It is just a cluster of little houses and one *estaminet*, whose patronne is glad to welcome her English visitors and to show them the memorial stone by the wayside.

Retracing our steps along the road through Auchonvillers, now rebuilt, even to its church—who does not remember the old sunken road where booby traps abounded?—we came to Mailly to find it little changed.

The protective sandbags round the old church must have served their purpose well. There seems to be no sign of damage. The brewery, in whose vats we bathed one bitterly cold March morning, still adorns the main street. Its vats now hold a more congenial brew.

From here to Colincamps is but a step. Distances, somehow, seem to have shrunk since we shed our equipment. The long, straggling village street is almost without sign of life. There is not even a murmur from the dingy bar of La Jeunesse Dorée.

The church, restored, stands guard at the end of the road. No longer is there an unsightly gap through its clock tower. And in the orchard behind, where our guns used to roar, the blossom is on the trees.

From here to Courcelles-au-Bois, which looks much the same, I find my old billet, but not the puttees I lost there, and which were the cause of much officious inquiry. On an old wall here there is even a trace of one of those revue posters which someone had plastered up to brighten the weary way to and from the line.

Lastly, dear old Bus. Here, outwardly, time has stood still. The old church, the *Mairie*, the *château*—everything is the same. There are many old friends, too, some of them very old. They have not forgotten us, and it is a happy reunion.

They have a warm welcome for '*les anciens soldats de* Leeds,' who spent so many months in their midst. And there is no heartier greeting than that of the children, to whom the Pals are a familiar name and, by now, something of a tradition.

The youngsters of war days have grown into men and women who run the village today. There is one corner of France, I do believe, where Leeds, for many years to come, will be something much more than a name. We leave Bus reluctantly, but with the hope that we may meet its good people again, and spend happy hours in its pleasant places.

This has been a wonderful pilgrimage of the Leeds Pals. It is not merely that we have covered the old ground and talked with people among whom we lived through many months of drama that seemed fated to have only one end.

We have encountered real friendliness—not the formal compliment of greeting acquaintances, but the true comradeship of those who lived together when the future was very dark. I am not talking now of the big centres in France. This is the story of the countryside—of Picardy, Artois, Normandy—the story of the villages we knew.

You must remember that when we quartered ourselves on this countryside, the Frenchmen of our age were away on other fronts. We knew the older folk and the younger.

Some of us think now of a Normandy farm where the grandfather—veteran of 1870—carried on while his two sons were fighting for France. He welcomed us to his barns and outhouses, made clean as a pin for us. His sons died.

Today, we meet his grandsons. They were babies when we first met them. They are fine fellows now these Normandy farmers, carrying on the ancient tradition of their line. Their handgrip is good to know. It is reserved, as they tell you very quietly, for their friends.

This serene land of Normandy is another of the unchanged areas of France we used to know so well. It never felt the harsh hand of the invader, and today I doubt the little villages of Forceville and Neuville—our first French billets—have more than three new buildings. Life moves very slowly in these parts.

Here is the very house of the classic story of the Pals when they first arrived from Egypt. I doubt if the 'decorations' of the room have changed! Colonel Taylor, of many happy memories, made a tour of billets to see if his troops, newly-arrived from Egypt, were settling down to the rigours of this Norman winter.

He comes to the house I have spoken about, and in the big room, inquires if his men billeted there are comfortable. 'We're all right, sir,' replies one bold private, 'except that we're lousy!'

'Lousy!' exclaims Col Taylor, turning to the RSM—we used to call him 'Ting, Ting,' as every Leeds Pal knows. 'He says he's lousy, Sergeant

Major! Well, you're lousy. *I'm* lousy, we're all lousy! What does the man want?'

I know this is true. The private concerned is with us today. The Colonel and the RSM have passed on. But this is where we remember them.

Do any Leeds Pals recall Airaines, the little town where we spent the first night on our march up to the line? It looks very much like Wetherby, and it is a good deal sleepier. The roads are so quiet that an occasional motor car creates quite a sensation in the main street.

Here is the Hotel de l'Ecu, which, I am told, means the Crown Hotel. Don't you remember it—and the cinema next door? It was on the stage of the cinema that some of us caught colds which, nearly—but not quite—prevented our early entrance into frontline warfare.

It was here, too, where we bought our first Maryland cigarettes, the mail and the Army supply having failed to reach us. The same tobacco shop, near the cinema, still sells them.

Vignacourt is the same today as it was then, but the Pals were only birds of passage, and there is none we can find to recall us.

In this land of memories, do you wonder that we have lived much more than a weekend since last Friday?

—Pte Lance Grocock, West Yorkshire Rgt, writing in April 1935.

*

Once a year, on April 25th, to be exact, I drink a silent mental toast to an episode of long ago. This toast is coupled with another, to the welfare of my old pals Bill, Bert and Alf, whose interpreter to the world, in picture and story, I am honoured to be.

Through the years I have never forgotten this date, in whatever part of the world I have happened to be; but this year, being in England, I felt the thing to do was to go to Belgium and celebrate this anniversary on the exact spot.

It was at 4am on April 25th, 1915, that the First Royal Warwicks, as part of the Tenth Brigade, went over the top, between Wieltje and St Julien, in the famous initial gas attack. At about nine o'clock on that same morning, yours truly was firmly and rudely informed by a shell that the attack had no further use for his services.

Now to revisit the Western Front and get the full measure of acute remembrance by doing so—it is most necessary to conjure up the past as vividly as possible. I am sure there are many who do not find it hard to do this.

Those names alone seem to be tattooed on the mind, and carry such a wealth of memory. Zillebeke, Zonnebeke, Langemarck, St Julien, Boesinghe, Hooge and so on. What stories they radiate! What stories of death and destruction, anguish and endurance. What monuments to courage and sad fraternity.

To get myself into the right mood for the pilgrimage, I re-read a few chapters of my own *Bullets and Billets*, a book I wrote long ago. In it the march of the Tenth Brigade, from Bailleul, via Locre and Vlamertinge, up into the Salient is dealt with.

Perhaps a few of my recorded impressions may be of interest. I excavate some, from the moment when we left Ypres, and journeyed onwards:

'At a little after midnight we left the field marching down the road which led towards the Yser canal, and the village of St Jean. The whole Brigade was on the road, our battalion being the last in the long column. I now knew what had been happening in the last 48 hours.

'The Germans had launched gas in the war, for the first time, and had by this means succeeded in breaking the line on a wide front to the north of Ypres. The second battle of Ypres had begun. We were making for the threatened spot, and were going to attack at four o'clock in the morning.

'We were marching in pouring rain, and darkness, down a muddy mangled road. Shattered poplar trees sticking up in black streaks on either side. Crash after crash! Shells were falling and exploding all around us, and behind, the burning city.'

I decided to traverse that very road again, or rather, trace out where that road once was, as nearly as possible. I would go to Ypres for a start.

Having landed in Belgium, I slowly dribbled along by train towards the famous city. A city whose very name still seems to burn. I was in one of those humble little dawdling trains with a small asthmatic engine.

Inside the carriage an ostentatious notice requested me not to spit, in four different languages. Looking out of the carriage window at the peaceful scene, as you find it today, it seems incredible that there ever was such an infantile mess as that war, yet pigs and hens, strolling in and out of old rusty corrugated iron dug-outs, and battered concrete gun emplacements bring the sad fact home.

This part of rebuilt Belgium has lost nothing of its old fashioned character in the rebuilding. The scar of the world's operation has healed amazingly. The stitches scarcely show. The farms, cottages, *estaminets* and churches look just the same as when I saw them before the war.

There is that same old flat land sliced up into well-kept fields. The long straight cobbled roads, the poplar and willow trees. The red tiles, and green shutters, the clean quiet rural order of things that was there before that thunderous massacre began.

The most discernible relic of the war seems to me to be the retention of innumerable curved sheets of old rusty, corrugated iron, which the thrifty Belgians have put to considerable and varied use.

On arrival at Ypres, I left the station, crossed the Place de la Gare, hitched up in a hotel and began to make my plans. I determined, as nearly as possible, to go through the geographical movements that my battalion had made, between dusk on April 24th, and dawn on April 25th.

I left the city and went along the road that leads to Vlamertinge, until I came to the now much altered field, where once, in pouring rain and darkness, we had rested after our long march.

It was here that I had sheltered under a mackintosh ground sheet with a very close friend. A man I had first met, in those clammy mud ditches, in front of St Yvon near Plugstreet Wood.

He was a lieutenant, and I will only allude to him by his initials GSM. 'Mac' was what I knew him as. We both sat in that drenching torrent watching the Cloth Hall and Cathedral burning, and listening to the thunderous crashing of shells in various parts of the wrecked city. Not a very cheerful view, but the best available at the time.

Mac was trembling so violently that I wondered what was the matter. All the more so as he was a man of the most determined courage. A courage more magnificent for the fact that he detested and despised the whole idea of war.

As we sat there in that sodden field his condition got worse, until he confided in me that he felt convinced he was 'for it.' It was obvious that he was suffering from an intensive premonition, I tried to talk him out of it, but to no avail. Here I will once more quote from *Bullets and Billets*.

'At about 11 o'clock, an orderly came along the field with a groundsheet over his head, and told me the Colonel wished to see me.

'"Where is he?" I asked. "In that little cottage place at the far corner of the field, sir."

'I scrambled out from under the sheet. "Where are you going to, BB?" asked my St Yvon friend.

'"Colonel's sent for me," I replied. "Well come back as soon as you can."

'I left, and never saw him again. He was killed early the next morning. One of the best chaps I ever knew.'

Having approximately located where we had sat that night, I started off on the road leading to St Jean, and did all I could to relive that ghastly march we had on the way to the attack. What a road it had been.

Punctured with shell-holes, littered with war debris, and strewn with dead men and horses. Now here I was again, in 1935 with serenity on all sides. I passed through St Jean and Wieltje, both smouldering ruins on that awful night, and came at last to the scene of our attack, and my lucky escape.

On the left Pilckem, in front of St Julien, Zonnebeke on the right, I remembered every detail clearly. The confusion, the death laden atmosphere and the appalling casualties. It was around here that in the space of a few days our battalion had been nearly wiped out.

Bland-eyes cows gently meander over those fields today, and the villages are filled with children who have scarcely heard of those past terrors, and who cannot understand them if they have.

Even that profuse array of cemeteries must appear to them as an accepted part of a natural landscape. What a lesson that whole salient is! What a pitiful monument for the 20th century to leave behind.

The results of years of mud, blood and destruction, along a curved line, that at the best, only surged back and forth a few miles in either direction. And for what?

I left the site of these meditations and turning to the east, proceeded round the Salient, via Hooge and Zillebeeke. I particularly wished to re-enter Ypres by the Menin Gate. Many a cemetery did I visit on the way, and gaze upon those endless ranks of stones. Daffodils, violets and pansies, as their companions, trembling in an April breeze. Many a time did I read the inscription, 'A soldier of the Great War. Known unto God.'

The Ypres Salient seems more like a being, than a tract of land. The custodian of the most poignant necropolis the world has ever made for itself. It was nearly eight o'clock when I returned to the city, and got my first view of the Menin Gate. The great memorial, I think, looks its best in evening light.

I observed it from a distance, then closely, reaching it from the east, the side on which the lion rests. I entered through the great arch, and saw those monster panels, closely packed with names. A heading for each regiment with its grim record below.

On the south wall, to the right of the steps that lead to the ramparts, the Royal Warwickshire Regiment has its large, allotted space. I began reading, pausing in memory at names I knew so well. I read on, and then ... there he was ... Mac. Ennobled now by the inclusion of his name, in this Gate of the Graveless.

After 20 years I had come back to Mac. I stood, and gazed, and thought. Suddenly the lights were turned on within the Memorial, and as the new clock, in the renovated Cloth Hall tower struck nine, the Last Post sounded ... the following morning I left Ypres and once more crossed the Place de la Gare, on my way to the station.

An old rusty, battered tank stands in that square, as a souvenir of angry days. Inside it a group of young and happy boys were playing. Laughter rang out from within those shell-scarred iron walls. What a joke it was! What fun!

'I say you chaps! Wouldn't it be fun if there was a war, and we could drive a tank in it! Come on! Let's pretend shall we!'

—CAPT. BRUCE BAIRNSFATHER, WRITING IN JUNE 1935.

Mac was Lt Gilchrist Stanley Maclagan who was a famous British rower. The Oxford University cox steered the Leander Club to the gold medal in the coxed eight at the 1908 Olympic Games. A member of the Stock Exchange before he was commissioned into the Royal Warwickshire Regiment, Maclagan was thirty-five years old when he was killed and was one of three members of the victorious men's eight to die in the First World War.

*

Little did I imagine 19 or 20 years ago that I should one day be strolling across the shell-swept ridges of the Somme with perfect freedom of movement or be worshipping in a beautiful church on a delightful summer morning in what then was a battered and shattered Ypres.

I have listened to people confessing their inability to understand why anyone should ever wish to return to those scenes of other days with their harrowing memories of 'destruction, mud and death'.

Yet one fancies that of the many who became familiar with those stricken areas between the years 1914–1918 very few have not felt a longing to see them in their more peaceful and normal setting.

Only such as were 'out there' can appreciate the desire to go back just to look once more on acres which must remain 'forever England's' and to walk again in thought with gallant comrades whom one knew and loved, and who now lie sleeping in the soil of France and Flanders.

We expected many changes and found them. Towns and villages that once seemed destroyed beyond all recognition and renewal have been beautifully reconstructed, and miles of devastated territory that could not so much boast a blade of grass have been transformed into fertile and smiling landscape. Peasants are toiling, cattle grazing and little children are playing in fields where men had a rendezvous with death.

It would be better to call it a pilgrimage. Mere curiosity or sight-seeing seems strangely out of place in the old battle zones. He has a peculiar make-up who can read unmoved the list of nearly 60,000 names inscribed on the Menin Gate Memorial, representing Britons from the Homeland or overseas to whom the fortunes of war denied a known and honourable burial.

'To the Armies of the British Empire who stood here from 1914–1918, and to those of their dead who have no known graves,' is the inscription.

The spirit of the true pilgrim is best enshrined in a verse by John Oxenham engraved on a tablet set up in Newfoundland Park, overlooking Beaumont Hamel:

Tread softly here, go reverently and slow
Yea, let your soul go down upon its knees,
And with bowed head and heart abased, strive hard
To grasp the future gain in this sore loss;
For not one foot of this dark sod, but drank
Its surfeit of the blood of gallant men,
Who, for their faith, their hope—for life and liberty,
Here made the sacrifice—here gave their lives,
And gave right willingly—for you and for me.

Leaving Victoria, one recalled those tragic departures of wartime. Now, an excited throng of holidaymakers, happy and expectant, crossing over to the Continent. Then a slow procession of khaki figures moving slowly toward the train and here and there some heart-broken wife bravely checking the tears, or an anxious mother bidding goodbye to the laddie she may never see again.

Boulogne to Doullens via Étaples and St Pol. It was never my lot to do other than pass through Étaples, nor did I ever crave a closer acquaintance with this British base. I knew it by repute, and millions will always associate it with 'The Bull Ring,' loved by none and hated by all.

St Pol was generally considered to be a friendly town, but one remembered a night in 1916 when we detrained in pouring rain and on that dismal occasion its greeting was less cordial.

Doullens I visited many times. It was here, on a morning in March 1918, where Statesmen and Army commanders gathered in anxious consultation, and where that momentous decision was reached to unite the Allied forces under a single command.

Most of the villages in the area bring back memories both grave and gay. Candas, Beauval, Fienvillers, Puchevillers, Toutencourt, Varennes, Acheux, Leauvillers! All of them concentration centres for divisions moving into the Somme sector, and it was to these quiet villages that those same divisions were withdrawn—or what was left of them.

The troops were accommodated in barns and outhouse, some of them minus walls or roof or both. The famous inscription still stands boldly out on a number of these billets. 'Cellar for 10.' Cafés and *estaminets* were crowded with men sipping the French wines and syrups, oblivious of the shattering experiences they were so soon to suffer, or forgetful of the carnage they had been fortunate to survive.

Seated in the kitchens of the different farmhouses would be groups of Tommies revelling in eggs and chips with the odour from the inevitable cesspool floating in through the open door. The story is told of an amusing episode which I believe happened in Forceville. One of my unit, having ordered his *pomme de terre*, found himself provided with a knife but no fork.

Holding up the first-named in his hand he called out, '*Kamerad*, *madam*.' Looking somewhat puzzled, the good woman disappeared and finally returned with a second knife, much to the private's embarrassment. He mused silently for a moment, and then brandishing the knife triumphantly aloft shouted, 'Fiancée, *madam*.'

Let it be recorded to her everlasting credit, *Madame* grasped the situation. With a, '*Oui*, *oui monsieur*,' she bolted into an adjoining room and emerged, equally triumphant, bearing the missing fork in her hand.

Today the villages are deserted and the *estaminets* empty, save for an occasional yokel who lurches in for a glass of wine and lurches out again. On this last visit, the friend who accompanied me was desirous of looking up a family he had known in Fienvillers.

After much questioning and diligent searching, we ran these friends to earth. Judging by the astonishment that appeared on their faces, they seemed to think we had dropped from the skies.

The little girl whose scalded leg was treated by men of the Field Ambulance is now a married woman, but still carries in her handbag a snapshot of herself, taken when she was a child, standing in the midst of the English soldiers who were delighted to render first aid.

A halt was made beside a hamlet whose memories are not altogether pleasant. The people who kept the farm were by no means kindly disposed to the troops thrust upon them, and never lost an opportunity of showing their displeasure.

Events reached a climax when, during the bitterly cold spell of February 1917, we found the well barricaded and bolted against our use. The furies were loose next morning when our unwilling hosts discovered the said well piled high with stones and refuse—the work of some nocturnal avenger.

The perpetrator was never found, nor was the slightest attempt made to identify him. All felt that, though the action was rather mean, yet in this instance it was richly deserved. The well is still there, and apparently existing in a state of uselessness.

On to Mailly-Maillet, Auchonvillers, and Beaumont Hamel. The last named was to have been taken in the first Somme offensive of July 1916, but the attacks of the Eighth Corps, under General Sir Aylmer Hunter-Weston, were defied and repulsed. Everything round about is pretty much as it was on that fateful July morning.

Nature's healing hand has been at work, but the long and winding lines of trenches and gaping shell-holes are all there. Relics of battle lie around. Broken and rusty rifles repose on the parapets, and here and there a steel helmet. The very stillness of the scene becomes eloquent. Nearby is the Newfoundland Memorial in the form of a caribou perched on a high cairn, its noble head raised proudly over the ground where so many Newfoundlanders went to their death.

Wandering across No Man's Land of 1916, and avoiding the barbed wire lying in the long grass, we came upon the bronze Highlander erected on the site of the old German frontline. This is the memorial to the 51st Highland Division which eventually wrested Beaumont Hamel from the enemy on November 13, 1916.

Dipping into the valley and pausing on the outskirts of the village itself, we took the main road to Hamel and Beaucourt. Beaucourt-sur-Ancre was the final objective of my own division on November 13th and 14th, 1916, and a simple but noble obelisk on the roadside testifies to those who struggled and fell here.

Albert, the gateway to the Somme and the home of the 'Leaning Virgin.' Possibly no town on the Western Front had a more tragic war history, and none has emerged from its bitter experience with greater dignity.

Its busy streets, flanked on either side by rows of well-built and prosperous-looking shops, constitute safe and congenial thoroughfares for the post-War traveller. Albert has been described as a town of cafés. It was reputed to have contained well over a hundred before the War, but today there must be nearly twice that number, a gigantic total for a country town of such dimensions.

As is the French custom, groups of people were sitting round the small tables invitingly placed outside the cafés, on what appeared to be an ordinary day, and in the evening the raucous cries from a loudspeaker could be heard at a distance of a hundred yards. Other days, other ways!

No longer has the pedestrian to grope his way forward in the brooding darkness in an unsuccessful attempt to negotiate piles of broken masonry, or rush for cover from the jagged fragments of a bursting shell. Passing through the area during the retreat of March 1918, one's heart sickened at the sight of the helpless refugees who were compelled to vacate their homes a second time.

Vehicles and transport of every description were piled high with whatever furniture and odds and ends their owners could hastily scrape together. Old folk or little children were trudging alongside gazing hopelessly upon the ranks of passing troops.

In his *A Fatalist at War*, Rudolf Binding says: 'It is practically certain that the reason why we did not reach Amiens was the looting at Albert and Moreuil. In Albert I saw it myself. The two places contained so much wine that the divisions which ought to have marched through them lay about in rooms and cellars. This was quite unforeseen. No other troops had been ordered up, with the result that the enemy gained fresh footing.'

Be that as it may. Albert was eventually delivered from her martyrdom, and once again she is a peaceful and hospitable town. The Cathedral, with its handsome facade, has risen from the dust, and making our way inside we noticed portions of the old ruins cleverly built into the new walls or exhibited as detached souvenirs of a cruel vandalism.

Its imposing tower once more supports the figure of the Virgin holding in her outstretched hands the Infant Christ. 'The Leaning Virgin of Albert' became world famous and was for long the cynosure of wondering eyes. It was declared, and by some believed, that its fall would mark the conclusion of hostilities. I understand that the figure fell from its precarious position in April 1918, but the war dragged on until November.

A short distance out of Albert, at a spot that was known as Tara Hill, I turned aside to inspect the Bapaume Post Military Cemetery. Captain H. A. Taylor says that, 'the beauty of the British War Cemeteries is, probably, the dominant memory of every visitor to the old battlefields.' You find them everywhere, and all are tenderly cared for.

Pausing at Flatiron Copse Cemetery, I tramped along Death Valley towards Mametz village. Scattered here and beside the uneven track were all relics of the war—steel helmets, empty jam tins, German water bottles, old boots, and pieces of shrapnel and high explosive.

From Mametz to Fricourt, where my companion and I hoped to catch a train for Albert, we were greatly disappointed. The service consists of two trains daily in each direction, and the second and last had departed for Albert some 10 minutes before we arrived.

Saying little, but thinking much, we pushed on to an appetising dinner and a night's repose. Seven o'clock the next morning found us *en route* for Havrincourt, via Achiet-le-Grand. Havrincourt we never liked.

My first visit was paid at the end of 1917, and much to our disgust, happened to coincide with a very spiteful gesture on the part of the enemy artillery. 'Must have known we were coming,' muttered a young hopeful.

Flinging ourselves forward in the darkness toward what looked like the entrance to a dug-out, a batch of us found ourselves reclining in a family vault which had evidently been torn asunder in some previous bombardment and whose gruesome contents were lying about in all directions.

Needless to relate, the company beat a hasty retreat and promptly set out in search of 'a better hole.' The village now boasts of another sanctuary, and a beautiful edifice it is.

During the divisional occupation of this sector there occurred one of the most touching incidents with which I was ever associated.

The Field Ambulance was resting in Nurlu, and towards midnight a dozen men were detailed for the line the next day. When the name of 'WH' was called, he suddenly shuddered, and whispered, 'I'm not coming back this time.'

One sought to dispel such an unhappy and dangerous idea from his mind, but without success, and seeing that he had never been given to thinking gloomily, his utterance became very distressing.

Early the following morning the squads proceeded 'up the line,' and in the evening word reached us that he and another had been hit, and both were then lying at the casualty clearing station before being sent down to the base.

Two of us immediately set off for the clearing station and found our friends in the same ward. As we drew near to his bedside, 'WH' greeted us with, 'What did I tell you?' Once again, we did our utmost to cheer him, and besought him to think differently, but without effect.

Somehow, we were not surprised when news came through two days later that he had died of wounds in hospital at Abbeville. The day after his friend also succumbed to his injuries in the same hospital. These lads were two of the nicest in the unit, and their passing was a real sorrow to us all.

Passing through Beauchamp, we took the field track to Ribécourt. This was a village into which the enemy seemed fond of flinging his gas shells, and the air was often thick with their obnoxious and deadly fumes. It was not uncommon for 20 or 30 men to be marshalled together and by the aid of a long wire or rope conducted to the dressing station in Havrincourt.

Much was being said these days of the coming German offensive, and on the morning of March 21st, 1918 the storm broke. The first wave of attack on the Naval Division front on the Flesquières salient made little or no impression, but the line being broken to the north and south made withdrawal from this area imperative, and thus began that extensive and desperate retreat which at more than one period threatened the Allied cause with disaster.

Ypres and the immortal Salient! For a week or more the route had lain through old haunts and familiar places, and every inch of ground covered had awakened memories and stirred the emotions.

Yet Ypres had been present in our thoughts from the outset, and when at last it was entered an atmosphere peculiar to itself immediately became apparent. Notwithstanding the fact that the entire city and its environs are absolutely new there is an air of grimness about the locality which will cling to it for many years to come. In view of its War history this is not to be wondered at.

It came to acquire a reputation more sinister than any other sector along the whole British front, and when troops were ordered to proceed there, they were few who did not dread the harrowing experiences that awaited them.

There were periods when Armentières enjoyed intervals of comparative quiet, and when even the old Somme battlefields lay still and peaceful, but not so Ypres. From October, 1914, to October, 1918, it was a city of deadly peril by day and night, and it is said there was hardly an hour that shell or a bomb did not fall within its boundaries.

For four long weary years the district round about was the scene of hundreds of major and minor engagements fought under the vilest conditions imaginable, and each of them constituting a supreme test of physical endurance and moral stamina.

'The Ypres Salient,' wrote Sir Philip Gibbs, 'was the ground on which the quality of British manhood was put to the test, most often, in most frightful conditions, against heaviest odds, during the years of war. Every yard of it is sanctified for our race by the heroism of our men who defended it by their bodies and souls.'

The Menin Gate, Hooge, Hill 60, Pilckem, Passchendaele, Gheluvelt, and a dozen other equally ill-famed names will be associated with exploits that rank as second to none in the annals of British military history.

Battered by shells, deluged with bombs, smothered in poison gas, the city was tenaciously held against everything, and from the moment the advanced cavalry patrols of the enemy retired in October 1914, to the day when the last shell dropped into it on October 14th, 1918, not a single German soldier set foot in it unless a prisoner.

The Rue de Lille leads into the Grande Place with the Rue de Menin on the right and the Rue de Beurre on the left. As though by instinct we turned along 'Butter Street' and continuing for a few hundred yards noticed a Union Jack fluttering gaily in the breeze and beneath it the welcome sign, 'Manchester House; B. Davis, Proprietor.' and without hesitation decided to make this the temporary home.

So far attention had been restricted to different points within the city itself and if areas farther afield and the battlefields proper were to be visited the time remaining must be devoted elsewhere, and having a little over two hours on hand before morning worship, we set out for Duhallow Farm via Canal Bank and Essex Farm.

The day was ideal for the purpose, glorious sunshine, cloudless skies, the lilt of birds, and unspoilt beauty all around. The tall poplars lining both sides of the canal were clearly reflected in the waters below, and at intervals along the banks numerous fishermen were sitting or reclining lazily in the shade contentedly holding rod and line.

It seemed utterly incredible that such undisturbed tranquillity should prevail in a region where 20 years ago the waters were stinking and stagnant, the stunted trees gaunt and ghostly, and where the only peace was the peace of death.

Leaving the canal bank at a point opposite Murat Farm we joined the Ypres-Boesinghe Road at Essex Farm Cemetery close to which is the memorial to the 49th (West Riding) Division, and nearby is the spot where Colonel McRae composed his famous poem 'In Flanders Fields.'

About half a mile along the same road in the direction of Ypres stands Duhallow Farm Cemetery, deriving its name from a popular Irish hunt. Duhallow Farm marks the site of a main dressing station hence the large number of graves to be found in its vicinity, and from October 19th to December 6th, 1917, it was the headquarters of my particular unit.

Looking back across the years it is doubtful whether one good thing could be said in its favour. Long before the day of relief arrived every individual had come to loathe the place, and the Field Ambulance eventually departed from it without a single regret.

The worst feature of all was the incessant raids carried out by enemy bombing machines, and night after night and all night through squadrons of aeroplanes would hurl their death-dealing projectiles on every hand.

It has been stated there were more bombs dropped in and around Ypres in a single night than were dropped over England all through the War! When men came down from the line for a brief respite, if they were fortunate to survive the ordeals of St Julien and Passchendaele, the 'rest' proved to be an almost equally nerve-racking experience but minus the mud.

Perhaps the following story was inspired here. 'The trenches were so full of water,' grumbled the regimental growler, 'that if you got right down into them you'd have been drowned. Then the enemy opened fire, and if you put up your head you were in danger of being shot. At that moment I remembered what the padre had said about "When in danger look up to heaven." I did, and hang me if there wasn't a blessed aeroplane dropping bombs on us!'

During one of these air-raids the cry of 'Stretcher bearers' was heard above the noise of exploding bombs, and hurrying to the scene of disaster we sighted an artillery dug-out that registered a direct hit. The majority of its occupants had been killed instantly, and the three who remained were carried into the dressing station where a few minutes later they too passed away. It was afterwards discovered that a group had gathered to celebrate a comrade's birthday, and on the morning of that fatal day the one concerned had received 11 welcome parcels from home.

Duhallow is associated with another sad incident. It was here where we laid to rest the body of a fellow student and a general favourite of our college days. He and another had been hit in front of St Julien in the act of carrying a wounded German officer to the aid post.

The other young fellow, himself the son of a Methodist minister, was killed outright, our friend being wounded in the knee and elbow.

The fate of the officer was never known. It was presumed that the force of the explosion flung him into one of the huge shell holes that lay on either side of the duckboard track and he was there drowned.

CL was quickly conveyed to the dressing station, but succumbed to his injuries the same day. On a cold, damp morning in November, 1917, we bade farewell to one beloved by all.

We thought as we hollowed his narrow bed.
And smoothed down his lonely pillow;
That the foe and the stranger world tread o'er his head,
And we far away on the billow.

Neither the foe nor the stranger have trodden o'er his head, for the grave is exactly where we first made it, and shows not the slightest sign of having ever been disturbed. Like all the others in that cemetery, and indeed in all the cemeteries, it has been beautifully kept and carefully tended through the interval of years.

Gazing again upon that sacred spot we wondered what might have been if the one whose name is inscribed there had been spared to enter the ranks of the Methodist ministry.

But it was not to be and with something of a wrench we turned thoughtfully away and quietly tiptoed on to the road.

Of all the areas traversed and places visited this was the most touching, and after making such a journey it appeared strangely fitting to enter the little English Church in Ypres and remember Him who said: 'I am the resurrection and the life; he that believeth In Me, though he were dead, yet shall he live.'

—Revd S. Gibson, forces chaplain attached to 7th Bn, Durham Light Infantry, writing October–November 1935.

This article was edited from a five-part series recording Revd Gibson's return to the battlefields.

18

1936

I could fill a book with the drama of the Somme as, footslogging over it in my storming way, I rediscovered it.

For though the Somme is at peace with itself and the world, relics and echoes of the days that you and I both knew still abound. You can neither avoid them nor mistake them.

One moment the Somme will display its war wounds and fangs naked and unashamed; another, and it is at pains to hide them, and you need a keen and trained eye to detect the old ravages. It will be another 20 years before we can say goodbye of this blood-soaked Somme, that it is still so heavily scarred.

It was to see how the years have dealt with the Somme since that scarlet first of July in the third year of the Great War that I crossed over again on the old leave boat a week ago and went back 'up the line.'

Many an echo did I find of those 16 Fusilier battalions who were cast into the 'blood bath,' as the foe called that titanic offensive. And it was the same with the 13 battalions of the Durhams, and the eight of the Borders, who, again and again, went into action between July 1st and the last act in that mighty theatre in November. There's a grand participation for you—nigh on 40 battalions from the North East alone!

Now come back with me and see the way of things over there today. I have an absorbing notebook for you. You come across the paraphernalia of our fun and games of 20 years ago in the most unexpected places. By the Longueval-Hébuterne crossroads, you pause in mild surprise at a huge roadside shell hole containing another mixed stock.

Then, on the Le Boisselle-Contalmaison road, they have dumped yet more of the old wire that we put out in No Man's Land to keep the neighbours off, while so much of it is in permanent employment, looped to our own iron pickets as a fencing to the fields, as, long before my pilgrimage was ended, to have ceased altogether to be news.

At Auchonvillers, as I made my best way to a Fusilier's Thiepval, I all but tripped headlong over an unexploded 'five-nine.' Frankly, we don't like the look of it, and as we are not yet tired of life, we will leave it where it is.

Alike at Flers, and 'Monty-Bong,' some diehard has raised the shells we didn't have time to loose off to the 'dignity' of a seat on wayside milestones. One of these days someone will get hurt.

Every one of the woods, too, is still giving up its dead. They are taking them all home to a last abiding rest in London Cemetery that faces High Wood. There, hundreds of wooden crosses await replacement by the familiar grey-white headstones. Each week they are burying opposite the Bois Feureaux, as the French call it.

Only the few are identified. I tread softly down the rows and above the colourful flower beds is the boys' final home, I read 'An Unknown Soldier of the Northumberland Fusiliers.' Over there it is 'Durham Light Infantry.' Do you see, now, why the Somme still lives tragically on, why not for many a year yet can we bid it that final farewell?

High Wood, where I paused awhile with the newly recovered slain, is thick with undergrowth again, and wild roses grow on its fringes. Many of the trees have grown to a good height, and a barbed wire picket aslant in the ditch was the sole offering of Armageddon.

The old drives and paths are back again in 'Devil's,' where they've put up cairns to mark the crossing trench lines. And so once more do you tread your Campbell Street, your Regent Street, your Princes Street and your Rotten Row.

Just as I was about to try conclusions with a couple of shells in the new 'Devil's'—finest of all the recovered woodlands—'Danger,' I read 'it is forbidden to touch any war material.' And remembering my brute of Auchonvillars, I desisted in time.

Many a rent and blasted veteran reared its gaunt head in 'Devil's,' but whereas these are purposely retained, the same echoes in Trônes and Bernafay Woods live on because none has bothered to chop them down.

The fact, however, that you can see through Bernafay in this instance has no connection with the soldier's Somme, they have merely filched from it for pit props in the northern mines.

Talking of our woods, it was at 'Devil's' that I met Northumberland-on-the-Somme in the person of Mr William Winn, for 14 years a cemetery gardener in our Picardy Dormitories. His family now lives in Gateshead. Not a little of my Somme scrapbook was based on information he gave me.

Then we crossed the border and were introduced to Mr and Mrs Hanslip, both true Scots. But we were still in Longueval, where Mr Hanslip resides as 'Super' of all the Silent Cities in that burial area, and guardian there, with Mr Winn, Mr Bullen, Mr Thompson, and other fine types of ex-servicemen, of Northumberlands, Durhams and the Border boys slain. I hope it will be a consolation to their relatives to learn that these warriors are cared for with a solicitude whose match it would be hard to find.

That torrid Sunday noon-day, in the Café Tabac at Longueval, where I suddenly remembered I had taken no 'rations' for many hours, and where your humble scribe forsook his duties to visit the 'cookhouse,' we Britons outnumbered even the natives. It was a real English reunion.

Even Albert has not entirely covered up the old sores and fissures. You come upon them in this street and that, but no estate agent publicises them as 'commanding sites.'

The largest of them is on a big corner near the station; another is the pre-war grotto, ghost of the days when Albert was a second Lourdes, from which they found the money to build the Cathedral which the guns of both sides were so soon to raze. Each is unsightly in its neglect and decrepitude.

In another respect Albert has changed for the worse since I was last in these parts, in 1930, when the Lord Mayor of Birmingham bade farewell to his city's battlefield godchild. The English colony has broken up and gone. Except for the cemetery gardeners only one remains, finding a living among the natives and the tourists with a taxi.

One who once ran cars over the Somme from Albert now owns a baker's shop somewhere in the Midlands; another has turned his back on the town and runs a French filling station; Capt. Almack, who went back as an exile to eke a livelihood from a florist's shop, is back again in Blighty.

But what's this legend calling to me outside my hotel?—'Tea as Mother Makes It?' Is it merely an enterprising effort by the owners to draw the itinerant Briton?

Normally the French simply can't brew tea, so I was dubious as I put the sign to the test of truth in advertising. Surprisingly enough, the tea won, for the pot they gave me in those small hours as I set out to gather my raw material for this narrative was certainly up to 'mother's' best standards.

But 'Tea Better Than Mother Makes it!' is how ex-Chief Despatch Rider C. Smith, mine host of the Prince of Wales Café in the shade of the vast Thiepval Memorial, improves on the old saw. And then, as a timely afterthought to catch the eye of the thirsty pilgrim, 'Beer, Cool and Fresh, Like Father Takes It.'

'Father,' however, in the person of your humble and perspiring scribe, was in no physical trim for aught but lemonade.

For dozens of those rehabilitated Somme villages, and at practically every compass point, the massive Thiepval pile is etched out as a great beacon on your skyline. You do not ask your direction on the Somme; you take it by Thiepval.

I'll say it is so high from base to platformed summit as the Queen Mary from keel to masthead, and I won't even bother to check up on my figures. Workmen regilding the flagstaff on that lofty eminence were as dwarfs in the sky.

In its shade ex-Chief Dispatch Rider C. Smith keeps the Prince of Wales Café aforementioned and he will proudly show you the dais which King Edward (as Prince of Wales) and President Lebrun used when his majesty unveiled the memorial in 1932.

As I tried to get you an unusual picture of this immense creation of Luytens I thought of those 5th and 6th Warwicks fighting it out on the Leipzig Redoubt, one of the keys to stubborn Thiepval.

There's so much in my scrapbook, I've told you nothing yet of La Boisselle, highlight of the Tyne and ranking side-by-side with Thiepval. After the beautiful little memorial to the Tyneside Irish and Tyneside Scottish brigades at the junction of the Albert-Bapaume and Contalmaison by-roads, of which I am giving you a picture, only the vast crater lends La Boisselle any note of distinction.

Containing 60,000lbs of guncotton, and fired beneath the German frontline on July 1st, 1916 it blew a cavity 100 yards across by 90 feet deep. A shabby village, this La Boisselle, with a church spire like one of those Welsh women's national hats—all 'high hat,' in fact, stuck unceremoniously on the squat body of the church.

Because of the nation's disregard of summertime, Contalmaison would have you believe you have an extra hour in hand in your search of the Somme, that you should not take any notice of the church clock. With neither railway nor post office, they stick to the old time, a state of affairs which is repeated in villages similarly situated as to communications.

So in two hamlets, no more than a mile apart, you may find two entirely different times.

All that my itinerant notebook tells me of Contalmaison that was familiar to most Tynesiders who arrived on the Somme is of the village geese that, unchecked, peck and strut over the church steps of the ruins that remain in parts and the house that looks suspiciously like a converted orderly room.

You recall the scores of old army Nissen huts in which the peasants of many of these villages live, and say that in a land of economy there is nothing bizarre in living in an orderly room.

Our North Eastern pilgrimage draws to its curtain. But we must go to Fricourt, where, at the onset of the Somme 'push' the 9th Fusiliers used the bayonet to good purpose....

I find there a field ablaze with the blood red of the Flanders poppy—hundreds and hundreds of them—and industrious French land women milking the cows in a cowshed perched at an alarming angle in a steep bank over a line of our old dug-outs.

Across the way at the big aircraft works at Méaulte they are building an airplane 'for the next war,' as a cynic told me in Longueval.

Hullo, what's this? Just another of those immense yellow, blue and white French signboards that give you your direction and shout the village you are entering. Nothing niggardly about these. This is the very place we have been looking for. We are in Gueudecourt which the Durhams have good cause to remember.

In one quarter of the hamlet they have made half-hearted attempts at rebuilding, but having dumped the new bricks, have washed their hands of the whole thing, and will have none of it. By the refuse heap is an orange, green and blue marquee put up for local whoopee.

Time enough to look in on the mayor—for he and I are old friends—and toast each other in his excellent white wine and eat his homemade cake. Finally, my friends, walk quietly with me into the AIF Burial Ground between Flers and Gueudecourt, and mark the many unknown Durham lads in this peaceful dormitory.

I look at another stone, and it commemorates 2nd Lt F. Barrie George, of the Durham Light Infantry. He was only 19 ... Albert Communal Cemetery extension too. In the first grave I see lies Pte W. Wyatt, of the 'Fifths.' Near him is almost a whole row of Fusiliers, together in death as in the fight from which they found no return.

It is one of the most colourful cemeteries in the Somme. Here, too, rests Brigadier General Barnett-Barker DSO and bar, son of Major John Barnett-Barker, late Northumberland Fusiliers. Turn around, and the great gilded figure of the Virgin and Child atop Albert Cathedral beckons to you. With such a symbol I will leave you.

—Pte Victor Hyde MC, writing in June 1936.

Hyde was a member of the Ypres League, author of war stories, and freelance journalist who made a number of journeys to the Western Front in the 1930s, revisiting the battle scenes and reporting back on his findings for regional newspapers across England.

*

The scene is a shell hole at Passchendaele. A private of the King's, who has just helped carry a casualty to the advance dressing station, has set to reminiscing, and, as he is by way of being a bit of a poet, has produced on a tattered scrap of paper this illuminating verse:

Search the ground round 'Lousy' Wood,
Search the place where Combles stood,
And many a Crimson trail will tell the tale,
Of a 'Saturday night brigade.'

My unknown Liverpolitan, with a leaning to literature, was writing of his Somme of a year earlier, which he had quitted for the even greater quagmire of 'Passion Dale.' ('Saturday night brigade' was the pre-war label applied to the Territorials).

And now, as we mark the 20th anniversary of that first and greatest battle of the Somme, in which no fewer than 13 battalions of the King's—a greater representation than any other county regiment—took their share, that vivid verse runs once more through my memory.

If you care to join me, we will 'Search the ground round "Lousy" (Leuze) Wood.' There's still some good shooting to be had there, but it is of rabbits and partridges now, and except for that wide shooting drive, 'Lousy' is thick and dense again.

Only Bernafay and Delville ('Devils') of the Somme woodlands live in the past. Five big trees that were in the throes of their rigor mortis those 20 Julys ago, still rear up out of the new Bernafay like grotesque aerial masts, and you know that a war once passed that way.

Bernafay has the appearance of many matchsticks stuck in the ground, with green heads sprouting on them. You can see, slatwise, right through the wood. In 'Devil's' now a permanent bit of Empire red on the Picardy map, those same torn and gaunt stumps, dead, and shot away long before the last act of that 1916 shambles, make a grim and ghostly contrast betwixt and between the brave new foliage.

A warning against touching any war material reminds you that those trees are not the only relics remaining in 'Devil's' today, for a spate of souvenirs awaits the curious. On other parts of the Somme where it is not purposely retained, as in 'Devil's,' they have a forthright way of dealing with these 'overs.'

An enterprising French firm has acquired the sole 'explosive rights' in the ammo still found, and as soon as they have collected a nice fat dump—no hard task even now—they put a match to it and rend the air with another miniature Somme cannonade.

In the semi-sunken road between Contalmaison and Pozieres, at minute intervals I heard the unmistakable sound of explosives popping off. When the last reverberations had died away, 'That's the dump merchants up to their games,' I said. And so it was. They'll take it and fire it all in time, except the 'Devil's' arsenal.

On the same 'front' as that memorial park, on the very ground where the 55th (West Lancs) Division fought, the King's graves have a distinguishing mark all their own. 'They win or die who wear the Rose of Lancashire,' runs the inscription, encircling the red rose on a metal disc, placed in the floral beds. This unusual emblem is below all the headstones of the King's and the Royal Lancasters.

In Guillemont Road cemetery it is prominent also on the graves of the many unknown soldiers of the King's scattered over this silent city. Of the identified dead, two of the first names I read recorded Rifleman R. H. Price and Private A. Boulton, both King's lads. In Albert communal cemetery extension, in the front of those parade ground lines, Private S. Holland, of the East Lancashires, rests close to two famous brigadiers, for in the placing of the graves there is no distinction in rank.

This is one of the most colourful of all the scores of Somme cemeteries; each line of graves, dressed by the right as on earth the warriors beneath them dressed by the right, is treated with a different floral scheme. At Thiepval over 2,000 of the slain of those 13 battalions of the King's who trod their Somme have their last resting place; they are part of the vast army of the missing.

In the shadow of that monument Thiepval itself is still largely as I left it. Of the *château* there is no more sign than existed at the end of the battle. And that was precisely nothing.

They could not rebuild Thiepval, so razed was it. Just three or four houses, a shanty, and the church. That's all. And a lot of shell holes and the 'Café of the Heroine of the Ruins.'

You scent romance, and meet the lined and hardy Mme Doutart Marie Louise, first of all of the Thiepvalites to venture back to the stricken hamlet. Without a doubt she's the stuff of which heroines are made. What a story, too, she could tell of it, for in all Picardy, Thiepval was Devastated Village No. 1.

Half a mile away, across the Hamel–Pozieres road, Mouquet Farm has recovered far more than Thiepval has. The new Mouquet, running to a vivid, red-tiled farmer's home and an equally massive piggery and cowshed, is trim and peaceful again astride that ridge of death.

But of signs of life at Mouquet there were none; it was as stilted as before its defenders manned their hidden guns. In front of it, the French grid system spans the countryside in an unending chain of steel stanchions and wire.

Time, now, we searched the place where Combles stood. The new Combles, where the King's and the Loyals and the East Lancashires fought it out, is more a town than a village, spreading itself out in all manner of abrupt and unexpected directions, with an ugly filling station beplastered with petrol advertisements, the only blot on its escutcheon.

Many of our army Nissen huts, a trifle woebegone and seedy now, still serve as 'desirable residences' in Combles. And if you buy a 'blonde' there, it is merely their way of selling you light beer.

My final verdict after pilgrimaging into every corner of this Somme in its 1936 dress is that it will be another 20 years before, of that once blood soaked wilderness, we can write a final goodbye. For the 'crimson trails' of my shell hole Liverpolitan are still far too stark; for 'many a take' can they yet recall.

—KING'S REGIMENT SOLDIER, WRITING IN JUNE 1936.

*

It was a strange experience, and more disturbing than I expected, to revisit the western battlefields nearly 18 years afterwards.

Vimy did not mean very much to me as a soldier. In the attack on the Ridge I was 'loaned' to the Canadians for a few days to carry ammunition to the guns; and the blizzard cost me 12 valuable horses. That was my sole experience of Vimy.

But scores of Canadians who saw the Memorial unveiled on Sunday brought their tattered old trench maps and some of them enthusiastically reconstructed the battle for my benefit.

The French veterans who had fought in this sector before the Canadians took over from them were less articulate. They spoke of the past with dull resentment.

Several young civilians in Arras who were infants or children when the war ended would not speak of it at all.

'We are weary of the oft repeated tale,' said one.

'But I suppose you would defend your homes again if you were attacked?' I asked him.

'Yes, certainly,' he said after a pause; then shrugged his shoulders.

No sign of an aggressive military spirit among these young Arras workers! From Arras I motored through the old front areas up to the Ypres Salient, many parts of which I knew more intimately than the streets of my home town.

Though I had read about it a dozen times, the transformation seemed to me not less miraculous. When I looked my last on the Salient in April 1918, it was a vast, evil looking, evil smelling, featureless swamp.

Now it is a land of smiling villages and ripening cornfields. The trees have grown again, and the willows droop tenderly over the streams as if the willows and the streams had never been blotted out of existence.

Old women sit outside their homes in the sunshine knitting as if they had been knitting there all their lives. The peasants in the fields look serene and happy. No longer do their ploughs turn up the lurking menace of unexploded five-nines.

As I wandered rather at a loss about sleepy Zonnebeke and looked down into 'The Wood'—a wood once more made real by 'Nature's own sweet and cunning hand'—I felt almost too embarrassed to speak of the phantasmagoria of war to the lounging villagers.

I wanted to ask the old ones if they noticed how beautifully the birds sang. The singing of the birds—that is the subtlest and most touching change of all. At Passchendaele no birds sang. If it were not for the grass covered relics of the pill-box forts, which only a soldier could identify for what they were, and the regimented dead in the silent cemeteries, one could discover no trace or hint of those years of hideous destruction.

How lovingly those graves are tended: the German graveyards no less than the British. Their unspoken eloquence is greater than the eloquence of all the pacifist propaganda ever printed. Up in Tyne Cot Cemetery, on the ridge of Passchendaele, lie 12,000 young soldiers. 'Nineteen years of age' appears like a ceremonial refrain.

Seven thousand stones bear only the inscription: 'A soldier of the Great War.' Not a button, not a badge, to identify them when they were found. We used to collect the remains of men blown to pieces by high explosive and bury them in sacking: it was often difficult, I remember, to shape the sack to the semblance of a human form. Here they are at rest.

From the great stone facade of the Memorial one may look back over the softly undulating landscape to the houses of the new Ypres on the distant skyline. It is a spot of heavenly quiet. The lawns and green paths are made of English grass seed. There are masses of roses and peonies and hydrangeas and gay flowering shrubs.

'I like looking after them,' said a sturdy English gardener who has lived in the Salient since 1918. 'I should miss these lads if I went away.' He told me that the pilgrimage to Tyne Cot continues unabated. In the summer 1,500 people visit the cemetery every week. Many of them are young men and women and English schoolboys.

'These youngsters,' he said, 'forget all about sightseeing when they come inside this place. They look at the graves, they see the thousands of names on the memorial, and they go away very quietly.'

I, too, went away very quietly. Before I went, I signed my name in the visitors' book at the entrance gate. It was just a greeting to comrades, some of whom lying there were the friends of my youth.

From Tyne Cot on to Passchendaele village, where it appeared obvious, as one turned first towards Ypres and then towards the 'enemy' lines, that unless the Ridge (the real one, not the false one) had been gained in 48 hours its conquest could have only the barest tactical significance. Did Haig (after the war) ever have a look at the ground?

Back to Ypres by way of St Jean, along the road up which we dragged the guns yard-by-yard into the stinking mire. I recognised the St Julien crossroads. There, one chill autumn day in 1917, I witnessed the bloodiest shambles of men and horses in my war experience. Now the spot is occupied by an *estaminet*.

A few kilometres further on, the deep, damp, damnable dug-out at St Jean, down which I once dived urgently with a leave pass in my pocket. An *estaminet* occupies this spot also.

In the Grande Place, at Ypres, where the half-completed Cloth Hall is slow raising its delicate facade, hundreds of Canadian pilgrims had just arrived.

With them I walked out to the Menin Gate. A grand memorial. It impressed me more, I confess, than the more pretentious memorial at Vimy Ridge. It has solid character. The sweep of the arch is magnificent. And that noble lion of unforgettable dignity and strength, gazing calmly out over the Salient; he is truly on guard.

There were many beautiful wreaths, and many simple bunches of flowers, bearing little personal messages of warm remembrance; messages that transformed the masses named on the walls into living personalities.

A talk with *Madame* at Skindles—the Skindles that carried on spasmodically with food and drink under bombardment—ended my own brief pilgrimage. Yes, the rusty howitzer and the dilapidated tank in front of Skindles were a shocking eyesore. Yes, Ypres was a handsome town again, and fairly prosperous now, though rich Belgians no longer lived there, and the old trade had gone.

Yes, the Belgians had rebuilt well—more rapidly and more thoroughly than the French. No, the English did not forget Ypres, or the war; nor did the steadfast Belgians. Ah, the war was indeed terrible, but what friendships sprang through it and the good God knew what brave men lived and died here.

Thus *Madame*, *très gentle* and inclined to be mystical over Belgium's inferno. I understood *Madame* and I began to feel mystical myself. Mysticism is still war's deadliest attraction. Even perhaps in this great new civilised era of poison gas.

—SOLDIER A. J. CUMMINGS, WRITING IN JULY 1936.

Cummings served as a front-line artillery officer during the war before taking up a career in journalism as a political commentator. He was a fierce critic of those war correspondents he felt acted as morale-boosting cheerleaders rather than reporting the reality of life on the frontline.

19

1937

There is no sentiment left in the Belgian landowner for the battlefields today. Even Hooge crater, scene of the great German liquid fire attack, has been turned into an ornamental lake and swimming pool.

Yet some at least remember. The day I signed the visitors' book at the Menin Gate there were over 50 signatories before mine, and every one was a Belgian's. Most Sundays, too, they visit our cemeteries.

The more indigent of the natives are glad enough to turn an honest franc or two over the 'souvenirs' we left behind, and which can still be found aplenty if you know where to look; the fact that 50 civilians have been killed in this way at Zillebeeke alone does not deter them.

Their 'markets' are the war museums at Hills 60 and 62, and their reward according to the desire of the owners for the particular souvenirs they have to offer. The builders, many of whom are out of work, trade in other ways, and sell the derelict war material for scrap. It's an ill war that blows nobody any good.

At Hill 60 last month a machine gun was dug up and added to an already imposing array of trophies, the same day a sniperscope followed it.

In Flanders at Hill 60 and Hill 62, and in Ypres itself, are war museums each large enough to start another war and, according to the way you look at things, each the most potent argument against the repetition of such a catastrophe as you and I are recalling today.

Ted Moon is a veteran of the Royal Warwicks and is now a cemetery gardener under the Imperial War Graves Commission. His wife, late of the Old Kent Road, London, runs the café.

Ted can afford to smile now at the record he holds for an unbroken stay in the trenches. In 1915 he spent 92 consecutive days in the line at Hill 60 and The Bluff, at a time when neither was a health resort. He loved the place so much that he came back to settle there!

It's an altogether remarkable museum that he has assembled at Hill 60. If you want to buy it, it will cost you £1,500. Every exhibit has been 'scrounged' from the battlefields. They range from a gas alarm bell and a caseful of the earliest German helmets to Indian kukris, and the message carriers put into the collars of the German dog teams.

There's a soldier's 'housewife,' the razor long since beyond all shaving ability, old rum jars—remember the SRD—wicked saw-edged bayonets that ripped your vitals, miners' lamps employed in tunnelling under the hill, and enough pistols and swords to fit out a battle.

Even the telephones we used under Jerry's lines are still there. 'This telephone,' reads the inscription on one, 'was used to speak to the men working at the face of the British line.'

Another is preserved on the spot where it was last used—in the tunnels that are still open beneath Hill 60.

I saw again the improvised kitchens, wire beds, stretchers—yes, and even abandoned meals—and the rest that made up an underground frontline war. You can descend these tunnels sweltering in the noonday heat, and emerge with your teeth chattering with intense cold. In parts they are flooded, too.

Part of the German tunnels on the hill fell in recently, and by the railway cutting where the Brussels express now tears by again resembles an immense cliff fall.

At Hill 62, an hour's easy walk, but seemingly leagues removed when the Ypres Salient was an impassable quagmire, is another frightening arsenal, equipped with every weapon that was ever invented to kill. Here the owner is a Belgian, who does pretty well, thank you.

The old trench signs plunge you right back into the past. 'Vince Street,' I read, and 'Front Line' and 'Canada Trench.' 'Wind Dangerous,' warns another, and as if that wasn't enough, someone, for the benefit of a tourist, must needs go and sound the gas alarm and send me scurrying to the array of masks behind the museum's glass.

Over here are more of those *verboten* saw-edged brutes, dixies and trench cookers that served the *table d'hôte* of the PBI, and an aeroplane propeller. In another case are some choice lines in German stick bombs. A catholic armoury, rounded off with shells of every conceivable calibre. I'd just hate to lose my temper with the owner...

Hullo, what's this, 'Mr Asquith stated that the Government were introducing forced labour or conscription.' The same wartime newspaper, tattered but historic, goes on to cite Sir Ian Hamilton's Dardanelles despatches.

Among the many thousands of exhibits in the Ypres Salient War Museum—founded and owned by Mr L. N. Murphy, of 18, Lime Grove, Manchester—are the special badges given to the Liverpool Pals' Battalion, including one in solid silver given by Lord Derby to the first 100 who enlisted in the battalion. '*Sans Changer*,' runs the motto.

Murphy points it out to all the parties he conducts round this fearsome arsenal. He values the whole collection at two million francs (£14,000). If you care to buy it at this figure, you will be the owner of the most remarkable war museum outside Great Britain.

In another case are the badges of every regiment which ever served on 'Westfront'. Part of the curator's 'stuff' is to ask if you can spot the badge of, 'the finest regiment In British Isles.' You were King's or Pals or Liverpool Scottish, and say, 'yes.' You were South Lancashires and say, 'yes.' You were Lancashire Fusiliers, and the answer's just the same. So everyone's satisfied!

After a tour of the thousands of exhibits there displayed and upon Bairnsfather's famous 'Well if you know of a better 'ole go to it' while you are debating this, someone only needs go and sound the gas alarm, and you tarry no longer on the order of your going. They served the same trick on me on Hill 62!

In the trenches outside—still just as we left them—where that newspaper and, as recently as last year, Australian and East Kent caps were dug up, is another fearsome arsenal for you—a half-buried aeroplane, plane engine, coils of barbed wire, tin hats, water bottles, shells, rifles, boots, duckboards.

It's all grimly stark at Hill 62. The old trench scaling ladders up which we swarmed to go over the top; the wire we put in No Man's Land to keep the neighbours off; trench mortars and 'flying pigs'—they are there for all to see where the end of things left them.

So is the tunnel, except that it's impassable now, and dark as the grave. Remember how it ran from the British frontline, under No Man's Line to the German trenches in Sanctuary Wood?

Round the corner from Murphy's grim dump, an old tunnel and dressing station were opened a month ago at the Lille Gate and advertised far and wide as 'Lord Plumer's headquarters.'

As soon as I explained that the 2nd Army headquarters had never been within miles of Ypres they changed the description of the site to the one I gave them—for which, indeed, they thanked me—and an innocent mistake ended happily enough.

Now, in this place where our wounds were staunched and dressed yet another museum has sprung up. Gas alarms, rum jars (containing the 'SRD' which, according to Murphy, 'seldom reached destination,' or else 'soon ran dry'). Verey lights, pistols, wire cutters, machine guns, snipers' breast plates—they are all there.

The Belgian tenant whom I corrected paid 10,000 francs option on the site for the next 10 years, and charges you two and a half francs entrance money. At Hill 62, by Zillebeeke, where he 'rents' the tunnels beneath the hill, out of every 100 francs taken at the same flat rate of admission, 18 go back to the Ypres city fathers as a landlord's rake-off.

A third native, to attract the tourist who throngs Ypres from June to September, has opened a museum in the town of the Cloth Hall in the Grande Place, and undercuts at two francs. Here I found a German machine gun which fired as many as 1,500 rounds a minute!

Even at the Menin Gate there is a postcard and souvenir stand—for the benefit of the poor invalids of Ypres—but the greatest concentration of all is at Hill 60, where, in addition to the café and war museum—both in English ownership—and the native-run tunnels, a blind Belgian keeps a souvenir stall.

For a trifle he will sell you a Pals' badge or that of almost any Lancashire regiment you care to name. Yes, he has them all—the badges you and I left behind.

The most intense jealousy exists between the parties responsible for the various enterprises, and none has a good word to say for the others. But so long as they don't cheat the pilgrim—and despite the closest watch, I failed to detect any sharp practices—the Ypres council allows them to carry on.

The real—and only—culprits are the children. At Hill 60 and other places they importune the tourist with flowers they picked when they see you coming—in one case it was a miserable little buttercup—and then seeking your alms!

No, I'm not joking. Each time I went to Hill 60 there were two policemen with a sharp eye for this practice. Outside Tyne Cot Cemetery, and the Plugstreet Wood memorial, cafés have been opened, and when I tell you that 50,000 a year regularly visit these and the other places I have mentioned, you can judge the trade that is done.

Many of the coaches, which take as much of the money as any, won't even stop to let the passengers wash. I even heard one guide announce, 'We are now passing the Menin Gate.' Yes, passing it....

Such is one side to your canvas these two decades after. Yet there's such a lot more. Over 2,000 have been killed in and around Ypres alone since 1919, trying conclusions with 'souvenirs' best left alone. I told you it was still a sticky war in Flanders.

Our own dead, too, are still being found. In the case of such recoveries in Ypres identification is as high as 25 per cent: far higher than on the actual battlefields, where the bodies are less well preserved.

You find the inevitable echo of these tragic discoveries in Bedford House cemetery beyond Shrapnel Corner, where hundreds of wooden crosses await replacement with the permanent headstones. This is one of three cemeteries kept open for reburials.

Swing left to Zillebeeke and a huge roadside legend greets you 'Zillebeeke Lake—ask for a Rum!' Though you needed one there in 1917, you are not in the mood for one today. In the village itself, *Herberg* (*estaminet*) *du Slaughter* strikes you as grimly appropriate name in these parts. Again, however, you don't feel like drinking.

Come to Wytschaete with me and I'll show you the new church built over a former dug-out, and the modern band stand that plays to the 'White Sheet' peasants on Sundays. 'Stout and Scotch' announces the *estaminet* opposite, but they don't say whether you have to take them mixed or not!

Fifty thousand people make the pilgrimage every year to Hill 62 and Sanctuary Wood—about the same number who visit Mr Moon and his hospitable family—compared with the 8,000 who trek to Tyne Cot in the 'season' between June and September.

At St Julien I encountered a sergeant on the same errand as myself. He was up from Ostend for the day. We set to reminiscing and discovered many of the old pill-boxes where we of the Cockneys and the Worcester boys and other battalions were fighting in the mud two decades ago this year.

I showed him the cavernous Cheddar Villa by the roadside as you enter that hamlet, with 10 more in a cluster a few yards away, and the notorious Schuler Galleries, which was six pill-boxes in one. Many will vividly remember these brutes.

It is hard to say which is worse, the questions some of the tourists ask or the ramp of the 'Grand Battlefields Tour' from the coast resorts. With few exceptions—generally your old soldier—the people who see the battlefields that way have no real interest. Every day in the summer they come.

'Is there anything interesting here?' I heard one ask in Sanctuary Wood Cemetery. 'Only 2,000 dead!' answered the weary head gardener. It's questions like that that make our wonderful ex-servicemen exiles see red. You wouldn't believe the stupid things they say.

'How green the grass is!' commented another. 'What colour do you expect it to be?' was the reply she got. Well, what would you have said?

The trippers who 'do' the battlefields that way and find it all a great lark are swindled right and left. Nor are the coach owners the only ones to regard France and Flanders as get-rich-quick playgrounds.

Why, in Ypres they are actually charging two francs to see 'Lord Plumer's headquarters,' when they are no more than the miserable advance dug-out of a gunner major! Cassel, where Plumer so successfully directed the defence of the Ypres Salient, is miles away.

That's the kind of thing that's going on if they get half a chance. What would an Empire's million dead say if they knew? Yes, we both know the answer, don't we?

In Ypres, where your true Yprian—the type who sign the book at the Menin Gate—are above that sort of thing; little boys play hide and seek in the tank in the station square, while the more agile use it as a ready made grandstand when there's a gymkhana or other whoopee in progress. The German gun, too, comes in mighty handy for the same purpose.

Between the Cloth Hall and Menin Gate, Ypres still bears some of the old scars. The former, only partially rebuilt, with props and rubble behind and a brave new face in front, is like a make-believe film set.

In St George's Church, in the British colony, I counted as many as 88 separate regimental plaques. Even the choir stalls, lectern and pulpit are dedicated in this strangest and most historic of English churches that isn't even in England.

As you radiate from Ypres by any one of the many bus routes that girdle the battlefields, the babel of the women passengers' voices drowns even the roar of the bus as it speeds and crashes over the cobbles.

At Passchendaele, where the Roulers bus deposits you, except for the beautiful stained glass window in the church erected in memory of British arms, there is little to see. Yet astride the ridges tens of thousands fought and died.

A chicory factory has displaced the acrid fumes of cordite; Paradise and Hooge cafés angle for the trade of the itinerant tourist, and ice cream tricycles clang their noisome way over the pavé, hoping you will 'stop them and buy one.' In the local furniture shop, an economical mademoiselle takes her Sunday ease in the best easy terms chair in the window.

Yes, the passions have gone, and only the echoes of Passion Dale remain. But what echoes! It takes Mr Parminter and 10 other gardeners to maintain Tyne Cot. Above those sloping lawns and 12,000 graves, 34,000 more are named because they are not named on any grave.

The first person I spoke to in Ypres was a Bedford man, and one of the first of the many British men to return to the country where they fought. Mr L. R. Potter has been a waiter at the largest hotel in Ypres since 1921. He knows everyone in Wipers, and is a mine of information.

Mr Potter joined the St John Ambulance at Rushden in 1914 and served in the Ypres Salient at Wieltje and St Jean, where he experienced the first German gas attack of April 1915. In 1917 he went to Italy as a sergeant in the RAMC and returned to serve on hospital ships, including the Asturian before it was torpedoed.

After further service in Calais, he joined the Ministry of Munitions after the war as a gas expert engaged on the battlefields. He told me many things of interest.

It was Potter who gave me news of the new British memorial to be erected in St Martin's Cathedral, and to take the form of a stained glass window over the south porch. It will commemorate the 250,000 who perished in the trail to Passion Dale.

The cost, £2,000, has been subscribed by the British Services, and the window will be unveiled in 1938. The cathedral itself was rebuilt by 30 men in eight years, and a remarkably good job they've made of it.

The cemetery gardeners include several from the East Midlands. Working in the Kemmel and Messines group I found Mr L. A. Golder, whose English home is Eydon Hall, near Byfield, Northamptonshire, and who served with the machine gun corps in the war. In the same group of 'silent cities' is Mr G. R. Hoyles, who served as a private in the Northamptonshire Regiment.

If you are going back for the first time, your strongest impression will be the new mobility, and the speed with which you are transported where last you crawled. For four francs, and in less than 20 minutes, the women-conducted buses will race you back from Passchendaele to Ypres where, these 20 Julys ago, it took you and me and the rest who were embroiled in the Passion Dale picnic all of six months in the other direction.

Despite all the museums and trenches and tunnels and dug-outs and dressing stations and pill-boxes, it's difficult, terribly difficult, to realise that almost every inch of this ground was fought over, backwards and forwards, score upon score of times.

Many of the new trees have grown to a surprising height—the tallest in Zouave Wood are 30ft high now—and everywhere are signs of agricultural activity. A new canvas, in fact, has been daubed over the old. Yet every foot is embedded deep in English history.

The noise of the machines cutting the crops reminds you of a cluster of machine guns with silencers, and a car raising the dust of the adolescent Flanders, of a shell burst or gas cloud. Then you remember....

You look upon this grim pill-box, and upon that, menacing and cavernous even in their decay, and fight again your fight to capture them. One hundred and eighty of these concrete monsters are ours now by right of acquisition, and only another war will shift them.

Yes, it's still a sticky war in Flanders, even when they don't sound that cursed gas alarm...

—PTE VICTOR HYDE MC, WRITING IN JULY 1937.

20

1938

The notice board at Victoria Station states that, for the Channel crossing the sky is cloudy but the sea is calm. On reaching the pier at Dover, the sea is anything but smooth, while the former part of the weather report is problematical as a thick haze hangs over the water.

With a choppy sea, quite a number of the passengers seem engaged looking for submarines, judging by the way they are hanging over the side of the boat. Others are content to sit on deck with handkerchief held tightly over their mouths. It reminds one of a Town Council heckling meeting, where a variety of things are liable to be brought up.

There are quite a number of men passengers on the same quest as I am, namely, to revisit the 'playing fields' of our youth, on this occasion we enjoy more freedom on board than we did in days of yore, and no destroyers are present to escort us across the Channel.

Twenty years or so ago, the Customs Office at Calais was not in the slightest interested in what we carried, and, strangely enough, it showed as little interest in my pack on this occasion. The Customs officer told me not to take it off my back, put his mark on it, and showed me where to get the Hazebrouck train.

The only ex-serviceman who entrains with me is an ex-Captain of the General Staff, and he is going to St Omer. I don't remember much of St Omer—Highland Light Infantry privates weren't on GHQ!—but I have one indelible memory of Hazebrouck.

On leaving Calais to go up to the line for the first time, we got issued with rations, including our water bottle full of tea, at that time it took days to travel what takes hours now. Feeling thirsty on the journey, I drank my tea. Now, cold tea with milk is bad enough but cold tea with both milk and sugar in it is about the most thirst inducing drink one can think of.

Crawling along, we eventually reached Hazebrouck, and my 'first' class coach (8 *chevaux*—40 *hommes*) stopped opposite the trunk of the engine water trough. The HLI didn't usually drink water, but I created a precedent! The water trough is still there, but whether on the same spot I know not.

I have to detrain at Hazebrouck for Ypres, and wishing to get some French money, I go into the town. The banks are closed, and I ask a Frenchman where I can get a pound note changed.

He either doesn't know, or more probably doesn't understand my French! However, a voice from a café across the street cries, 'Jock, what you want?' and I go into the café to find it full of young French soldiers down on weekend leave from the Belgian frontier.

The *Madame*, who hailed me, had been there in 1914–18, and is keen to show, even at this late day, her appreciation (?) of what we did for France during the War. Her appreciation takes the form of offering me 150 francs for £1, leaving her only a paltry 26 francs to go and come on should the £1 drop during the night.

I bid her '*bon jour*' four times before I eventually get her up to 165. On the spur of the moment, without considering how much loss of sleep it will entail, I stand drinks to the 15 soldiers in order to cement the Franco-Scottish alliance! The soldiers are all infantrymen, some being in khaki, while others are in the blue grey uniform we knew so well in the old days.

The train to Ypres is composed of coaches of about 1890 vintage, and the speed of the train is in keeping. At Abeele, the Belgian Customs station, we detrain to pass through the Customs. Apparently, I am the only 'foreigner,' and that being so, I get the full blast of the inspection. Unfortunately, I have a small bottle of Scottish sal volatile, which an officer holds up like a fisher showing off a 3lb trout he catches in Cameron.

After some discussion, I am told I have to pay, but as I intend returning next day, I tell them to keep it for me. Unfortunately, I did not go back, and so the Belgiques will have something to pour over their Christmas pudding!

Leaving Abeele, the line runs on towards Poperinghe. Gone are the elephant huts of 'Siege Camp' and others the names of which I forget. The town itself is unrecognisable. It is built up, but, like all Flemish towns, it is dead quiet. What a contrast to 1914–18, when there was the continual rattle of limbers, guns, ammunition waggons, the tramp of men, the whine of a shell, the crash denoting its safe arrival to earth, or bricks, or men.

The long, straight road to Ypres is silent, too. The only traffic I see is a tandem, with a couple pedalling along gaily. The potholes are no more. There is no camouflage in the way of screens linking the trees to hide movements of troops. It is unnecessary, too, because there are no prying Jerry observation balloons watching for a target.

The trees are thriving. The old War veterans, towering above the post-War ones planted to replace the big casualty list, seem to stick out chests, as much as to say to the saplings, 'Before you came up, chum.'

Ypres at last, and what a transfiguration! For nearly five years the rumble of gunfire was synonymous with Ypres. Today there are taxis standing in the Station Square, but one never took a taxi in Ypres. Firstly, because it wasn't done, and, secondly, because there was none to take. The only reminder of war is a disabled tank and a field gun.

A short walk takes me to the centre of the town. There stands the majestic Cloth Hall while the Cathedral is again a Cathedral and not a heap of smashed masonry. The eastern end of the Cloth Hall has not yet been rebuilt, but the ruins of it are there.

The rubble has all been cleared away, and, though hard to believe, the Square of Ypres is easily the tidiest and cleanest I came across. It appears as though it is cleaned by a Hoover, so tidy is it all.

In place of a military policeman at the junction of the Lille road, there stands a gendarme. I have less qualms about going up to the latter than I had to the former. I ask the way to the British Legion Club and, fearless of the wrath of his 'Inspector Beveridge,' he takes my arm, and we march across the Square to the Legion rooms.

The clubrooms are spacious, and kept spotlessly clean by ex-Sergeant Reeder, of the Lancers, and his capable Belgian wife. The latter greeted me in excellent English, and escorted me to a room. After a wash-up, I come downstairs, when she shows me through the house. In front is a huge office, with poppy wreaths hanging on one wall, and a map of the battlefields on another.

Behind is a big, bright tea-room, which opens through French windows on to a lawn, on which are perhaps a dozen tables all set for tea. A trellis, covered with red rambler roses, screens it from other eyes. Upstairs are reading, writing, smoking, and ladies' rooms, while above these again are bedrooms.

Sgt Reeder is a busy man. He goes to all the cemeteries by car to lay wreaths, and at Armistice last year, he told me, he laid over 1,600 poppy wreaths. Each year the numbers tend to diminish. His wife has also her work cut out. During the season they provide thousands of teas for parties from England and Scotland. The Saturday I arrived, she had had 272. She is helped by her daughter and a Belgian maid.

To anyone going Ypres way, I can thoroughly recommend the Legion Club. High tea, bed, and bacon and egg breakfast, cost me, including 10 per cent service tax, 43 francs—approximately *5s 6d* in Belgian money. It's a wonder the place is not packed with Aberdonians!

Saturday night is very quiet, and is like all other nights of the week, except Sunday night when the town and shops are busy. At 8.30pm I wend my way along the cobbled street to the Menin Gate that wonderful memorial, primarily for some 60,000 missing in the Ypres Salient before August 15, 1917, but also the Cenotaph for all those British and Colonials who laid down their lives in 1914–18.

It is massive, but wonderfully designed. It weighs over 20,000 tons, it is shaped like a huge, covered hall, with a gateway at either end, in the dome is a circular opening showing the sky, while on either side are two huge electric lights.

The latter are switched on about 10 minutes to nine at night to light the Hall, and when the first peals of the town bells begin to herald, the approaching hour of nine, two *gendarmes* stand in the roadway, and all traffic is stopped. On the walls in the Hall and on the walls of the staircase leading to the battlements are inscribed, under their respective regiments, the names of all those who have no known grave.

Dead silence prevails as the two buglers—members of the Ypres Fire Brigade—step forward. As one bugle, the notes of the 'Last Post' sound, and echo through the Gate. There is no hurry to get the 'Call' finished. These two Belgians sound it better and with greater sincerity than any buglers in the British Army could do it.

Standing there, one feels, that those 60,000 are again standing to attention and, having heard it, they lie down, content in the knowledge that they are not forgotten. How impressive it all is.

Among those assembled to pay silent homage are Britishers, Colonials, French, Belgians, Americans, men, women and children of all ages and classes. Each night brings new faces, but many of the Ypres inhabitants are ever-present.

When the last echo of the notes of the 'Last Post' have died away, an Australian who is standing near turns to me, and with tears glistening in his eyes, says, 'My God, Jock, I thought I was a hardened digger, but I guess I'm wrong. The way these chaps sound that call got me completely.' He isn't the only one who feels like that. We all do, and find a curious lump in our throats as we try to speak.

One feels honoured standing there in that Gateway, shoulder-to-shoulder, as it seems, with those countless thousands of Britishers, whose light will never go out. It is all so simple, yet so full of sincerity.

I salute those two Belgians. Night after night, year after year, they are in their places, and put such depth of feeling behind their sounding of that call. In wintertime, when a biting icy wind sweeps through the Gateway, driving onlookers to shelter, these two stand bare-headed and sound it as deliberately and correctly as they do in summer, I salute them, too, for having done it without reward.

That, however, has been remedied now, for the British Legion rightly felt that they should receive some small recompense, and so a sum of money has been set aside to give a small gratuity to these men, so that the 'Last Post,' the close of day call of the British Army, shall resound through that wonderful Memorial so long as there is a British nation.

The Aussie and I climb up the stone staircase to the ramparts. We tread softly lest we waken those who sleep, but look on the panels as we go, for the names of those friends we knew—names which are now indelibly inscribed on the walls of that Gateway, standing sentinel o'er the blood-drenched roadway, which leads to Menin, to Passchendaele, to Zonnebeke, to Gheluvelt, and the dawn.

Retracing our steps, we pass through the Menin Gate and walk back to the centre of Ypres. It is a silent city, although the hour is but 9.45pm. The cafés are empty, and pedestrians are few and far between.

My Australian friend, like many more who came over for the unveiling of the Villers Brettoneux War Memorial, has got to return without having achieved his wish. The Australians are naturally very sore over the postponement of the ceremony and have been badly let down.

I return to the BL Club, where I find one of the gardeners from Tyne Cot Cemetery. We have a long talk. He has been in France and Belgium since 1914 and is married to a Belgian. The gardeners get a month's leave each year, with free travel.

Many of them—some 70 per cent of the 600 odd in France and Belgium are married to French women—have not re-visited Britain for years, but they all say they are to go there when they retire.

I am up betimes next morning (Sunday), and set out for Boesinghe at 7.30am. Boesinghe was some two or three miles behind the front for most of the War, except in 1914 and early '15, and for a short time in 1918.

It was in ruins all the time, and when we came out on rest from Pilckem, Langemarck, or Houthulst, we lived in dug-outs on the Yperlee (often miscalled the Ypres Comines) Canal bank, or in huts at the T-shaped crossroads, where the long part of the T leads to Elverdinghe.

All is changed now. The church is rebuilt. A convent stands where we ran a crown and anchor school! The inhabitants are of no help in finding old landmarks, and one has got to rake one's memory for the old familiar places, and very unsatisfactory it is.

Over the pont, or bridge, of the canal I wend my way along what used to be a road which was a veritable death-trap at sundown, Further on I enter the first cemetery I come to. I can hardly recognise the place—Artillery Corner.

Twenty odd years ago, when we buried some of our comrades there, we felt that, both literally and figuratively, it was the last of them. We could hardly have thought otherwise. It was centred in a sea of mud and slime, broken wire, and all the heterogeneous paraphernalia of war. It was continually under fire, and, on at least one occasion, the burial party didn't all return to their posts.

Today that burial ground is not a cemetery—it is a garden, and such a garden. Flowers bloom there in profusion. It is a typical British cemetery. Headstones are all alike, with one exception. There is one solitary wooden cross of a named soldier. Why it should be there I was unable to ascertain. I came across only one other wooden cross in the 23 cemeteries I visited.

One can enter these gardens at any time of the day or night. The gates are never locked. At the entrance to each are two plaques—one in English and the other in French—stating that these pieces of ground have been gifted to Britain in perpetuity by the French (or Belgian) Government.

I pass out through the gateway, and join the Langemarck road after crossing the Ypres-Roulers railway line. Pilckem Ridge looms in sight, and instead of having to make a run for it at the crossroads, I take a photograph of the neat and tidy *estaminet* which now adorns the corner. The aspect from the Ridge is entirely changed. Gone are the pill-boxes over on the left front. Everywhere is waving corn, wheat, barley, or cultivated ground of some description.

The whole plateau to Houthulst and Poelcappelle is cultivated. Cattle and horses are grazing peacefully, while hens, chickens, and ducks are everywhere. I pictured an apoplectic Staff Colonel revisiting this area—scene of so much bloodshed and countless battles—and being confronted with hens cackling on the battlefield, 'Brrrmph, Brrrmph, Sergeant Major, remove these dammed hens—poultry on a battlefield; never heard the like; what?'

There are wire fences in Langemarck now; thanks mostly to the thousands of old iron stakes and yards of wire which adorned the ridges in the War years. A short distance from Pilckem I was reminded of a play done by the Dramatic Society. A cow had been dissatisfied with grass feeding, and had broken through the fence. It is standing in a field of corn practically unobserved, as the corn is about four feet high.

I enter Cement House Cemetery. Perhaps it is invidious to single out one cemetery as being more beautiful than another, but here there are red roses in full bloom, and what a sight they are! In one row of headstones alone there are perhaps 60 of these rose trees, with, at least, a dozen blooms per head.

There are dozens of other flowers besides, but the eye is drawn to the roses, which seem to overshadow all other flowers. On opening the visitors' book, which is to be found in a stone safe in every cemetery, near the entrance, I find that the last name written there is WD Campbell, St Andrews, 8/9/37! Let me explain the reason why all that time should elapse between his entry and mine without any names between.

In the first place, with the advance of time, visitors are fewer, and probably not all of them enter their names; secondly, there are many who visit them annually, but, having entered their names on the first occasion, do not do so on succeeding visits.

I reach Langemarck, but not the Langemarck I knew. I am getting down-hearted, as I had hoped to be able to find an old shell-hole or breastwork or pill-box where I had had 'bed' and breakfast, but no! It begins to dawn on me that as this part of the line had been stationary for four years, its destruction was practically complete and therefore the greater the change.

Further south, where the position of the frontline varied from year-to-year, or where fighting was practically non-existent (where the Guards Division held the line!), there is little change and old scenes remain.

I enter a shop in Langemarck and ask for wartime views of the village. The *Madame*, who fled to Poperinghe on the entry of the Germans, told me she had none; she had never seen any; and they were never asked for. She directs me to Houthulst, and in front of the church I see a signpost.

The names of the places mentioned on that sign will re-awaken memories in many ex-Servicemen: Pitscottie, Dairsie—pardon me, that was Bannockburn days—St Julien (spelt St Juliaan), Zonnebeke, Ypres (Ieper), Houthulst, Klerken, Staden, and Bixschoote.

A kilometre east of Langemarck stands a foreboding looking building—clumsy and unsightly. It is the entrance to one of the biggest German cemeteries in France or Belgium. It contains over 80,000 dead. Entering the doorway there is a porch, on the right of which is a sort of annex railed off.

In the annexe are two huge Nazi wreaths with the Swastika prominently displayed, accompanied by wide coloured ribbon of brilliant hues. Out through the porch is a miniature courtyard surrounded by high stone walls. On the walls are more wreaths. To the right is an opening in the wall leading through an avenue, hedged six feet high on either side.

Every few yards there is an opening on the left to allow entrance to the cemetery proper. I make to go through the first of these openings, when I notice a movement at the far side of the cemetery.

I turn back, as the movement is that of an elderly woman and a younger one, both in black. They are at a cross. I get out and go along the road back towards Langemarck. Presently, a car which I saw standing stationary some distance along the Houthulst road passes me, and I note there are two ladies in it. It is a German car.

Turning back, I re-enter the cemetery. All the graves are marked with creosoted wooden crosses, and each cross bears two names—one on either side. The German dead are buried head-to-head. The cemetery is looked after by a Belgian, and the grass is cut short. There are no flowers, but rows of small trees break the monotony of the row upon row of crosses.

At its eastern end is a bank, and I go along there. Mounting the steps, my eyes are dazzled by the scene. Here the grass is rank, with a goodly number of marguerites, but these are overshadowed by the thousands of huge red poppies swaying gently in the breeze.

It is truly a wonderful sight. Beyond the poppies are a series of large square cement blocks bearing names of German towns and regiments. There is also a wartime pill-box, with grass growing on top. My eye comes back to these poppies, and I say to myself that perhaps in these self-same emblems of our dead we could forge a link for peace.

That little wild flower blooms with as much beauty o'er the graves of the vanquished as o'er those of the victors. I walk back, thinking of these poppies, and as I emerge from the cemetery a car draws up, and two gentlemen get out. I see at once they are German, and that they are father and son. I wish them 'Good morning.' They reply rather gruffly, I think. I move off towards Houthoulst, but think that I am missing an opportunity of perhaps doing a service, and so I again turn back and re-enter the cemetery.

I run into them as they emerge through one of the openings in the hedge. I speak again, and this time they stop. I am pleased, because I wish to hear what they have to say and what their views are.

Conversation is rather difficult, as it hangs on my little knowledge of French and meagre knowledge of German, as neither speaks English, I gather the father, who is a doctor, is showing his son—25 years of age—over the part of the battlefield he was on in 1914–15. He, like me, recognises it only vaguely. I take them along to show them the poppies and tell them how on Armistice Day we associate our dead with them.

Between the road and the field of poppies is a stretch of stagnant water. I ask the doctor if he can tell me what it is there for, as there is no apparent reason for its presence. The water is about 30 yards long by two wide, and looks as though it were part of a canal. I was surprised at the result of my query.

The father turned to his son, and in a voice full of unhidden hatred, he spat out the information that it was symbolic of the Belgians opening the sluices of their canals and preventing the victorious soldiers of the Vaterland reaching the Channel ports! I could not understand entirely what the father said, but I grasped sufficient to let me know that these poppies will again be re-dipped in blood.

It is simply no use blinding our eyes to the fact. We do not understand the Continental mind (I was told so later by a Frenchman). Anyhow, I felt I should point out to the son that as his countrymen had entered Belgium without invitation, the Belgians were quite within their rights in doing what they did to stop the invader.

The father broke in, and in a torrent of language impressed, or tried to, on me that they (the Germans) wouldn't forget; and wouldn't be caught that way again. I don't know how tense the situation was in Downing Street on the eve of August 4th, 1914, but I did know that it looked as though the poor old HLI was to bear the brunt of it as usual, unless I could pour oil on troubled waters!

Taking the son by the arm, I turn him round, and pointing to these thousands of crosses, say how futile it all was, whether for the winner or the loser. I should have saved myself the trouble. He is not an individual, but part of the Vaterland, and the question of his becoming clay at the age of 25 is of little moment if it is in the interests of Germany.

By the time we reach the roadway again, we were getting more friendly. As I pass the unknown's grave in the porch, I pay my respects, and am saying goodbye when the doctor says he will run me to Houthulst in his car if I will come first to Lizerne, near where he was wounded in 1915.

I get in the back—it is a big saloon Ford—and off we set. The son drives, and we go down through Langemarck and Pilckem to Boesinghe, then along by Het-Sas (a sluice on the canal over which I had many times traversed when going into the Houthulst sector), and on to Lizerne. Here at the crossroads on the wall of a house is a notice to the effect that the invader (Germans) were held here in 1914, and got no further.

Turning right, we go down the Dixmude road. The car stops, and I notice a memorial. The doctor asks me to come out and have a look. It is the Belgian Memorial to the men who were gassed here in April 1915. It is a gruesome reminder of the horrors of gas.

There is a man tearing at his throat, while others are writhing on the ground in agony, trying to strangle each other. To us it was German frightfulness; to the German, retaliation for the opening of these sluices!

A little farther on the car stops suddenly at a side road, and the doctor gets out and examines the surroundings. It is here he was hit. On again, and as the car speedometer is registering 104 kilometres an hour, I mention Hitler. The son half turns, and, fortunately, there is no ditch, only rough ground slightly lower than the road.

The father pulls the wheel round, and with a jolt that nearly sends my head through the roof we regain the road! I laughingly suggest that there's no reason why, because he (the father) omitted to kill me when as a soldier I was in Houthulst Forest, his son should have a shot at me as a civilian.

They both saw the humour of it, and, for the first time, they laughed. We are skirting Houthulst now, and reaching the village, we stop. The signpost says 18 kilometres to Ypres, and they offer to drive me but I tell them I'm walking it.

They ask me if I have any food, and I say I don't require any, but the father jumps out, opens the back of the car, and presents me with six bananas and fills my sporran with cherries—another alliance cemented!

We shake hands, and they wave to me as I set out for Poelcappelle and Ypres. What would the Führer say to his minions hobnobbing with a Jew from Aberdeen!

Ayette is a lovely little village now, with no evidence of its rather hectic war experience, except for the presence on its outskirts of a British cemetery and a combined Indian and Chinese one.

In the centre of the village stands the local War Memorial. It Is enclosed by a railing which is practically hidden by a gorgeous show of red rambler roses. I have the choice of four roads here. I choose the Douchy one, although I would have liked to go to Moyenneville and Hamelincourt, but I must put in a step and get back to Arras before dusk.

The other roads lead to Courcelles and Achiet-le-Grand. It is only a kilometre to Douchy. I stop and speak with some farm workers busy hoeing neeps. They are needing rain for them, but other crops are excellent. On the outskirts of Douchy is a small British cemetery, and there is a small party of British people in it taking a photograph of one of the graves.

As I come out of the garden the gardener joins me and walks along the street as far as his house. He is a Devonshire man, while his wife, who is newly back from London, is a cockney. They seem quite content, although they feel a bit lonely in wintertime. The man has three gardens under his care, two at Ayette and one at Douchy.

I am sorely tempted to take the left road, which leads to Monchy-au-Bois, Foncquevillers, Hannescamps, Bienvillers, and Pommier, but I must turn back towards Arras. I take the Adinfer road—it's even in worse condition than when we held it in March 1918. No car would go on it as boulders are every few yards.

Much remains of the battle front here. On the bank on the side of a sunken field I note with pleasure the old funk-holes we inhabited when in supports. The sight of them makes me decide to make a return visit. I am taking a pick and a spade with me next time, because I spot what I take to be the funk-hole in which Jerry put his visiting card—a 5.9—when I was out wiring.

It buried my equipment, all of which I made good, except an entrenching tool, the cost of which was duly deducted from my pay, and which I am determined to recover next visit.

This area recalls many memories—the brighter ones, anyway—but of that more anon.

Adinfer is as dead as mutton. I see not a living soul, while Hendecourt is little better. The roads in the Highlands of Scotland may be bad, but they are drawing room carpets compared to the one I am on now.

Walking along the undulating road to Blairville I recall a burial party. It may sound strange, because these were common daily sights, but this one will always remain with me. In the soft fading light of a beautiful June evening I was returning alone to my company, which was in support behind Boiry Sugar Factory, when I met a party of Argylls coming down from the line.

They were a burial party, and had with them the bodies of three of their comrades who had been killed by a shell. The party were singing—singing softly and with feeling—and the song was 'There's a long, long trail a-winding.' It was to be 'a long, long night of waiting' for three homes at least.

I reach Blairville—a lovely little wooded village—and am surprised that there is no sign of the cemetery we made on the right on entering it. I wonder, because it was getting fairly well filled when I knew it. Three women I ask about it, and all tell me there never was one there, and they had returned to Blairville in 1919. I turn left in the centre of the village, and go to where a heap stood. In its place is now a pretty little church.

Again, near it, I see a café, with the proprietor standing at the door. I ask him in despair about the cemetery, and he confirms what I remembered. There was a British cemetery, but the bodies were all removed in 1923 to Berles-au-Bois British Cemetery.

On the left hand side of the road on entering Blairville there used to stand three guns of a six-inch battery. The other three were at Ransart. I mention this fact because one night on returning from a wiring party we came across country and, wading through corn, we landed on the three guns.

Now, there was one thing which got the gunners' goat, and that was making a track right on to his guns. It was so easily discernible from the air. The teams of these six-inch guns were no exception, and they didn't recognise us as HLI—at least that's not the name they gave us.

Strangely enough, on that battery were two gunners, one of whom belonged to St Andrews, while the other was in a St Andrews Bank until a year or two ago. The former is a St Andrews postman, who is now content with a double-barrelled sporting gun. He finds it slightly easier to load, but he is not able to follow the shot as he could when a six-inch shell was fired from a gun in his battery.

Looking from Blairville it is possible to trace many of the trenches, although they are all filled in. The subsoil is chalk, as all those who had the 'pleasure' of digging in these will remember. Today the trail of the upturned chalk is plainly seen zig-zagging through the fields.

While I am speaking to the Frenchman there is a sound as though a 5.9 has landed in the village, and in answer to my look of 'wind up,' he says it is only the underground tunnel caving in somewhere. During the German occupation of Blairville the village was undermined by a network of tunnels in the chalk.

Jerry had not time to ventilate them properly, and when we knew them it was impossible for a candle to burn after a platoon had slept in one of the galleries. Leaving the Frenchman, I retrace my steps, and turn left on the Bretencourt road.

I see the 'smoke' rising from the 'shell' and find on closer inspection that a house has caved in and, bar one wall and the rafters, has disappeared. It has not been unexpected, as the inhabitants were warned out a month ago.

I set off by car for Villers Brettoneux. The driver is an Englishman who has lived in Amiens since 1923 and is married to a French lady. Reaching Villers Brettoneux Cemetery, I enter it, and am accosted by a gendarme, who wishes to see my passport.

It satisfies him, and I make to go up the cemetery to the Australian Memorial, which is due to be unveiled three weeks later. The gendarme stands in my way and tells me I can't go further. I see no reason why I shouldn't, and he gets quite excited and begins to threaten me.

I note there is a military guard of French soldiers at the top of the cemetery, too. I rather resent his intervention but ask him to accompany me back to the road. At the entrance, I draw his attention to the plaque which states that the ground is British, having been gifted (in reality, paid for a hundred times over in blood) by the French.

I tell him that I should be escorting him off, and he gets real excited, and I thank my stars I haven't to take down, even in shorthand, what he says. It is really comical how strung up the French are over the Royal visit.

The reason is that while they are most anxious for it to take place, the memory of Marseille still lingers. I bid him *au revoir* with a sweet smile, but on looking back after the car had started, I see him still gesticulating wildly!

We make for the village of Villers Brettoneux (the memorial is two kilometres outside on the Corbie road). Reaching the centre of the village, we stop, and I go and look for an old billet. I find it because it was near the only cross streets in the place.

It is a two-storey house now, but when my billet it had only one room intact—i.e. nothing bigger than an elephant could come through the 'moth' holes in walls. In August 1918 we returned to Villers about three one morning for a 'rest.'

Three of my section spotted this room, so we at once started to make it a home once more. The village was badly messed about, and so far no civilians had returned to it. We began to salvage furniture, and by noon had a nice four poster bed, a set of china of various colour schemes, armchairs, ornaments, pictures, etc.

After dinner, served up on the best 'cheena,' we were having a siesta when we were awakened by the entrance of an oldish Frenchman. In a short time, there were three Frenchmen and four women, and we were treated to a real 'stair held row.'

One man claimed the armchairs as his. A woman said they were hers, and our laughter didn't help them any. We knew that they were both liars, as we had 'scrounged' them from different ruins.

However, as it was disturbing our sleep, one of our number threatened to shoot them unless they obeyed his injunction to '*allez*.' They eventually cleared out, and when we went along to draw rations later, we saw the 'owner' of our armchairs with a donkey and a cart. On the latter were two armchairs and a collection of pictures.

We watched, and as he proceeded along the street he went into another ruined house and came out with another armchair. That poor donkey was to have some load before he left Villers, and the stuff would naturally be all his master's.

Our 'rest' was short-lived. Nine o'clock next morning saw us away up the line again. The old *château* in the village has been left as a ruin. The courtyard is chokeful of long grass, and it serves as a reminder of what the whole place looked like.

From Villers we make for Dernuin, passing Crucifix Corner and Hangard Wood. The latter place saw fierce hand-to-hand fighting before the Canadians got Jerry properly started to run. Striking the main Amiens–Roye road, we proceed as far as Le Quesnel.

It is as sleepy as it was when unoccupied by civilians. I enter the church. It used to have two gaping holes in its walls, but these are patched up. The organ has been shifted, but it is still the same one, for some of the pipes have the old shrapnel marks on them.

I reach Bellenglise. It is rather a charming little village, and has contrived to rid itself of all reminders that it was once the scene of History with a capital H. I turn down a road to the right, which brings me to the canal, and I inspect the bridge.

Now, on September 29th, 1918, there were two bridges, some 80–100 yards apart, but I only see the one I am at. Of the two, the one nearer St Quentin went up in the air as our first wave was approaching it, but we caught the German sappers in the act at the other, and this had much to do with the success of the attack.

I make inquiries, but am informed there was only one bridge. Fortunately, I am not downhearted, because I am beginning to realise that the average French civilian knows or cares very little about the wartime aspect of his home villages.

However much I try to convince myself that this is 'my' bridge, something tells me I'm wrong. I go down the road towards Vermand, turn and come back slowly. Sometimes I say 'Yes' and sometimes 'No,' but definitely 'No' as I approach the bridge.

The road rises before meeting it, but the road we rushed was quite flat, while the bridge itself was slightly to the left as the road reached the bank of the canal. I see another road slightly to the north, but it swings south at the canal, and merges with the Vermand road beside the bridge.

Disappointed, I go up the village to the left and look for the entrance to the Hindenburg Line. As usual, no one is able to direct me, so I forage about for myself. Reaching a corn field, I see a white heap, with bushes growing round it. Skirting the edge of the corn, I reach the heap, as usual well protected by nettles.

Removing some loose lumps of cement, I uncover a hole about a foot in diameter. I peer down, but all I can see is that the sides have caved in. I clamber on top of the pile of cement blocks, and I am able to get my bearings from the road which leads to Magny-la-Fosse. I am definitely satisfied that where I stand is the entrance to the tunnel down which we chased some stray Jerries.

On referring to my wartime diary, I find that it had 72 steps down into the bowels of the earth. On the 'first floor' were assembly rooms, dining rooms, and kitchens. Down below that were wire beds by the score. The third floor had a hospital with full equipment (I had 'captured' a syringe and some tablets, only to lose them later), while down at the bottom of the shaft was a light railway running parallel with the canal and one at right angles with the exit, as we found later, in Le Tronquoy.

Most of the Germans escaped along this tunnel. The whole place was electrically lit and was a marvellous structure. Today it is all caved in, which seems rather a pity. I am certainly to revisit the spot and try to squeeze into the tunnel. I'll roll a kebbuck of cheese down in front of me, as I've no doubt it will be a rat home now. There was quite a number of them, 'permanent boarders,' in 1918.

I write up the remainder of my day's tramp and experiences and find myself not at all 'happy' about the bridge at Bellenglise. Unfortunately, it is one of the few places I haven't got a trench map of, and after studying an ordinary map, I decide that, much as I would like to see St Quentin in daylight, I must return to Bellenglise in the morning.

There are so many villages I wish to revisit that I will require to allow more time for the Somme. It is 3am ere I get to bed, and as I am down at breakfast by seven, it's costing me about 10 Francs an hour to sleep—extravagance!

At eight o'clock in the morning I set off for Bellenglise again, and on reaching it I go straight to the canal bridge. Crossing it, I turn sharp right on the road I noticed last night and follow it along the bank for some 80 yards, and then out across country.

At the high bank on this road I turn about, and lie down near the centre. I soon get things in their proper perspective so far as they concerned me on that eventful Sunday morning in September 1918.

Waving crops, trees and the rebuilt village do not change it. This is definitely the road we 'sauntered' along when attacking the canal, despite the fact that there is no bridge practically opposite it at the canal bank.

Strange how, as I sit on the grassy bank the old memories of that misty morning and then gloriously sunny day come back. Strange, too, how it is the lighter rather than the grimmer side that my mind dwells on. Perhaps it is because, as I sit, the whole countryside is so peaceful that the sordidness of war seems incompatible with the beauty around me.

Strange, but it is in sleep that the stark horror of screeching, crashing shells, the screams and groans, the nauseating fumes of gas and burnt cordite, and of squelching over disfigured and shattered but still bleeding, breathing bodies, asserts itself.

I see my platoon—we were attached to the Staffords—going forward in extended order. What a motley crew we were. Above our equipment we had lifebelts on to enable us to ford the canal. Whenever I see the Michelin tyre man, he reminds me of that Sabbath day! The white lifebelts made us practically invisible from any distance in the thick mist.

So thick was it in parts that about a dozen of us lost touch with our flanks. We congregated at this bank and peering through the mist we noted we were pretty near the canal. Our artillery barrage hadn't opened out properly.

We were making use of the thickness to make our 'visit' as much as a surprise one as possible. Then it thinned considerably, and we saw our flanks coming slowly forward, while at the same time the German machine gunners on the canal bank saw them, and us, too. Suddenly, the canal bank became an inferno—our guns had opened out, and nothing could live long under their murderous concentration.

A machine gun from the far side of the canal was trained on this bank on which I now sit, but it was firing a shade too high, and 'plupping' into the earth over our heads. Only one of us had the 'courage' to stick his arm up, and he got away with a lovely 'blighty' one—he was a Highland Light Infantryman, of course!

The canal was dry when we reached it, so that there would have been no need for lifebelts, even apart from the fact that we got the bridge before Jerry put it 'up a kye.'

One of those humorous interludes occurred here. Perhaps it sounds paradoxical, but, while one didn't, and couldn't be expected to, laugh uproariously, even in an attack sometimes something happened which caused a smile, though only a fleeting one.

There was a scramble to reach the far side of the bridge as there was a bank there which afforded one a breather in comparative safety. A not too popular NCO landed head over heels in the slimy bed of the canal (it was slimy, too, as I afterwards 'tasted' it). He looked a picture, complete with lifebelt and mud from head to foot.

I walk towards the canal, and instead of going round to the bridge, I take a left incline, but find no sign of any bridge or of an old foundation of one. I ask a man with a horse and cart, but he never heard of another. The canal is busy. There are many barges on it, loaded principally with coal. They are making for St Quentin.

Recrossing the canal, I turn left, and go into the farmyard. I ask the help of the farmer, and he leads me down through his steading to the east bank, where he shows me, hidden by grass, a piece of masonry. It is all that is left of 'my' bridge.

The reason the inhabitants know nothing of it is that the village was in ruins throughout the war, when the Germans had thrown the bridge across. Then before the village again became inhabitable after the Armistice all traces, except what the farmer showed me, has been removed. The farmer tells me that there is only one entrance to the tunnel on his farm, but it is in the middle of a field of corn. I didn't let him know I had already 'discovered' it.

Passing through the village of Bellenglise, I cross the main St Quentin road and enter La Baraque Cemetery. It is hidden from the road and contains only some 50 graves. I open the visitors' book, but there are few names in it.

There is a tinge of sadness, a feeling of loneliness, as though these 50 have been forgotten. And yet I don't know. The flowers are beautiful, and I feel that in their profusion of blooms, they, at least, are determined to compensate those who rest here for the failings of us humans. It is truly a garden among gardens.

Back in Amiens, I enter a bookseller's to get some Penguin books I see in the window. I assume English is spoken and ask for the books by their name. The assistant tells me in French to wait a moment, and leaves me, to return by the street door with a gentleman.

The latter asks me in the English of a Frenchman what I want, and when I get the books, I turn and say good-day to him. He accompanies me to the street, and he tells me the shop isn't his, but that they usually get him when a British customer comes in.

He points across the street and says, 'That is my pub across there.' I look across and see an up-to-date café with the name 'Thompson' in big letters above it. I say to him, 'Are you English?' and he replies, 'Yes, did you think I was a Frenchman?' I admit I did, and he laughs.

He tells me he has been in France since 1916. We speak about the War, and judge my surprise when he says, 'Were you in the HLI?' I reply, 'Yes,' but can't place him, not even when he says he was in the 'Skins' (Inniskilling Fusiliers).

They were in the same Brigade until the Brigades were reduced to three battalions in February 1918. 'You don't remember me?' he asks. I don't, at least not until he asks me if I remember playing football against his battalion. Then it all comes back to me.

Before the 'Skins' left us we played a football match with them at 'P' Camp, near Woesten, in Belgium. Most of my battalion's regular team were doing field punishment Number One, or waiting on a court martial, so I 'volunteered' to play inside-right.

The reason for this outstanding act of bravery on my part was that, knowing the 'Skins' were a tough lot, I had high hopes of at least getting a broken limb in the match. Unfortunately, I came out of the engagement unscathed, except for bruised shins, which only merited the award MD (medicine on duty) when I visited the doctor. (I never wear the award—the ribbon of the number nine clashes so with the colours of those of the other pot lids!).

My football display was such that I was never again asked to dishonour my battalion on the football field. Incidentally, I never volunteered for anything again, except when I had the good fortune to stand behind a teetotaller at a rum issue, and I volunteered to take his share.

But to get back to Thompson. He played inside-left for the 'Skins,' and as 10 goals were scored in this match, he and I had many opportunities of passing anything but complimentary remarks to each other.

Thompson was really a very fine player and played regularly for Division. After the Armistice, he tells me, he played for the Army in a number of exhibition matches in French towns. The French got quite keen, and a team was started in Calais.

They approached him, and he signed as a professional with them. Two years later he was transferred to Lille, and after four years with them, Amiens bought him. He played regularly for them until 1933.

He tells me he played for France a number of times against touring teams in Paris. Retiring from active participation in the game, he settled down here in Amiens. He seems to do well and is known by all and sundry as 'Jimmy.'

I am glad I went back to the battlefields. Perhaps sentiment entered into this visit much more than it did in those days of some 20 years ago. Sentiment was taboo on active service, at least with Infantry.

Yes, I am 20 years older on this visit, and in the reawakening of the memories of my last 'visit' I am able to appreciate more fully than I did even then that the Infantry was no place for a man of 30 years of age or over.

In my Company there were quite a few from time-to-time, but the majority of the personnel were aged from 17 to 20. I am afraid the latter didn't understand the older men, who had responsibilities at home, and who, naturally, had many thoughtful moments.

They had to put up with a lot from the younger ones. I admire them now, looking back, and marvel at the way in which they stuck with it.

Another thing which will disillusion many of the older generation is this, that to the majority of the Infantry—i.e. 17–20—the question of fighting for a righteous cause was never heard of. We did notice that we were often called on to go 'over the top' on a Sunday, but assumed that that came under the heading of 'military strategy'.

We didn't even enlist for the defence of King and country. We enlisted simply because others did so; we were sent to France because we'd no option (and at 17–20 few of us would have taken advantage of an option); we found ourselves in the trenches, and that was all there was to it.

Rarely, if ever, did we picture what we would do when the war was all over. We never looked so far ahead. When our rations arrived in the trenches, we used to eat most of them straight away, just in case!

The youths of 17–20 of today are shaping their lives, planning their careers and picturing the heights to which they may rise. The only heights to which we could rise didn't bear thinking about!

We did find something which was worth finding. We found that something so elusive in peacetime—comradeship. What a truly wonderful thing it was to arise out of the 'glaur' of war. Comradeship must not be compared with friendship. The latter could never survive the tests to which the former was subjected. It is a deeper and far finer thing than friendship. Comradeship was international. It was extended to friend and foe alike.

I felt, when speaking to those gardeners who tend the Silent Cities, as Kipling calls the cemeteries, that there is still that comradeship in them—a comradeship kept evergreen by their proximity to those who lived that comradeship, but whose voices are now stilled.

—Pte Alfred W. Keith, Highland Light Infantry, writing in June 1938.

These extracts are taken from a ten-part series chronicling Keith's journey along the Western Front to mark twenty years since the end of the war. He returned the following year for another tour of the region in the weeks before the outbreak of the Second World War.

*

During the most critical days of the recent Crisis (if, God grant, the past tense be justified) it so happened that I was on Pilgrimage to France. Yes, 'Pilgrimage' is a word better suited than 'Holiday.'

Prior to the commencement on July 1st, 1916, of the Battle proper I had been serving on the Somme. Serving in a Line Battalion of one of the most famous of County Regiments. In these days the War, in retrospective, seemed quite a Gentlemen's War alternating with tours of trench duty and visits to billets (mostly barns) in the villages adjacent to the line.

To this district then by means of a trusty cycle I made my way. Very little changes are to be seen in some villages and great was my joy to find one old friend (Madame Perin) still alive and well in Bus-lès-Artois. A flood of reminiscences, old faces appeared at memory's window, names long forgotten returned to the mind and—in silence was drunk a toast 'Peace in our time, O Lord!'

Then the walk to Bertrancourt, Colincamps with its avenue of trees (which used to shelter our 18 pounder batteries) still standing albeit with many vacant spots and many scars. *La Sucrerie*! Here used to be the entrance to the main communication trench and here still remains our cemetery. Our cemetery for alas even in those 'quiet' days we—the Brigade (together with our neighbours next door in 'Ocean Villas'—the 4th Division) steadily contributed to War's grim harvest!

A typical September afternoon with a beautiful sun and all around me the scattered groups of French peasantry busily engaged in harvesting the corn whilst I walk reverently along rows of headstones! Old pals, their faces come back and in many cases the manner of their death. This stone, for example, I know is erected over a small collection of fragments of all that could be found after a *minenwerfer* had done its task! No clean bullet hole here but a ghastly mess!

A tear or two that simply will not be held back and so on towards Beaumont Hamel where the New Zealanders perished in a gallant attack against impossible odds. On down through the valley of the Ancre now sleepily flowing in its natural colour and not stained crimson by the lifeblood of the cream of nations!

Up the steady slope so bitterly bought to the dominating ridge of Thiepval. Here to be seen for miles in any direction stands the Thiepval Memorial. Containing the names of those of the British Army who fell in the Battles of the Somme and who have no known graves it stands like some grim sentinel.

'Tread lightly,' it seems to say, 'this ground as far as you can see was once drenched in blood and almost every yard of it was at some time or another a Gethsemane or a Calvary for some simple-hearted child of God, either in khaki or field grey!'

Beautiful spots these cemeteries! Beautiful in their tragedy and alas as numerous as the countless small stacks of newly gathered corn. A few days later—Delville Wood and its cemetery wherein are countless rows of graves many bearing the same inscription, 'A soldier of the Great War known unto God.'

Yet even as I stood there the war clouds are gathering and the horizon seems black. But a few miles further and here is a cemetery of different pattern. Black crosses! And here a lady and a gentleman paying a visit to the grave of a brother (*Soldat* Franz Hoppen 102nd Regt.).

Seeing my Union Jack on the cycle they speak and the gentleman tells me that he was a German soldier too! Reverently I accompany them to the grave, here (was it fate?) we are joined by the one-armed French gardener, his arm was lost at Verdun. We gaze around us in silence, our eyes rather misty.

The German nation do not want war, the French do not want war and yet here as we stand in silence we realise that war might be commencing at that very moment! What of France itself in these days of strain?

Ready, resolute and prepared yet one heard only one comment—pity. Pity for German women and children who would surely be slain in the next war as ours were in the last, So, we realise that the world has progressed a little after all for no pity was expressed last time, only a burning hatred!

Last Sunday was a day of Thanksgiving but do not let us be too premature, rather let us make every Sunday a day of Intercession, a day when our Churches and our Chapels too are less empty and let us all take heed of the lesson of the last few weeks.

Pray for peace but whilst we pray for peace let us be ready and resolute, each trained to play a part of usefulness that Democracy be maintained. The more prepared this country is then it is my firm opinion the shorter would be any future war and therefore the less would be the harvest, the 'Grim Harvest.'

—SOLDIER W. C. J. WILLIAMS, WRITING IN OCTOBER 1938.

*

When I arrived in Erquinghem I went to the original house where I was billeted and was told that *Monsieur* and *Madame* Charles had fled some time in 1918 and had not returned.

But all the old billets and several of the inhabitants remembered me; they thought I had been killed. I showed them photos of the family, and they told me that the eldest daughter lived in another part of the village.

So we went there, and as we were motoring along, I saw a woman coming down the lane leading to the church. She was carrying a bucket and I recognised her immediately. I pulled up suddenly, called 'Marie!' and got out.

She put down her bucket and took a good look at me and shouted 'Arthur!' and we shook hands and made such a noise that all the villagers gathered round to find out what was happening.

She was delighted, and what memories came back to me! One of her first questions was whether I was married and had any 'pickaninnies.' I told her 'Yes,' and we found that both of us had two children. I showed her a photo of the band of the 16th RWF and tears came into her eyes as she looked at it. Then she took me by the arm to the cemetery adjoining her house, and showed me some of the graves of my pals.

I wanted to take photos, but it was too late, so we came back next day and they invited us into the little *estaminet* called the Excelsior, and we were taken through the bar into a private parlour, where everything was arranged for us, where they drank my health, and Miss Grantham's health because she is my employer.

It was all so simple and genuine that it impressed us very much. We clinked glasses with the usual 'Bon Salute,' and they would not take any pay for it. It was a great moment to think I was there after an absence of 22 years.

We went into Ypres and found the remains of 113 Brigade Headquarters of the 38th Welsh Division situated on the canal bank. There we found dugouts where I had actually been, still in a state of good preservation. I was impressed by the peace and quiet of the countryside and spoke to an inhabitant who was calmly fishing in the canal which I had known in all its horrors of bloodshed and shelling.

We then drove through Lens to Vimy Ridge, and on the way could not help comparing the long, uninteresting roads with that of wartime. As we rushed through it seemed impossible that troops could march along them with the cheerfulness that prevailed then. It seemed very wearisome, even when motoring.

At Vimy Ridge we found impressions of the shell-holes and barbed wire. The country had not altered except for the newly built farms and there were still remnants of the elephant dugouts the troops used during the war, also remains of gun emplacements which the farmers now make good use of for their implements.

What impressed us very much was that all the battlefront lands were covered with British cemeteries, one practically every mile beautifully kept and a credit to the War Graves Commission.

We had now passed Bapaume Ridge and were in the Somme district, arriving at Albert to find the town entirely rebuilt. We proceeded to

Mametz Wood and discovered the sunken road leading to Danzig alley. Here I stood in much different circumstances. A peaceful and beautiful scene now prevailed.

I remembered how this wood was attacked and taken by the 28th Welsh Division, consisting of the RWF and Welsh regiments. In these sunken roads are the impressions of dugouts plainly marked in the chalk banks. We stood where the actual frontline trench used to be (it is a stubble field now), where I had stood 20 years before on July 20th at 4.30 in the morning.

I remember we had to attack this wood and run down a very steep embankment where there was no shelter from the guns, where many of the boys were caught and simply mown down. I ran down with them, and they were being killed round me, but by good fortune I was saved.

Now on this calm and beautiful day I did exactly the same thing, and at the bottom of the embankment found a British hot water bottle, the inevitable rum jar, and soles of boots, and a labourer in the fields told me I was the first British ex-servicemen he had seen revisiting that spot.

The Somme has not altered whatsoever although the courageous French have recultivated the country and built their houses again. For one can still see signs of the horrors of the war days, one can relive again incidents sad and sometimes happy.

My pilgrimage gave me deep satisfaction and a long felt wish has been accomplished. One consolation remains in mind - our boys, our comrades, lie in perfect peace among peaceful surroundings, respected and revered by all French citizens who carry on their task of reconstruction in the hope of forgetting those terrible years of 1914–1918.

—Cpl Arthur Williams, 16th Bn, Royal Welch Fusiliers, writing in November 1938.

After the war, Williams was employed as a chauffeur for Miss Grantham who worked for the Voluntary Aid Detachment in Chester. Following her retirement, she travelled to see the battlefields where many of her patients had been wounded with Williams as her driver.

21

1939

I've been 'up the line' again. Not, I must admit, under the same conditions as when I last went up. A 10 horse power car certainly reduces those long, endless marches to mere trifling trips.

Nevertheless, I recently returned from visiting the old frontline of 1918. Everyone told me that there was nothing left. Everybody said that I would never recognise the places again. Don't believe them. The landscape hasn't altered so much, and, provided you know where to look, there are plenty of traces of the Great War.

Naturally one doesn't expect to find the towns and cities in the ruins they were when we left them. It is out in the quiet, unfrequented spots that the war is still visible to those who can recognise it.

The old barbed wire still remains to be seen, supported by the inevitable picket stakes which we laboriously humped up from somewhere behind. Only now they mark the boundaries of the little farms dotted all over the countryside.

Incidentally, the general opinion amongst the farmers is that the German wire was better than ours. Each farm, too, has its share of corrugated iron shelters—'elephant shelters' they were known as—scrounged from a nearby dump we had left behind.

The show places are all there to be seen, of course. Vimy Ridge, Sanctuary Wood, and the others, but these, to me, did not seem to hold the same significance as did the two straggly grass-grown trenches that I discovered in Pacaut Wood, near Merville—the German frontline of April 1918, and, a few years away, the English line—memories of nights in that same line when the Verey lights used to swish up into the darkness and fall to earth behind us. We knew then that Jerry wasn't so far away.

I picked up a German helmet near these lines, the owner of which must have copped a real one, as it carries a large jagged hole just where his left ear must have been. Before me, as I write, lies a small piece of cordite which I picked up just outside the wood. Every old soldier will remember the artillery bags of cordite with which we used to light our fires.

The farmer, on whose land I found it, showed me his back garden covered with it, and although it was pouring with rain at the time, I picked up a bit, put a lighted match to it and it flared up immediately, just as it did 21 years ago.

It was the same farmer who, on returning to his farm in 1919, discovered hidden among the trees of Pacaut Wood, two corpses, a Scottish soldier and a German. Each one had transfixed the other with his bayonet. Had one only the time there are heaps of souvenirs to be found there, as the place has hardly ever been visited since the Armistice.

Further along our old line, on the banks of the Canal d'Aire (which we mistakenly used to call the La Bassée Canal), I discovered more of our trenches, and it seemed to me that, in the event of further hostilities in that part of the world again, they would not require much preparation beyond clearing away the grass and deepening a little.

How the memories flocked back as I stood there again. Incidents which I had forgotten came back to me as though only a few months had passed. Just behind was the farm where we discovered a cow, left behind by the occupants when the Germans advanced before Merville in April 1918. Two of our fellows crept out in the night and milked it, bringing back as many full mess-tins as they could carry.

I told this to a French peasant who walked along the canal bank while I was gazing around me. To my surprise he showed great interest, and then told me that it was his mother's cow. The farm belonged to her in those days—now it is his. With true Gallic humour, his wife suggested that the time was now ripe for paying for that milk.

Arras, of course, has been practically entirely rebuilt, although here and there in the Grande Place, one can see gaps in the rows of houses which have never been filled in. The Cathedral, too, bears thousands of shrapnel scars on its ancient walls.

Along the Arras–Cambrai road. A hell-spot once with its memories of 'toute-suite' shells (you heard the sound of the gun and immediately on top of it the explosion of the shell) and the droning of German planes searching for it to lay their 'eggs' on the two streams of traffic which nightly packed the road once it was dark.

Over to the left is Freuchy. Having spent five days (and nights) in a queer kind of blockhouse on its outskirts, I was anxious to explore the place again, and it did not take me long to discover the same blockhouse.

It had fallen in considerably and was overgrown with weeds, but I could not fail to recognise the spot where I stood on sentry one night for nearly six hours, the remainder of the section being employed on fatigue.

It was just after Jerry's advance, and we had retreated to this post which was in a small copse. In front of us someone had thoughtfully strung up some wire and tied a few old cans to it. These used to tinkle in the night breeze and send us into a cold sweat of apprehension, which wasn't lessened any by our officer, visiting the posts, informing us that our nearest post on the right had disappeared. They were captured by Jerry and never seen again.

Along the road again, past Happy Valley (there is a British cemetery there now) to the Scarpe, and through Fampoux (a Jerry plane nearly got me there in March, 1918) to Roeux. Roeux was the first place where I went into the line, and where I saw my first German.

Anyone who was at Roeux during '17 and '18 will remember Mount Pleasant cave, a tunnel which ran from the reserve line, about 500 yards in the rear, to the frontline. It had originally been dug out before the war for the chalk stone which they use such a lot for building in Artois. I felt sure that the caves would still be there, but was not prepared to find what I actually did.

Upon enquiries in the village concerning this cave I was told to see M Dumont, who is the local cycle agent and agricultural implement maker. Dumont proved to be a keen young fellow of about 35.

He made me exceptionally welcome when I told him what I had come to see, and, producing a bunch of keys, directed me to follow him. Round at the side of his house was a complete dug-out entrance, the door of which he unlocked, and, after lighting an acetylene lamp, we entered and slithered down about 20ft of loose chalky rubble and there I found myself back again in Mount Pleasant cave.

It was then that he told me the extraordinary story of the cave. During the crisis of last September when we were all busily engaged in trench digging in our back gardens in England, the villagers of Roeux decided that they ought to make some provision for their safety.

Some of the older inhabitants remembered these chalk caves, and, as they had been of such service to the British troops during the war, they felt that here was all the shelter they needed. But how to get in?

When we retreated from that front in March 1918, the ends had been blown in and sealed so that the Germans might not have the use of them. Then someone remembered that the well in his farm passed right through the tunnel into the earth below. That gave Dumont an idea.

He descended the well (I have seen the iron rungs clamped down the sides) and, sure enough, he found a small opening which led into a passage.

Coming up to the top again, he took a long thin iron bar with which he pierced the earth near his own house.

When he felt it go right through he detailed a friend to stand inside it and, at regular intervals, tap it with a hammer; then he descended the well again and entered the passage. The ringing sound of the metal guided him to where the iron had pierced, and, having made contact there, they commenced digging a shaft, which was the one I entered by.

Can you imagine my feelings when I recognised the caves as being in practically the same condition as when I left them. My regiment was the last to leave them, and for 21 years they have remained there untouched.

In places there have been some falls of chalk, but not enough to impede our progress as we wandered from one tunnel to another. Naturally Dumont is as proud of his cave ('*Mon Plaisir*' they call it) as a mother of her first-born.

The old wire beds we used are still there. Though the wood had rotted, the wire is still sound. A mouldered gas-proof curtain flapped across my face as I passed along. The kitchens where the cooks held sway are still there.

The signposts on the walls are as clear today as when they were put up. Actually, there is quite a labyrinth of tunnels down there and each one ran to a different part of the trench. All along the walls are the names of soldiers who occupied it. The first name I spotted was W. G. Loudon, 2nd Bn, Seaforths (my own mob). I wonder what happened to him.

Everybody who spent any time down there at all wrote his name on the walls. My name is down there somewhere, but I could not find it, unfortunately. At one time the Artists' Rifles occupied it, and they have left many artistic souvenirs on its chalky white surfaces.

I spent over two hours down there and would have loved to have spent a week. At every step I discovered something which I remembered previously. In our time the place was lit at intervals along the walls by electric lamps, the power for which was generated by a dynamo, and the wires are still there, though Dumont told me that they removed the dynamo themselves. He was also most excited when I explained how I had been one of the last in there during the war, and was certainly the first British soldier to return.

When we occupied Mount Pleasant it was the eve of the German attack. We knew it was coming, but of course nobody knew the exact day. Instructions had been issued that, when the attack materialised, two rings on an electric bell would be heard in the cave. The first meant 'get out'; and, at the second ring, the entrances were to be blown in.

One afternoon the bell rang. The excitement that ensued was indescribable. Imagine practically a full battalion of men endeavouring to get out through two or three entrances which were no bigger than a yard high by two and a half feet wide.

Fortunately there was no second bell. I have since thought that it must have been the work of some practical joker. We had few such down there. The dynamo was in the charge of an elderly Royal Engineers sapper, who had been so long down there that he was too 'windy' to come up.

One day one of my company, having found an old German hat, scrounged a German groundsheet which he slung around his shoulders and then crept along to the dynamo station, where its caretaker was stretched out on his wire bed snatching 40 winks.

He gently prodded the slumberer in the shoulder, at the same time uttering some guttural gibberish which certainly sounded like German. The old sapper opened his eyes and, with a wild yell that the 'bl___ Germans' were here, he leapt off his bed and scuttled off down the passage, and we saw no more of him that day. All this came back to me most vividly as I stood beside the remains of the very bed on which he had slept.

We had always imagined that Jerry had taken over the caves from us when we left, as nobody seemed to know if the proposed blowing in of the entrances had actually taken place, but Dumont assured me that there was no trace of German occupation down there at all, so somebody must have done his duty after all on the day we got out so hurriedly.

Later on in the year, when it was our turn to advance, the Germans were pushed back far behind Roeux, which is probably the reason why the caves were never reopened, and thus they stayed until last September.

It was interesting to learn also that the Germans occupied Roeux until they were pushed out at Easter, 1917. Dumont's mother was in the village all the time and, when the Germans retired, she, along with others, was forced to retreat with them. She could certainly have told us some interesting yarns had we but had the time.

The Great War is by no means 21 years old over there. In fact, when talking to the French people who experienced it first hand, one feels that it was only a few years ago, it is so fresh in their memories, and it certainly proves how wrong were the scoffers who told me that there was 'nothing left to see.'

—PTE WILLIAM EDWARD PETHERS, 2ND BN, SEAFORTH HIGHLANDERS, WRITING IN JULY 1939.

Pethers served as a teenager in Roeux in 1918. After the war, he became resident conductor of London Palladium Orchestra and for almost forty years was musical director of Coventry New Hippodrome Orchestra. At one time he was the personal conductor to the movie star Gracie Fields.

*

The *Maid of Orleans* doesn't carry very many passengers as she glides across to Calais on a sea as smooth as the proverbial millpond. Half an hour out from Dover a gentleman approaches me and asks where I am making for.

He himself is on his first visit, since the war years, to the battlefields. He served with the Royal Engineers' 51st Division, belongs to Arran, but now lives in Oxford. The Customs at Calais are 'nae bother at a'. The officer puts his mark on my pack without my having to take it off, and I join the Lille train. This time I go past Hazebrouck to Armentières .

En route a number of new and strongly fortified blockhouses can be seen from the train. They form the northern part of the Maginot Line and have a formidable expanse of wire entanglements in front of them. The stakes are embedded in concrete well below ground and rise to a good height above. It looks as though Adolf's tanks will 'hang on the wire' all right.

On reaching Armentières, I detrain and go back towards the pill-boxes but one is not allowed near enough to get a photograph. I cross the frontier at Le Bizet, but see no sign of the *Douaniers*. I put my pack on the Ypres bus, and take another bus which goes via Neuve Eglise, Dranoutre, Locre, Westoutre, to Reningelst. I am tempted to get off at Dranoutre where, for a short period in the war, we got 'bumped' continually all night for a fortnight, thus depriving us of our beauty sleep.

Reningelst is back to normal, and I recall it at once as I notice the houses on either side of the steep decline into the village. The cemetery here records mostly the graves of Canadians who fell in the early part of the war.

Via Hallebast and Dickebusch I reach Ypres again. My friends at Haig House are hale and hearty. After a meal I go out as far as New Irish Cemetery, St Jean and return in time for 'Last Post' at the Menin Gate. When I reach the latter about 8.40pm I find already a large number of people have assembled.

At the approach of 9pm, all traffic is stopped by two Belgian policemen, and when the hour has struck, the strains of the Last Post resound from the walls. There is a tenseness even more pronounced than last year.

The air is sultry, and those present paying homage to the 56,000 Britishers whose names are inscribed on the walls, are fully conscious of the proximity to a possible catastrophe greater than the holocaust of 1914–18.

Can it be possible that the great sacrifice made by those heroes only some 20 years ago is on the brink of being obliterated by one, the magnitude of which is beyond human conception?

Those we are honouring in giving all it was possible for them to give made that sacrifice in an effort to make death on the battlefield an impossible death for their sons and their sons' sons. But the sickle is being sharpened again, and its blade will be drenched not only in the blood of soldiers, but of women and children indiscriminately.

The echoes of the Last Post fade away. 'We have remembered them at the going down of the sun,' but we must remember them in the morning, and in our pride of their memory let us not fail them as the war clouds gather round us. An inscription I saw on one stone later on in my travels is suitable for insertion here, it read: 'For freedom—'tis better to have fought and died than never to have fought at all.'

I overtake the two Belgian buglers as they go home. Both saw service in the last war with the Belgian Army, and both are proud to sound the Last Post in the hallowed hall of the Menin Gate.

Monday morning I set out along the Gheluvelt Road. I pass White Château on my left. Here were Haig's HQs in the early days of the war before the house was destroyed. Today it is again a *château*, with its original owners in occupation, and where Lady Haig stays when with the yearly Scottish Pilgrimage to the salient.

On along the straight stretch of road, passing Hellfire Corner—there are no shattered horses, limbers or lifeless bodies lying there today—I tramp.

Before reaching the top of Hill 62, I notice a small café at the side of which is a notice inviting visitors to come and inspect the old trenches. A modest charge of two and a half Francs allows one to walk through the old trenches, or creep into deep and evil smelling dug-outs.

There appears to be little change here. The barkless and lifeless stumps of trees still stand, the old revetment necessary in these trenches for this part of the line has prevented them falling in. Duckboards—or bits of them—are noticeable under the mud.

In every traverse are old rifles, grenades of all kinds, equipment, etc., lying just as one would expect to see after the attackers have passed forward. Here lies a steel helmet, the wearer of which must have been numbered among the dead, for there is a jagged hole four inches long where a piece of shrapnel had torn through.

In Ypres I was told these trenches were the only ones worth seeing, and I thoroughly agree. If anyone who was never in the war wishes to sample trenches, then go to Sanctuary Wood. The Vimy Ridge trenches are a Hollywood adaptation compared to them. The Canadian Memorial at Vimy is wonderful, and so is the underground labyrinth, but the trenches—impossible.

Only at the entrance to the Sanctuary Wood trenches is there a semblance of 'show.' Laid out for inspection is a collection of all the various paraphernalia of war—field guns, shells, 'minnies,' 'tattie mashers,' jam tins, Hotchkiss and Jerry machine guns of all descriptions, wire cutters, etc.

There is a soldier's holdall laid out, complete with button stick and razor. There is a familiarity about the latter which, although encrusted with rust, feels, by its sharpness, to be uncommonly like the one the Government so kindly gave me, and expected me with its aid to keep my hirsute growth in such a condition that it couldn't scratch the butt of my rifle when I put it to my shoulder.

The rifles are not in a condition to defend a trench, while the Lewis guns have a stoppage not mentioned as a likely one in action. From this heterogeneous collection of 'old iron' I pass into the café, where there is a museum with another very interesting collection of headdresses worn by the opposing forces in 1914 before the advent of steel helmets.

Sabres and other cavalry equipment adorn the walls, while in glass cases are official photographs taken in the Salient during the war, many being of Sanctuary Wood and the surrounding area, and depicting some truly gruesome reminders that we are only clay. How commonplace were these sights to us, yet today, looking at a photograph, one's flesh creeps.

There are two opposing forces on Hill 60 still. A Britisher from Old Kent Road staked his claim a few years back, and with his Belgian wife purchased a piece of the ground wherein were some trenches and dug-outs.

Then a Belgian, seeing money flowing in to the Britisher, decided to start in opposition hard by. He purchased adjoining land with some remains of trenches, made new ones, and, on notice boards prominently placed, declared in rather broken English, his part to be the one and only. The 'war' continues, but the Britisher, who felt the draught to start with, is finding things brightening up again.

The trenches are in good condition and look fairly original. The various types of death-dealing influences are to be met or seen in the trenches or on the parapets. Very realistic among the implements of war are two rum jars. What makes them more realistic is the fact that they are empty! It was only a Sergeant Major or Sergeant who ever saw a full rum jar!

From Hill 60 I cross the deep railway siding, a little to the north of Battle Wood, and make for the Hollebeke–Ypres Road. A few hundred yards down it and I cut across some fields to Bedford House.

The *château* remains a ruin, and is surrounded by a large British cemetery, part of which, until recently, was used for interring any remains found in the Salient since 1925. (This cemetery is now closed for that purpose, any new burials being made in Cement House Cemetery, Langemarck).

There are some 500 graves here, marked by simple wooden crosses. These, however, are being replaced by the familiar Portland headstones. Most of the crosses record the resting place of an unknown British soldier.

In only seven cases did I find that the body had been identified. In the whole cemetery there are nearly 5,000 graves.

Joining the main Armentières road, I turn back to Ypres, passing Shrapnel Corner safely. On the right is an old iron dump with a conglomeration of iron in the shape of shells, machine guns, bicycles, horseshoes, carts, etc.

The road leads me into Ypres by the Lille Gate, only slightly less famous than its nearby neighbour—the Menin Gate. The ramparts here bear testimony to its subjection to shell fire, but in the moat, which extends right round, there are water flies by the hundred, and, judging by the number of 'Isaac Waltons,' a considerable number of fish.

Just over the bridge which spans the moat there are a number of dug-outs leading to tunnels in the ramparts. They have been commercialised, and only last year the proprietor, beginning to find business slackening, created a new dug-out, aged it artificially, and today there is a notice to say it was the one-time headquarters of Rawlinson in 1914!

Instead of going into the town I walk round the path by the side of the moat outside the ramparts. The powers that be have started to repair the latter, and to erase what seemed to be an all time reminder of the siege of Ypres.

It will take a considerable time to repair, as the walls are high and the bricks are being laid four deep. Much of the water has been drained from the moat, and platoon bridges have been thrown across to give the workmen access to the wall. With the lowering of the water level, some gruesome sights are being revealed.

Perhaps they should not be classified as gruesome, as they are past that condition. It is quite common for the fishers to hook a skull or pelvis, but the inhabitants are so accustomed to these that they cause no comment. I walk over one of the workmen's bridges, and count five skulls, together with quite a number of bones.

This bridge is placed practically on the same spot as one used during the war by our troops to evade the Menin Gate road. A hole was cut in the ramparts to allow access. If the moat should be drained completely, a tremendous amount of shells should be salvaged.

The Belgians say that the fact that the ramparts are being repaired after all these years is a sign that a new war is not far distant. They, by the way, don't think a war is so near at hand as do the French.

Back in Haig House I have a long chat with Sgt Reeder and his wife. The latter belongs to that well known village Wytschaete. She had trying experiences during 1914. When the Uhlans rode in, they simply billeted themselves as they pleased.

At nights she and her father had to barricade themselves in an attic. German officers took the house. In the village they plundered everywhere.

The local butcher was off to the Belgian Army and his rather stout wife was left to look after the shop.

The Uhlans marched in and demanded the carcass of a newly killed pig. In return they gave her a signed receipt and told her to present it to the German authorities. As it was written in German, she didn't understand it, but on translation it read, 'The pig we took is not nearly so fat as the woman from whom we took it.'

At Armentières I await my friend from Haig House, who is motoring to Lens, depositing wreaths at various cemeteries on the way. He takes me via Bois Grenier Orchard Cemetery, a small but lovely garden.

As I sign the visitors' book I note the following touching message, written in a rather shaky hand, and dated the day previous to my visit: 'My son, your mother is always thinking of you. This is my 12th and last visit. I feel we will all be meeting again soon.' I quote the words, not out of vulgar curiosity, but because in them I feel that there is the voice of a mother—any mother who lost a son.

Back in Arras I put my pack on the Bucquoy bus, and after a talk with two Londoners of the Rifle Brigade, who are heading north, I set out on my next lap. Reaching Ficheux, I leave for the road and make for the railway embankment. Mercatel is over on the rise just beyond.

I ask a French woman who is in her garden if there is a path down to the part of the embankment to which I wish to go. She replies that there isn't, but she will get her husband to show me the way. The husband turns out to be an Irishman!

Wounded with the Leinsters during the War, he remained in France in 1919, and got to his pre-War occupation of mining. Owing to an accident last year he had to stop work but is now waiting for the result of a tribunal fixing his disability. He tells me the miners get good pay, and there is evidence of it in the fact that he has bought his house and a small piece of ground.

He leads me on to the railway, and we walk down it until we reach the tunnel through the embankment. Near it are still two of the dug-outs which we occupied when in support to the frontline just over the embankment at Boisieux. The tunnel has been made up into a permanent structure and is used by the farmer.

We used to get good shooting practice lying on the slope of the embankment every morning, when Jerry used to come swooping down over the frontline. It was no pleasure when we were in the trenches and were the target of his machine gun. Our rifle fire didn't seem to worry him much, but he rose to a more comfortable height for everyone concerned when we got the Lewis gun trained on him.

It was on this banking near to the level crossing that one of my Section decided, one night, that it was time he was wounded. Unfortunately, he did not make a good job of it. However, I advised him to make for a Casualty Clearing Station, which he did.

Some three weeks later he returned to the Company, complete with a gold wounded stripe on his sleeve! He never attempted to repeat the dose and came through the remaining six months of the war without losing any more blood for his country!

Back to the Bucquoy road, I continue on my way. Here again I recognise an unhealthy part close to Boiry. There is a high bank extending, on the eastern side of the road, to perhaps 40 yards. The line ran round it, forming the sharp apex of a salient.

At night, when the 'fair' was on, with Verey lights going up everywhere and a strafe on, it seemed impossible to get back to Bretencourt, a small village some seven kilometres from the line, for chips and eggs from some civilians who stuck it. The chips and eggs were certainly cold by the time they reached us, but we heated them up, and I'm sure the smell wafted across No Man's Land must have proved very trying to Jerry.

This bank was a good guide on the return journey for the heroes who risked death for the delicacies referred to, for their figures were silhouetted on the skyline. No doubt, when the Guards took over from us the practice would be discontinued. A Guardsman always asked permission to do anything, but every man in the Highland Light Infantry was trained to use his own initiative.

As I walk towards Hendecourt, the air becomes oppressive and the distant thunder gradually comes nearer, making a grand background to the part of the line I am in. So far, the rain has kept off, but I begin to feel big drops. Reaching Hendecourt, I speak with the farmer whose farm is in the centre of the village. The 'barrage' has increased, rain falls and lightning is flashing all round.

I am invited into the farmhouse, and glad I am of the shelter, for the storm breaks and the rain comes down like the monsoon. Forked lightning dances everywhere, and so loud and continuous is the thunder that we can't hear each either speak. The farmer's wife produces a bottle of French wine and some cakes, so we make merry!

After an hour's delay, I set off again in a much clearer atmosphere. The road to Adinfer is ankle deep in water at places and the water is white. Those who served round about here won't be surprised. The subsoil is chalk, and my shoes, by the time I reached Adinfer, are like tennis ones.

I reach Douchy and enter a café there. The village, of course, is now a village again, and not a brick heap covered with nettles, as it was when we, the Guards, and the 2nd Division knew it. The café, like all the houses of the smaller villages, was rebuilt by Italian labour.

French labour was so scarce that some thousands—roughly 150,000—Italians were employed. Most of them have remained in France, preferring the freedom of France to their Italian regime. Recently they pledged their allegiance to their new Motherland.

The *Madame* in the café tells me that along with her mother and little brother they fled from the village as the Uhlans entered the north end. This was in 1914, and all they took was the clothes they stood in. Her father remained behind to look after his café, but he, with the others who stayed, were taken to the other side of Cambrai by the Germans.

In the morning I go to the cemetery—a large one—and find the gardeners busy scrubbing the stones. The head gardener tells me I am the first Britisher to visit since August last year.

I drive to Puisieux, where I pay off my driver and set out on foot. Reaching Serre, I leave the road and take to a farm track. The old barbed wire hangs about, and stakes are still in the ground. I trip over one, and while what I say would bring a blush to the cheeks of the present-day sergeant majors, the wartime ones would probably have asked if I thought I was still in the Band of Hope!

The track is familiar, and lying everywhere are bombs, boots etc. In the long grass I notice the barrel of a Lewis gun, and as I poke, my stick catches in something. I pull, and when I see what I've done, I cover the next 100 yards as only a soldier can! It was the pin of a Mills bomb that came away. I didn't hear any explosion. I expect it was too encrusted with dirt, etc. to go off, but I never liked them with the pin out!

They have been doing their twice yearly collecting of war relics at Martinpuich. As I enter the village, there is a dump on the roadside of shells galore. A rough and conservative estimate would place them at 1,000—the majority unexploded!

One I noticed had my regimental number on it! Had I known that, I wouldn't have spent so much of my time hiding behind blades of grass or ducking every time a shell came within a thousand yards of me.

Besides the unexploded shells, are countless muskets, driving bands, pieces of shrapnel, which, if they'd found a billet, would have made one lose one's head; bombs by the dozen, some with pins out, some not; bayonets, steel helmets, and even iron rations.

I continue on my way, and reach the south western end of High Wood (Bois de Fourcoult is the proper name), lying opposite the side road to Bazentin-le-Petit. Now, the wood is surrounded by a fence of barbed wire. It is about eight feet high, and the wires are taut, making it impossible to scramble through.

I come to a gate into the wood. It is padlocked, and barbed wire is twined about it, too. However, I get over it, and have a look about. The undergrowth is fairly thick, so I decide to get back to the road, and go further along, in the hope of getting easier access.

On the right of the road, halfway along by the side of the wood, is a small cemetery, named London Cemetery, so called because the 101 men buried therein belonged to the 47th (London) Division. At the side of it is a wooden gate and a board which says, 'Extension to London Cemetery.'

I climb over the gate, as it is locked, and walk alongside the wall of the latter. At the end I see a sight which recalls the war years. There are hundreds of wooden crosses—row upon row, plot after plot. In the first two plots, 'A' and 'B,' stones have replaced the crosses. So far there are no grass borders, although in the first six plots flowers have been put in.

Plot 'K' has just been commenced on; the long grave trench is open, except for eight places filled in. From a gardener in a neighbouring cemetery, I meet later in the day, I learn that four were buried in the early morning.

The bodies had been found near Mametz Wood, where woodmen are working. None of the four could be recognised, other than that they were British soldiers. Identification was made from the equipment beside the bones.

I return to the gate, enter the London Cemetery, and scan the list of names which is given there of those buried in the extension. The list is partly typed and partly written in ink. Those under the latter are the more recently found remains. My eye catches the name of one of my Company. He was posted missing after a raid.

I go to pay my respects and find his grave in plot 'H.' There is the strip of aluminium giving his name and regiment. There is no regimental number. Something makes me kneel down and look closely at the plate. It has been stamped out DLI (Durham Light Infantry) instead of HLI. I leave a note drawing attention to the error. The extension contains nearly 5,000 graves, all of which have been added in the past few years from finds in the Somme area.

I proceed along the road past the 47th Division Memorial. A little past it I see a farm steading. A man, whom I take to be the farmer, is busy in the farmyard. I had been previously told by three different Britishers that he allowed no one into High Wood (hence the high fence)—and would shoot if he did find anyone in it.

Remembering these facts, I continue on my way to the end of the wood, where I take a farm track along its east side. This takes me to the 1st Black Watch and 1st Camerons Memorial. On the eastern side of the cross is the Cameron badge and an inscription, while on the opposite side is that of the Black Watch.

I go a little further along, hoping for a gap in the never-ending fence, but there is not one. I come to another locked gate, with barbed wire above it, so it appears hopeless. Retracing my steps, I note that the field opposite has had a hay crop and has been raked. The rakings are on the edge of the track.

There are pieces of shrapnel, a bomb, and numberless bones. On the wood side are again funk holes, with an old petrol tin brazier in one, ammunition pouches still with ammunition in them, a few steel helmets, and coils of rusty wire.

Back on the road the spirit of the HLI asserts itself, and I go along to the gate leading to the farmstead. It is locked, but I hail the farmer. He looks up for a minute, then starts to dig again. I shout to him again. This time he sticks his spade in the ground and makes his way across to me.

After asking directions, during which time we speak through the gate, I ask about his crops and his farm generally. Then I tell him I hardly know the old wood, and he there and then unlocks the gate and invites me in! Not content with that, but he offers to lead me through it.

He is a man of 65 or thereabouts. He leads the way—we must go single file for there is an abundance of wire, here and there a dud shell, and in most places the path is overgrown with brambles and wild roses.

He talks in French—too rapid sometimes for me to pick him up—but I learn his farm is 450 acres, of which about 120 is taken up by High Wood. He has five horses, 49 head of cattle, and 15 pigs.

He stops suddenly, and I bump into him. It is the remains of a tank which impedes our progress. Further on, if one didn't know better, one would never dream that this had ever been other than a lovely, wooded glade. Wild roses are blooming profusely, with wildflowers of every description.

My guide leads the way across a rather undulating piece of open ground. The undulations have grass growing in them now, but at the time of their origin, one wasn't concerned with the beauties of the scenery!

Our next stop is an uprooted pill-box. It lies on its side, and around it the farmer tells me he has found a number of bodies—mostly German. The farmer lifts up a long stick—one sees them everywhere—and starts probing the ground. He tells me he has come on quite a number of bodies and shells by this means, especially during the rainy season, when the ground is soft. He is unsuccessful this time—the ground being too hard.

The pill-box is now a fox's lair. I ask him how they come to be here again, and he says he thinks that probably the older ones had found their way back to the wood after the War. He wishes his photo taken, so I get him seated on top of the pill-box, and he smiles like a hero.

On we go through heavy undergrowth, my guide, in his thick trousers, leading the way, regardless of my bleeding face, hands, and legs. A branch of a thorny rose springs back as he passes it, and I get it full in the face, another catches my knees, and I tell him that I'd rather go through barbed wire. He laughs, and I only realised later why. It gets denser and denser, and we have virtually to fight our way through.

We pass one or two machine gun emplacements, and at last a fairly wide path, which leads to another gate. We stand talking for a while. He thinks war is coming, but, like the rest of the French, doesn't seem to be worried about it.

He thinks that we should fight rather than continue the way we are doing. I bid him goodbye, thanking him for his kindness. It is exactly one hour and a quarter since I cried to him in front of his farm.

It is difficult today to believe that here around Ors heavy fighting took place. The whole countryside is the antithesis of war and destruction. Even on November 3rd, 1918 there were few visible portents that on the morrow the slow moving waters of the canal would become red with blood.

Across the canal are still the same hedgerows from which belched forth death. The only consolation, if it can be counted as such, of the battle here on November 4th was that all those killed were identified, and so none was buried as 'an unknown British soldier.'

Strangely enough, there is no sign of a German cemetery, although from Ors to La Folie we took heavy toll. Perhaps they were taken to Germany after the armistice. My French friend tells me that Hitler has issued an order that all German soldiers buried in France are to be disinterred and taken back to the Fatherland for re-burial.

If that is the case, then I am afraid that the Führer, while he may have served in the war, is determined to keep alive their 'Hymn of Hate.' The German dead who lie in France or Flanders, have no greater honour than to lie where they fell. Their transfer to their own country, at the instigation of a leader who is leading their sons to the same fate, is quite unworthy of their sacrifice.

It might be to Europe's benefit if Hitler would visit the military cemeteries in the war area. Would that, instead of Berchtesgaden, his retreat were situated in, or close to, the London Extension Cemetery at High Wood, surrounded by the wooden crosses—even today still increasing in number, although 21 years have passed since the 'ceasefire' was sounded.

If he looked out over that sea of crosses, row upon row, and plot after plot, he would pause and reflect. In the twilight he might see the march of over 7,000,000 ghosts of those who were once flesh and blood. He might see a vision of the millions maimed, crippled, blind, insane.

He might see the faces of millions of little children as they ask their mothers why their fathers never came home. This is not a matter of sentiment, but a question of hard facts. Has he forgotten the horrors, the sordidness, the hell of it all?

If he has then he is worse than his predecessor, Kaiser Wilhelm II. The latter didn't know what the lighting of the match was to bring forth. Hitler, on the other hand, has sampled it, and knowing what lies ahead for not only his own countrymen, but those of the world at large, he is an even greater criminal if he precipitates a world conflagration.

One thing Hitler has taught us. It is that sabre rattling is common to the German, whether he be of high birth or a painter. He may try to make black white and say the Allies deprived Germany of her monies etc., but let him be under no illusions of what's coming to him and his country if he carries on with current tactics.

The last war was never fought as a war to end all wars. It wasn't until we had won that that commendable idea was suggested. This time, if there is to be a this time, that will be one of our main incentives, and being so, should be a factor in our favour.

There will be no Doorn for Adolph and his minions. If they think that, as a reward for spilling the blood of millions, they will get to end their days cutting and chopping wood, they will get a rude awakening. The more likely end of them will be shuffling coals for a 'gentleman' who, they will find out, is a taskmaster far superior to themselves.

Yes, it would do Hitler a world of good. He would find in those cemeteries that friend and foe lie side-by-side, and are tended by men who knew war, but who have long since forgotten any enmity which may have existed during the war years.

The English chauffeur at the hotel tells me he is going to Chuignes with a message, and if I care to come on the run, he will be very pleased. We go out the Villers Brettoneux road through Villers and Warfusée to Proyart.

Halfway between the latter and Chuignes we turn off the main road, taking a side one, the surface of which is far from smooth. On the left side of it are still the remains of gun emplacements. Then turning up a farm track we arrive at a rambling cottage surrounded by trees.

Dismounting, we go through a garden gate between two hedges, and before us is 'Big Bertha'—or most of 'her' anyway. This gun fired on Amiens in 1918. It was captured by the Australians, who had a piece of the muzzle sawn off and sent to Sydney. It was the largest gun captured, having a calibre off 15 inches.

To give an idea of its size—each shell weighed nearly a ton, while its range was nearly 30 miles. Its original purpose was for firing across the Straits of Dover 'when' the Germans got the Channel ports.

Made at Krupps, its base weighs 960 tons. Its recoil was minimised by coming against a cylinder of glycerine. It is said that when the first shell was fired, the concussion was such that 19 of her team were killed.

It had been wonderfully camouflaged by hedges, in which the muzzle was hidden. The present day owner is a Spaniard. He has a café and sells souvenirs. Then at the cost of two francs one can enter the long German dug-out which housed the gunners and see practically every type and size of shell used in the Great War. There are also some very fine stereoscopic photographs to be seen.

As I passed Longueau railway siding in the afternoon in the car, I saw three trains standing full of troops. My chauffeur friend said it was getting a common sight, and the destinations of the troops were unknown.

I have thoroughly enjoyed and benefited from my tramp over the battlefields. Repeated assurances that war is inevitable, either now or next year, have changed my views. The French are not any keener to have unnecessary bloodshed than we are, but they have never trusted Germany, and judging by what I hear, they are justified.

War will be more costly to the French than to us, but they are prepared to face the cost. Surely, if it should materialise, we, at home, will stand up to it with equal calmness.

I am sorry that my tramp is at an end. I have received innumerable kindnesses from all classes, and, without wishing personal aggrandisement, I feel proud of these kindnesses, for they are given me, not because of who I am, but because I am a Scotsman.

I have been asked many times if Scotland will help France again if need be. My answer has always been in the affirmative. People will perhaps think France is getting the 'wind up' over the situation. Far from it. They are fatalists, and as things are as they are, and if war should come, then we will all require to join that 'Union.'

Those of us who served in the Great War soon became 'members.' I am afraid that, had we not, then we would never have stuck it as we did. I often wondered, as I tramped over the old familiar ground, if the wounds of 1914–18, healed in some places, healing slowly in others, will all be reopened. I wondered if the names Beaumont Hamel, Arras, Albert, Cambrai, Ypres, St Quentin, Le Cateau, Villers Brettoneux will again be Press headlines.

How much of the scrap metal of the battlefields will again find its way back to these fields via the munition factory and gun? Will those poppies at High Wood be re-dipped? Will the tramp of British troops echo again through the streets and highways of France?

An Aberdonian doesn't usually let money slip through his fingers, but I must admit that what I had heard and seen prior to reaching Arras made me refuse to take on the bet.

The steamer sails out of Boulogne harbour. The sea is calm. The statue of Britannia—unveiled last year to the memory of the landing of the British Expeditionary Force—stands high at the end of the pier.

I wonder if I shall see it again sooner than I intend? As it recedes from view, my thoughts go to those who lie in 1,760 odd gardens or whose names are inscribed on the Memorials to the missing. I hear the 'Last Post' at the Menin Gate, with its message to those who rest in France. I feel that their appeal—

To you from falling hands we throw
The Torch—be yours to hold it high;
Take up our quarrel with the foe.
If ye break faith with us who die.
We shall not sleep, though poppies grow in Flanders fields

—will be answered if necessary. We shall not let them down.

And so, once again, *au revoir* to France.

—PTE ALFRED W. KEITH, HIGHLAND LIGHT INFANTRY, WRITING IN JULY 1939.

These extracts are taken from a ten-part series chronicling Keith's journey along the Western Front twelve months after recording a similar return visit to mark the twentieth anniversary of the war ending.

References and Sources

Introduction

John Masefield, *The Old Front Line* (London: William Heinemann, 1917)
Capt. Maurice Edward Mascall, *The Civil and Military Gazette*, 10 February 1915
Rudyard Kipling, *The Times*, 5 December 1919
Unknown, *Nottingham Evening Post*, 5 May 1931
Unknown, *Sheffield Telegraph*, 6 August 1925
Maj. Charles Emil Salvesen, *The Ypres Times*, October 1935
R. H. Mottram, *Journey to the Western Front* (London: G. Bell & Sons, Ltd, 1936)

1919

Scottish chaplain, *The Scotsman*, 18 June 1919; 21 June 1919; 28 June 1919; 5 July 1919
Field officer, *Lancashire Daily Post*, 10 September 1919

1920

Maj. Charles H. Fair DSO, *Memories*, journal of the Old Comrades Association of the 19th London Regiment, 1920, via hellfirecorner.co.uk
Lt-Col. George Rowlandson Crosfield CBE DSO, *Widnes Examiner*, 19 June 1920
Revd George Kendall OBE, *Sheffield Daily Telegraph*, 23 June 1920
Revd Leslie Napier Forse, *Fleetwood Chronicle*, 1 October 1920

1921

Sapper Frank Heathcote Briant, *The Clarion*, 27 May 1921
Soldier, *Lewisham Borough News*, 3 August 1921

Capt. Bruce Bairnsfather, *Daily Graphic*, 11 October 1921; 12 October 1921; 13 October 1921

1922

Sgt William Holt, *Todmorden and District News*, 24 February 1922
Soldier, *Belfast Telegraph*, 12 May 1922

1923

L/Cpl Andrew Glen, *Leeds Mercury*, 24 September 1923
Sgt Alex Potter, 8th (Service) Bn, Norfolk Regiment, *Eastern Daily Press*, September 1923

1924

Australian soldier, *Lancashire Daily Post*, 21 July 1924
Lt Samuel Worrall MC, Royal Garrison Artillery, edited from *Eckington, Woodhouse and Staveley Express*, 27 September 1924

1925

Vernon Bartlett, *The Brighter Side of European Chaos: A Journalist's Scrapbook* (London: Heath Cranton Limited, 1925)
Soldier, *The Scotsman*, 17 October 1925

1926

Raymond Bridgeway, *Leeds Mercury*, 29 June 1926; 2 July 1926; 6 July 1926; 13 July 1926
Revd T. B. Stewart Thomson MC BD, *The Scotsman*, 8 July 1926
Lt Ernest Matthews Channing-Renton, *Cornish Guardian*, 10 September 1926; 17 September 1926
Former officer, 6th Bn, North Staffordshire Rgt, *Rugeley Times*, 31 December 1926

1927

Soldier, *The Times*, 19 July 1927
Capt. Ferdinand Tuohy, *The Sphere*, 9 July 1927; 23 July 1927

1928

Pte Percy Waddington, *Nottingham Journal*, 6 August 1928
Lt Ralph Hale Mottram, *Daily Mirror*, 9 August 1928
Anonymous, *West Lothian Courier*, 10 August 1928

1929

Soldier H. C. P., *Lichfield Mercury*, 16 August 1929

1930

Soldier, *Hull Daily Mail*, 15 April 1930
Officer DS, *Evening Despatch*, 28 May 1930; *Sheffield Daily Independent*, 30 May 1930
Soldier J. B. M., *Belfast News Letter*, 4 August 1930

1931

Revd C. P. Robertson MA, *Montrose Standard*, 14 August 1931
Revd Tancred Ambrose Agius, *Somerset Guardian*, 4 September 1931; 18 September 1931
Infantrymen Henry V., *Forest Hill Examiner*, 4 September 1931; 12 September 1931
2Lt Andrew Lawson Ingram, *Aberdeen Press and Journal*, 10 November 1931

1932

Pte Lance Grocock, *Leeds Mercury*, 1 August 1932; 2 August 1932; 3 August 1932

1933

Pte Arthur Wilson, *Sheffield Daily Independent*, 31 July 1933

1934

Officer, *Western Daily Mail*, 24 August 1934
Corporal 1435, *Liverpool Daily Post*, 9 November 1934

1935

Pte Lance Grocock, *Leeds Mercury*, 22 April 1935; 23 April 1935
Capt. Bruce Bairnsfather, *British Legion Journal*, June 1935
Revd S. Gibson, *Sunderland Daily Echo and Shipping Gazette*, 14 October 1935; 21 October 1935; 11 November 1935

1936

Pte Victor Hyde MC, edited from *Sunday Sun*, 28 June 1936; *Sunday Mercury*, 28 June 1936
King's Regiment soldier, *Liverpool Echo*, 30 June 1936
Soldier A. J. Cummings, *London Daily News*, 31 July 1936

1937

Pte Victor Hyde MC, edited from *Liverpool Echo*, 29 July 1937; *Sunday Mercury*, 1 August 1937; *Northampton Mercury and Herald*, 6 August 1937; *The Kentish Express*, 13 August 1937; *Sunday Sun*, 29 August 1937

1938

Pte Alfred W. Keith, *St Andrew's Citizen*, 16 July 1938; 23 July 1938; 6 August 1938; 20 August 1938; 27 August 1938; 3 September 1938; 10 September 1938; 17 September 1938

Soldier W. C. J. Williams, *Nuneaton Chronicle*, 14 October 1938

Cpl Arthur Williams, *Chester Chronicle*, 12 November 1938

1939

Pte William Edward Pethers, *Perthshire Advertiser*, 8 July 1939

Pte Alfred W. Keith, *Fife Herald*, 19 July 1939; 26 July 1939; 9 August 1939; 23 August 1939; 13 September 1939; 20 September 1939

Index